BERLIN The Wall Is Not Forever

BERLIN The Wall Is Not Forever

by ELEANOR LANSING DULLES

Foreword by CHANCELLOR KONRAD ADENAUER

THE UNIVERSITY OF NORTH CAROLINA PRESS · CHAPEL HILL

*Copyright © 1967 by
Eleanor Lansing Dulles
Library of Congress Catalog Card Number 67-17032*

To
THE PEOPLE OF BERLIN
whose decision in 1948 to resist
communist threats and promises
has been important
to free men everywhere

FOREWORD
by Chancellor Konrad Adenauer

It is useful and even necessary to keep the essential elements of the situation in Europe constantly before our eyes. This book gives a clear and comprehensive presentation of the development of the East-West confrontation concerning Europe and Berlin. The sister of former American Secretary of State John Foster Dulles, Mrs. Eleanor Dulles has been consistently a keen-sighted observer of the German question. She has clearly recognized the nature of the significance of this question for Europe and for East-West relations.

Mrs. Dulles has presented a prognosis in the English edition in her choice of title: *Berlin: The Wall Is Not Forever*. This title can be an inspiring message for us Germans not to lose sight of the goal of a general freedom for Europe—a freedom which alone can be the foundation for peace.

PREFACE

In this book I cannot answer the main question posed. I cannot say when the Wall will be breached. I cannot forecast when reunification will come. I can only state my firm conviction that the Wall will be dismantled in a meaningful period of contemporary history. Not at once, and perhaps not even at the same time, the Wall will come down and Germany will be reunited. The time and manner cannot be predicted. I have cited episodes and outlined influences that tend to bring a united Germany into the Western Community. I have suggested that the present division is not wholly in the Communist interest.

In referring to the major changes in the political situations and the destinies of nations, I have emphasized a number of uncertainties and have refrained from prophecy. Understanding must grow from early perception of what has already taken place.

In referring to heroic persons living and dead, I have endeavored to express my appreciation for what they have done and for my opportunity to work for the reconstruction of democratic Berlin.

The conclusions in this book are based on more than two decades of work and study of postwar history. The discussion reflects several score of conversations in the summer of 1965.

Again in January, 1967, as the guest of the Free University, I visited Bonn and Berlin. I had the opportunity of talking with Chancellor Kurt Georg Kiesinger, Governing Mayor Heinrich Albertz, and other friends and members of the German coalition government. On my brief visit, I went to see the Wall, still grim in its stark outlines, crossed only occasionally by Berliners with special passes. On this last visit to the divided city I walked near the Teltow canal where, on the night of January twenty-sixth, two young men swimming to freedom were shot on entering the American sector. This was one of four shootings in five consecutive days. As a result, Western patrols along the border were increased.

It has been more than two decades that Germany has remained divided. Some of the people I talked with, particularly those of the older generation, expressed weariness. Some of the younger people saw hope and progress illustrated by the establishment of diplomatic relations with Rumania, by talks with Poland, Czechoslovakia, and Hungary. The spirit of change and of new types of action were clearly discernible.

The next months give promise of expanding relations. But, as always, emphasis is placed upon a continuing close co-operation with the United States.

In preparing the text of *Berlin: The Wall Is Not Forever*, as well as in my earlier work, I have had the assistance of hundreds of persons in Germany and at home. My former colleagues in the Department of State have been not only efficient co-workers but loyal friends over the years. These persons know, I hope, the extent of my gratitude for their help and advice. While their aid has been inestimable, this book is definitely a result of my own observations—many of them occurring after my resignation in 1962—rather than an expression of Department of State policy or opinion.

Throughout my study I have had the liberal and understanding support of The Center for Strategic Studies of Georgetown University. I am particularly grateful to Admiral Arleigh Burke and Dr. David Abshire for the continuing and generous assistance they have afforded me.

At crucial times I have been aided by Richard Wier, Mary Catherine McCarthy, Christa Thompson, Maria Garcia, and Patricia Azocar. They have helped me with many technical and pro-

Preface

fessional problems in putting the manuscript in shape and making it ready for the publisher.

Blythe Finke and William Allen were with me in Berlin, helping with many interviews and presiding over the informal suppers we gave so we could explore the contemporary scene and ideas of 1965. Blythe has been of constant help, giving me in many instances her spare time and her unusually perceptive judgment.

My son David Dulles and his wife Pamela Dulles have both advised on text and proofs.

Renata Goerz and Marc Catudal have helped me in various ways. They have reviewed the German translation by the Cologne publishers *Wissenschaft und Politik* and have also contributed by examining the English text. Their knowledge of Berlin has qualified them for this task. I also wish to thank Colonel Oscar Drake for reading the manuscript. Edward Joyce, of the American Mission in Bonn, gave me invaluable help at a late stage of handling the German and English texts. As always, Elwood Williams in the Department of State has facilitated my work and contacts.

Sydney and Jameson Parker served as skillful and knowledgeable critics at an early stage.

My good friend Professor Charles B. Robson, of Chapel Hill, North Carolina, gave invaluable support and help in substantive matters, both in reconstructing portions of the text and in filling in detail.

I have found the staff members of The University of North Carolina Press unfailing in their helpfulness.

I bear the entire blame for the shortcomings of this text. I can, however, express my genuine pleasure in the associations this work has brought me, and my gratification for the chance to tell the Berlin story and to recall many stirring events of recent years.

Eleanor Lansing Dulles
February, 1967

CONTENTS

	Foreword by Chancellor Konrad Adenauer	vii
	Preface	ix
I	Berlin Today and Yesterday	3
II	Historical Perspective on the Island City	22
III	The Wall	47
IV	The Relations of Divided Germany and Berlin	79
V	The East Zone—Twenty Years After	103
VI	The Vulnerability of Berlin	129
VII	The Strength of Berlin	146
VIII	The Young Men	165
IX	The Mood and the Method	179
X	The Germans Vote in the New Era	198
XI	The Wall Is Not Forever	209
	Bibliography	229
	Index	237

TABLES

1	The Flow of Refugees from the East Zone	56
2	Production of Selected Industrial Goods	111
3	Agricultural Statistics	121
4	Trade between the Federal Republic, Berlin, and the East Zone, 1965	143
5	United States Aid to Berlin, 1945–1961	156
6	West Berlin Balance of Trade and Goods and Services	158
7	West Berlin Industrial Production, Selected Indices	158
8	Official Results of German Elections from 1957 to 1965	201

BERLIN The Wall Is Not Forever

I. BERLIN

Today and Yesterday

Berlin is as important to Washington as any city—even one of our own—Boston, Chicago, Pittsburgh, or Denver. It constitutes a vital interest of the United States, and it has now held this position in our policy for almost twenty years. Its survival in freedom has been declared to be essential to the free world. We have committed the lives of American men to protecting the welfare and security of the city. We have spent time, energy, and hundreds of millions of dollars to support its economy, to encourage its people, and to make the city a brilliant example of democratic co-operation. We have risked war perhaps more often in Berlin than in any other outpost of American policy. Our commitment has been consistent, bipartisan, and broadly based. We stand firm.

In spite of these facts, few understand the vitality of the city, the complexity of the German problem, the significance of Berlin in halting the aggressive drive of Communism, or why the city is absolutely essential to us.

The explanation lies in a chain of agreements, in the determination of the people to resist tyranny, and in our realization of the Soviet aim to gain all Germany as a prize. It lies in the many intricate relations to the North Atlantic Treaty Organization, and in our involvement in Europe. If we lose Berlin, we lose Germany. Without Germany, Europe would be a slender reed. The Alliance would be gravely weakened. These interrelationships were explained by Soviet Foreign Minister Molotov: "What happens to Berlin, happens to Germany; what happens to Germany, happens to Europe."[1] They lie behind Soviet evaluation of the importance of Berlin, behind the NATO commitment. To an extent not widely realized, our own fate is bound up with this city.

In Berlin, more than anywhere else, the strengths and weaknesses of the Western alliance are tested daily. Here lies the key to the future of Germany, the linchpin of NATO, and the foundation stone in the structure of the Atlantic Community. Here the will to resist is probed by the Kremlin with a variety of means, while efforts to erode the Western commitments continue to be a major aspect of Soviet strategy.

The assignment to work on Berlin problems came to me as a surprise, although more than four years' work, from 1945 through 1949, on Austria and in Vienna had made me familiar with the issues arising from occupation, reconstruction, divided governments, and postwar treaty problems. When Jimmy Riddleberger[2] met me by chance in 1952 at the State Department flag pole on Twenty-First Street, he asked me if I could come to work in the German Bureau. He wanted someone to be responsible for all the major problems of Berlin. I immediately realized that the suggestion opened unusual opportunities. It was not many days before a transfer from another government job put me to work in the Berlin desk of what was then the Bureau of German Affairs (later the Office of German Affairs).

It had been decided that it would be useful to have one point of responsibility where economic, political, aid, public affairs, and other aspects of American concern for Berlin's problems could be co-ordinated. So, after some briefing on the policies on which I had done little since about 1949, I was on my way to Berlin and to my first meeting with Chancellor Konrad Adenauer in Bonn, Mayor Ernst Reuter in Berlin, and others in Germany who were dealing with problems I was to work with over a period of more than seven years.

---

1. Edgar R. Rosen, "The United States and the Berlin Problem: An American View," in Charles B. Robson (ed.), *Berlin: Pivot of German Destiny* (Chapel Hill: University of North Carolina Press, 1960), p. 203.
2. Ambassador James W. Riddleberger served in London in 1942 and 1943 and was associated with the European Advisory Commission. Afterwards he was Chief of Political Section American Military Government, Berlin, Germany, from 1947 through 1950. Subsequently, he was Ambassador to Yugoslavia, Greece, and Austria.

Between the Wars

Almost thirty-six years before this Berlin assignment, my personal involvement in European affairs began on a very informal basis. I was graduated from Bryn Mawr College in June, 1917, and sailed two days afterwards for France to engage in refugee relief. Thus it came about that I was in Europe during the peace conference. I was able to come to Paris from the arduous work and austere life in the devastated areas in late 1918 to be there when President Wilson drove in triumph through the city. I watched the crowds cheering him as I stood on the balcony of the Hotel Crillon. Among the staff working on the settlement were my brothers John Foster Dulles and Allen Dulles as well as my uncle, Robert Lansing, who was Secretary of State. I tried to understand the problems of ending the war with Germany, and began to realize that peace, too, has its dangers. The destructive elements in the Versailles Treaty became evident early in the course of the Peace Conference in 1918–1919.

I heard scraps of conversation about some of the clauses. I had studied no economics in college and did not understand why it was not feasible to transfer livestock, machines, and other material wealth directly from Germany to replace the devastation and losses in northern France. I knew vaguely that John Maynard Keynes and my brother Foster were both opposing the imposition of a heavy annual payment on Germany. They foresaw economic and political difficulties. I returned to my plain living and bicycle visits to the ruined villages, mystified by the complex problems of reconstruction and finance.

I knew from the conversations I had on these brief visits that many of the wiser men were troubled by the future prospects. I knew that Lansing had difficulty lifting the blockade which was causing untold hardship on starving Germans and that the Americans feared not so much for the damage being caused in one country but for the future relations in Europe and potential harm to international peace. The transfer of large sums between nations to pay for destruction or to meet war debts could severely strain the financial structure of the major trading nations. It was not until 1922, however, that I learned more specifically the meaning of the mistakes made in Paris which were to bring disastrous consequences. By then I had begun my studies of finance. I had also worked in American factories and with labor education, learning something of the intricate interaction of economics and politics.

In turning again toward Europe, I spent a year at the London School of Economics. I had the opportunity to listen to some of the finest intellectuals in Europe. I took a vacation in Germany, which was then suffering from runaway inflation. I visited many cities and forest-covered mountains. I could not visit Berlin. It was too far east—deep in Prussian territory. I had neither the time nor the money for the long train journey. There were no commercial planes in those days. As a student I walked in the Black Forest with a rucksack on my back. I met many German youths. Their tortured views gave me a strange impression of the coming struggles of a recalcitrant Germany.

The legacy of the war and of the treaty were causing bitter political attitudes. I was not prepared for the hard words of hatred from the young men—so young and handsome, eager to climb their beloved mountains and enjoy the beauty of their unspoiled countryside. In the high places of Bavaria, where some of Europe's finest landscapes delight the traveler, the realization of increasing psychological tensions came as a shock to me. I was in Munich in time to hear of the massive demonstration on August eleventh of antigovernment groups, associated with General Erich Ludendorff and agitating for revolt, at which Hitler spoke. This episode was a forerunner to Hitler's Beer Hall Putsch in November, 1923. I went back to my studies with new concern for Germany's political tendencies.

The city I could not then visit was to become a major focus of my working life thirty years later. It was to be more familiar to me than most American cities. Its fate was to be closely linked with American security, and it was to be a keystone in the arch of European policy. Before then, however, another tragic war would be fought.

The Nazi Years

It was in 1930, while paddling down the Mosel, that I first heard the young men speak of National Socialism. I realized that the

September election had given Adolf Hitler a fighting chance for power. Later, I spent some time in Berlin. I went to Nazi headquarters and met Paul Joseph Goebbels and a member of his staff at 14 Heddemangasse. Goebbels himself refused to talk to me—he stood silent, menacing. In an interview later at the Hotel Bristol, I talked with Hjalmar Greeley Schacht. I tried by questioning a number of people to discover the meaning of Hitler's new National Socialist party, particularly its economic program. Europe's monetary difficulties were mounting. My studies in Berlin, Paris, and Switzerland were focused on finance.

I had an apartment in Elisabethenstrasse with my friend Mildred Wertheimer of the Foreign Policy Association. I tried to console her when, as an American reporter with an appointment at the midtown Nazi party office, she was driven from the reception desk by black-booted young men, threatening her and screaming, "You are a Jew." She returned home white and shaken.

I could not stay in the city long enough to gain a comprehensive knowledge of the conflicting currents and insidious dangers of the new movement. My impression in 1930 was that the causes of National Socialism were mainly psychological and ideological and not economic. With time, however, there was little doubt that economic distress became a motive that turned many in the direction of programs Hitler invented. Political developments were not my field of specialization. To fulfill my obligations under my Harvard and Radcliffe grant, I was on my way to Basel to carry further my financial research at the Bank for International Settlements. My research and subsequent book were more concerned with the financial than with the political.

As I look back now on my talks in Berlin, I recall my sense of oppression and fear for the future. I did not find it easy, however, to convince those I talked with then, of the serious trouble that the city and its people were coming to. I had already seen grave signs that men with new power might run amuck. There was in the air a weird sense of defiance of decency which was not easy to describe. Several of my friends in Berlin and in Switzerland were alarmed. Among them were Alex Klieforth in the Embassy and Dorothy Thompson in her newspaper work. In 1930, too little of the changing attitudes of these German leaders was reported in America.

The psychological-political revolution escaped observation for the most part. It was only immediately before the outbreak of the war that the public awoke to the danger.

I was to visit Berlin again in the bleak, cold days of March, 1947. Secretary George C. Marshall was on his way to Moscow. Foster Dulles, acting for the U.S. government on the Council of Foreign Ministers, was with him. The conference was scheduled to bring agreement on treaties for Germany and Austria. Foster had requested, through the State Department, that I come from Vienna to Berlin to brief him on the situation in Austria. I had been assigned to Austrian affairs in the Department of State early in 1945 and was sent by way of Italy to Austria in June. I was at the time financial adviser to John G. Erhardt, who was Political Adviser for General Mark Clark.[3] In 1947 Austria was moving rapidly towards recovery while Germany was still in dire straits.

I flew to Germany with General Clark in his small army plane. I was installed in the Dahlem home of my friends, the John Holts, who were in military government. I learned that the American delegation would arrive the next day, and in the meantime I met some Berliners. On arrival, Foster was billeted in the army guest house on the shores of the Wannsee. He and I talked for several hours. I knew something of Soviet tactics in Austria; I knew less about recent Soviet-German policy. But the contrasts that I had noted were instructive and were to prove increasingly significant for me each year.

It was on this visit, riding on the S-Bahn elevated railway that circled the city, that I saw the large-scale Soviet loading of German equipment to be removed eastward from Berlin.

At this time I called on a noted sculptor who lived in a bombed-out apartment hanging over an abyss of rubble with only a curtain where the building wall fronted the street. We huddled over a cup of thin tea—shivering in the wind. Everyone was cold that winter—even the Americans. I saw people picking over the piles of stone looking for bits of fuel or searching for lost posses-

---

3. I stayed in Vienna from 1945 until October 30, 1948, making trips to Germany, Czechoslovakia, Hungary, Trieste, Italy, and Switzerland to note conditions in these countries.

sions. The city was a shambles, the future dark, the people crushed under the weight of despair. A few of the Germans I met during my short stay, such as Annedore Leber, the widow of a hero of the resistance in the July 20 attack on Hitler, and Hannah Reuter, wife of the man chosen for mayor—Reuter was not then permitted to govern—had a grasp of the task ahead. Some of them recognized the challenge of de-nazification and reconstruction and had the courage to face the future. I for my part was not sure, when I went back to Vienna, that Berlin had a future. The destruction had been so complete—the loss of men and morale so devastating.

A Year of Blockade, 1948–1949

A year later—while I was still in Vienna—the stunning news of the blockade came. In our sector and zone we set about, in haste, to prepare for the possibility of a similar contingency. A small stockpile was assembled mainly for the military and their dependents.

I tried, from a distance—with the picture of the dark days of 1947 in mind—to understand what was going on in Berlin. The will and determination of the people were surprising as was their rejection of Communist enticement with food and other offerings. Shocked by the brutality of the blockade into a strong resistance, they did not hesitate to reject Communist attempts at political bribery. We in Austria—where our supply lines were also vulnerable—began to appreciate the great achievement of the military airlift: we marveled at the degree of American success in transporting supplies. We were impressed by the new awareness of western freedom and fear of Communist domination in the city.

All through the long months of hardship, the Berliners cheered the incoming planes, landing every two or three minutes with coal, flour, and other necessities. It was at this time that out of the attempt to annihilate the struggling city there came a new political order. The supporters of freedom recognized the challenge, and the memories of the defeated Reich were partly swept away. The city was in the hands of men of courage as defeat gave way to a new victory. A moral as well as physical reconstruction was about to gain momentum. The Soviets had overplayed their hand, and the Communists had lost Germany to the Western world. The

German-American alliance of today was rooted in the defiance of the men of 1948. A corner had been turned, and Germany was moving in a new direction.

In late 1948 I returned to Washington. I was still working on the Austrian treaty in 1949.

Not until 1952—after my work in the State Department on Austria was over and when I was given the special responsibility for Berlin—did I go to Germany again. At this time I was charged with the task of finding out what the United States could do for Berlin. Now the Department's work was to be concentrated in one office and co-ordinated to achieve a more active program that would give attention to the special aspects of the difficult problems.

In 1953 the economy of the city was faltering, and production was at a low level. Some thought there could be only a small amount of improvement. Using a more optimistic approach, a many-sided program was initiated. This included continuing aid to industry, building up the stockpile, subsidizing housing for refugees in Berlin and in the Federal Republic, improving public relations, and varied measures not developed under other aid programs. The new attention to the city of Berlin was to be so comprehensive as to give a clear impression of the usefulness of an imaginative American and German approach to the needs and support which could be given. I was called on to expand and develop further the many-sided working arrangements with the authorities in Berlin and in Bonn. I was permitted to shuttle back and forth, two or three times a year—enough to keep me in close touch with the Berliners.

The visits I paid to Berlin have been variously counted. My passport shows more than thirty entrances into the city. Some of these were short trips in from Bonn, as I went back and forth from the Federal Republic to tie together negotiations there, with arrangements made in Berlin for various programs of construction and support. For this purpose I flew the Atlantic twenty-seven round trips between 1952–1961.[4] The arrangement for my transat-

---

4. I was transferred from the German Office in September, 1959. I continued to be concerned with Berlin's problems in the next years, and I kept close contacts with my friends in Berlin, the State Department, and elsewhere.

lantic co-ordination of programs in this case was well suited to the special needs of Berlin, since the three-cornered financing of many projects and the psychological subtleties of the resistance to Communist harassment called for a more responsive understanding of the moods and the attitudes which could not be easily reflected in cables.

One such time of special stirring developed early in 1953 and became critical in June. The events of that year were of particular concern to the Germans in the Federal Republic as well as to the Berliners. There were unexpected interacting influences just at the time when Eisenhower and Dulles in Washington shaped the foreign policy of the newly elected administration. The disturbing reports and rumors of trials and repression behind the Iron Curtain, the outward rush of refugees, and the death of Stalin, preceded the revolt of the East Germans in June. Speculation and uncertainty required new and increased support designed to inspire confidence in the firmness of the western position in the city.

Chancellor Adenauer

It was on the first of a new series of visits to Germany that I met Chancellor Konrad Adenauer. He invited me to a luncheon at the Schaumburg Palace in January, 1953. The only other guests were Sam Reber, American political adviser to the High Commissioner, and the skillful interpreter, Heinz Weber. Dr. Adenauer, in a cordial mood, clearly wished to get from me some preliminary sign of the nature of the man whom he was later to term the "greatest man he had known," his friend, my brother Foster. He apparently thought my visit to Germany an indication of Foster's personal interest.

The conversation turned to the several earlier visits Foster had made to Germany and to my travels in prewar years. He was amused that my first arrival in Bonn in 1930 was by Faltboot—a German folding rubber canoe. I told him I had sampled the Bernkastler Doktor, a Piesporter, and other Mosel wines on my leisurely cruise from Trier to Koblenz. He immediately called the waiter and sent him to the cellar for a rare Mosel wine.

Four weeks later, Foster came to Bonn. His visit underscored the intention of President Eisenhower and the Secretary to continue, and even to reinforce, the policy of supporting the reconstruction of Germany and Berlin. In his recent memoirs, Dr. Adenauer refers to the Dulles statement that the reunification of Germany, far from hindering, would expedite the unity of Europe.[5] This visit was the beginning of an association of outstanding importance to the future of Germany. Theirs was, through six years of contacts, an unusually close and warm association.

When in 1965 I had another of many talks with the Chancellor, he showed the basic qualities of wit, affection, determination, and firmness in which he needed to yield first place to no one. He reminded me again of his last meeting with Foster in Bonn in 1959. He recalled the message he received through my brother Allen in February—when Foster, after his second operation, took special pains to inform him that he had indeed been surprised by the unexpected verdict that his cancer had returned. Thus he corrected an earlier confidential and highly optimistic report on his health.

The general purport of Adenauer's 1965 conversation on NATO, France, Western defense, and the threats to Western democracy was on questions of power, politics, defense, and the future of the alliance. On all these matters he said he and Foster had thought alike. They had a similar approach to the methods and urgency of saving western values from destruction by Communism. He echoed opinions which I had heard Foster express and used many of the same arguments on the importance of the Western Alliance.

My contacts with the authorities in Bonn, Berlin, and elsewhere began in 1953 in the time of Mayor Ernst Reuter and continued through the years when Willy Brandt held the office as governing mayor. I counted the men and women with whom I was associated as my friends. I worked closely with Paul Hertz, intelligent, heroic, and untiring in devotion to principle. Hertz had been living for several years a comfortable and secure life on Long Island in 1949 when Ernst Reuter said, "Paul, you must come back to help me build up the city." He was a moderate but strong-minded socialist who used to debate hotly the merits of some of our suggestions. He was always fighting for the protection of the worker, for shelter for the homeless, better conditions for the poor.

5. Konrad Adenauer, *Erinnerungen 1945–1953* (Stuttgart: Deutsche Verlags-Austalt, 1965), pp. 308–13, German edition; pp. 430–34, English edition.

Some of the "impact projects" met with initial resistance from Hertz and from some financial officers in Bonn. They were obliged to ration sparingly the supporting German budget funds. We Americans, on our part, had to stress the over-all needs of the economy and the long-run interests of the city as well as propaganda and political issues. Without impairing these various considerations, consulting together, we developed a balanced and dependable program.

The reconciliation of American programs, which looked ahead to a time of greater prosperity, with the more austere approach to Berlin's needs based on the years of struggle and general misery, brought an effective compromise; and the result was an efficient and impressive use of funds. This was a special case of handling aid money—spearheaded in Washington by the Department of State, co-ordinated with the International Co-operation Administration (ICA) and the Department of Defense, justified before the Bureau of the Budget, and debated seriously in Congress. I had to follow these programs at every stage from the committees where we worked, with the Germans in Bonn and Berlin, through the Washington bureaucracy—through their authorization, appropriation, allocation, commitment, and disbursement. For these stages of the program, there was one central office in the Department of State. For more than six years, I was fortunate to be able to act in every stage of this process, to know the people, the problems, and the technical as well as the political realities. The work was most satisfying because I knew the people, the factories, the building sites, the conflicts, and the problems. From 1952 on, I was in touch with the relevant facts in Washington and in Berlin.

From the first days, until the Wall was built, I followed the meaning of the refugee flow. I can never forget my first visit to a refugee camp—Salzufer—an old warehouse, bleak and barren. Men, women, and children were crowded in, lying on straw, so close together that I had to pick my way with care as I walked through the large rooms with my friends—talking to the refugees in my imperfect German. They were fed, housed, and flown out to the Federal Republic at government expense. They were safe there from reprisals and kidnapping. A small percentage were allowed to stay in West Berlin. I made a practice of sitting in with the special committee that screened the refugees at the headquarters on Fischerstrasse,[6] and of talking with the wise Dr. Elizabeth Gerhartz, who gave the physical examinations.

The committee explored with the incoming people their reasons for fleeing to the East Zone and learned of political and economic conditions in their home towns. I saw their distress and their hopes as they waited crowded in large warehouses with their few bundles of personal possessions, anxious for their turn in line to board the plane that would fly them to the Federal Republic. They could not use the road.

In February, as the number of refugees increased sharply, we allocated fifteen million dollars of aid funds for housing to relieve the shortage, acute since war days, and becoming rapidly worse. I returned to Washington to report on the intolerable burden of unemployment in West Berlin, the imperative need for industrial loans, the larger need for worker dwellings, the desirability of accelerating the pace of stockpile accumulation, the importance of continuing demonstration of western support.

It was in early June that my brother Foster called me and said, "I remembered the things you told me about Berlin and its needs. In our meeting to determine what should be done with funds likely to lapse because they will not be spent on military items before the close of the fiscal year, I persuaded my colleagues to transfer fifty million dollars for the stockpile or related purposes."

The new funds were divided between the industrial investment program and the stockpile. They were *obligated* in Washington and tentatively committed in Germany in the next two weeks. I went to Berlin again to work on both of these programs.

Thus I was in Berlin on June 16, 1953. I was busy attending a meeting near the sector border to plan the expansion of the stockpile designed as a protection of the industry and living standards of the city in case of emergency. One of the late arrivals on the committee rushed into the room, saying, "The workers in East Berlin are in revolt. You can see the plasterers from Stalinallee running down the streets in their white smocks." We looked out at the commotion in the streets and then went back to work, not

---

6. Later moved to Marienfelde.

realizing the extent of the uprising.[7] Later that day, one of the German officials asked me to go with him to a warehouse where several thousands were given shelter when they were forced over the sector border.

I stood among the rioters on June 17—hearing their fiery plea for American armed support in a rebellion against the Communist regime, the desperate shouts for help, and the protests against Allied inaction. These youths had fled for their lives when the Soviet tanks were brought into East Berlin. Some, as the firing began, climbed the Brandenburg Gate at the sector border and tore the Communist red flag from its staff. An angry crowd shouted, "Why don't the Americans give us guns so we can drive the criminals out of our city." I knew of the hard decision of the American and British authorities not to give support on the night of the sixteenth and the morning of the seventeenth.

On the seventeenth there was even more violence than on the sixteenth. Soviet tanks rolled into the city. Men were crushed under the vehicles. Others were shot. The uprising spread throughout the Zone and lasted for several weeks before it was completely suppressed. Some 250 cities and towns were involved. Political prisoners were freed, garrisons were driven from their central posts. But in the end the Soviet occupation forces suppressed the revolt.

At this time, temporary barriers failed to keep out the more determined of the escaping East Germans who came over in scores. Though the Communists stopped the free access for the East, the measures taken were very different from the Wall of 1961. I talked to those who had come over at the Marienfelde reception center. They said that the crossing was difficult, but that they could find ways of getting across. No one could be sure when or if the border would be reopened. In fact, the obstructions were taken down in a few days. At this time there was considerable talk of the possibility of the Communist's successfully sealing off West Berlin. It was discussed pro and con, and the consensus was that such an attempt would be possible but that the propaganda aspects might loom large to prevent such a Soviet decision.

The June uprising led to the influx of Russian tanks into the city

---

7. "Flight from 'Paradise': The East German Exodus," *Background*, Department of State, Office of Public Affairs (June, 1953), pp. 1–8.

and their deployment along the sector border, and the barring of the street crossings with armed soldiers, machine guns, and barbed wire. Many hundreds swam the canals, jumped from roof tops, and stormed the barriers, fearing further obstructions that would make escape increasingly difficult. At this time Soviet policy was still directed to keeping Germany out of NATO and to winning the whole country—not yet firmly in the Western camp, or so they thought.[8] The revolt was crushed and surface calm restored, but unrest remained. We had to become increasingly active and affirmative in our programs.

The Food Package Program was one of the more controversial of 1953. It was designed by Allen Dulles, the head of CIA, by Foster Dulles, and by me working with my colleagues in other agencies. The thought was, somehow, to make a gesture to demonstrate our concern for those whose homes and jobs were in the Soviet zone.

Fifteen million dollars were allocated for this general purpose in July. The method adopted was to give out food packages to all who came to get them. To permit immediate action the supplies were borrowed from the stockpile already in Berlin, later replaced by shipments from America. The people who streamed into the city during the next weeks were making a gesture of solidarity with the West. They came in many cases from afar. Their expenses often exceeded the value of the gift.

The Communists, faced with this act of defiance, hesitated to impose obstacles for those seeking food, but they finally decided to harass, and even arrest, many of those traveling to Berlin. It was decided to halt the program to lessen the danger to the residents of the Zone. The funds remaining were spent in other ways for their benefit. Some of the subsequent programs were classified.

It was in September of this year that Ernst Reuter died. He had been a bold and idealistic man, opposing the Soviets when he thought it necessary and not yielding to the Western authorities if he thought they were acting against the best interests of the Berlin people. His death, from heart failure, like that of many others in these troubled years can be ascribed to overwork. He was succeeded

---

8. Stefan Brant, *The East German Rising* (New York: Praeger, 1957); Arno Scholz et al., *Panzer am Potsdamer Platz* (Berlin: Verlags, GMBH, 1954).

by Walter Schreiber as governing mayor. Otto Suhr and Willy Brandt were to come later.

With all these men, in the years from 1953 to 1957, I worked on the problems of increasing confidence, reducing unemployment, and expanding the social housing and other major facilities. Here, partly because of the Berliners' sense of planning, our dollars, the counterpart in German money, and the Federal Republic's appropriations were combined to accelerate reconstruction and an improved standard of living. The ease of operation and lack of friction or waste were gratifying. The number of unemployed declined from over 300,000 to negligible numbers. Production and the standard of living soared.

I had little to do with the intelligence community in Berlin, though some of the men who had their assignments from the Central Intelligence helped me to evaluate the situation and to understand the Communist tactics of harassment. In spite of my restraint and the obvious impossibility of my acting in a covert manner, I was accused in the East Zone press of starting the 1953 revolt. I was also credited with the building, or at least the planning, of the intelligence tunnel constructed under the East sector to monitor telephone calls. I would gladly have taken the responsibility but, in fact, I had not even been told of this ingenious enterprise.

While we built many buildings on a co-operative basis to fit the many needs of the city, probably the most satisfying project for some of us was the construction of the Berlin Congress Hall as a contribution to the Berlin Building Exhibition of 1957. This work, in which a number of distinguished American architects and lawyers participated, was the occasion for the forming of the German-American Benjamin Franklin Foundation, now responsible for the construction of the impressive Klinikum, also in Berlin.

The idea of memorializing the great American was welcomed by the Berliners, who in passing often stand before the imposing relief of Franklin to read the quotation from his letter to David Hartley: "God grant that not only the love of liberty but a thorough knowledge of the rights of man may pervade all nations of the earth so that a philosopher may set his foot anywhere on the surface of the earth and say This is my country." Before this inscription I saw a small boy standing in wonder—he turned to his mother and said, "Can I become an American?" Thus, the fine Congress Hall—with its many convenient meeting rooms, its daring roof, its wide vistas looking toward the old Reichstag, the Brandenburg Gate, the green Tiergarten, and the modern constructions in the Hansaviertel—represents the spirit and the constructive ideals of the Berlin policy for which we worked over the decades.

Concern for Berlin

Both my brothers, Foster and Allen, had always been most concerned about Berlin. Allen visited the city in 1945 while the ruins were still smoking. He met President Harry Truman at Potsdam. It was three years later, in October 1948, that Foster went in on the airlift to meet General Lucius Clay.

He had come to Vienna to talk with the occupying authorities and the Austrian leaders. I gave a luncheon for him on Sunday. Distinguished military personnel and leading American diplomats came to my house to discuss the blockade in Germany and the hope for a treaty in Austria. Unfortunately, neither he nor I could attend the luncheon, which was served in fine fashion by my loyal helpers Trudi and Relli.[9]

General Clay had called Foster from Berlin. It would help morale, he said, if the man expected to be the Secretary of State for Thomas Dewey, then candidate for President, would fly into Berlin along with a cargo of supplies. He left at 7:00 A.M. for Frankfurt. I left at eight in response to a request from Averell Harriman to come to Paris to confer on Marshall Plan aid to Austria.

Foster and I met that Sunday night in Paris. His mission had greatly impressed him, even though he had time for only a few hours in the city where the mounting effort was that of piling wheat and coal at Templehof Airport. He marveled at the effectiveness of the operation.

Then later, in 1954 in Berlin, he had one of his most interesting negotiating battles with the Communists. It is said that each time the Soviets began a long harangue over the need for a peace treaty with the East Germans and the impossibility of a rearmed Germany, he would take a penknife from his pocket and sharpen

---

9. Gertrude Rotter and Aurelie Rotter.

the pencils which lay beside his yellow pad on the conference table. Slowly and deliberately he would then expound the Western point of view, its program, and the legal position which must be observed—the importance of a proper handling of the future of a great nation.

In 1958, I persuaded a somewhat reluctant secretariat in the Department of State that there would be time for a short visit by the Secretary between the end of the meeting in Copenhagen, where the ministers of the NATO countries had been conferring, and his evening appointments in Paris. The arrangements of such visits by significant persons had been a regular part of my work.

The four hours in the city of Berlin were tightly scheduled. The impressive figures of Brandt and Dulles dominated the welcoming ceremony at Templehof Airport where the military plane landed. Here Foster reviewed the honor guard of the occupying troops, drawn up in formation.

The motorcade to the Schöneberg Rathaus drove over a well-planned route through the crowded streets near the sector border. Foster drove down Unter den Zelten [10] by the Congress Hall, an avenue that was to be named for him a little more than a year later, after his death.

At the Schöneberg Rathaus, the speech was timed so that after the solemn reiteration of the commitment to protect Berlin, the Freedom Bell rang out—carrying its noon message to the Communist areas surrounding West Berlin. The luncheon was held in a fine villa on the edge of one of the little lakes in the center of town. The little American flags at each place gave a cheerful note, and the toasts were brief and witty.

Crowds swarmed the streets outside to see the dignitaries come and go. Time was short, and the cars were waiting to take Dulles and his group of American assistants to the airport, where the Mayor bade good-bye to the group taking off for Paris. There was no doubt of the depth of feeling on both sides—German and American—in this short meeting, on a crowded schedule, undertaken in the interests of the defense of the free world.

10. *Zelten* is the German word for the tents pitched there by the Romans several centuries ago.

While the work in late 1958 and 1959 was somewhat overshadowed by the diplomatic crisis occasioned by the Khrushchev ultimatum of November, the programs for economic and cultural development continued. There was scarcely a break in the steady improvement of conditions; the moment of panic was quickly over, and the rise in production and employment continued unabated.

The brief survey of the work carried on for Berlin suggests, for those who may have forgotten some aspects of the Berlin policy from 1940 through 1959, the special nature of the problem, the variety of American effort, the warm response of the Berliners, and the quality of foreign policy as it bore on this unique problem. Many days and nights of hard work by hundreds of people in America and abroad went into creating this new Berlin. One person could only experience a part of the whole and could have only a minor share in the total program.

My official work in the Department of State, on Berlin, ended two years before the Wall. I was transferred to a different office. I was able to visit the city on various ceremonial occasions and as a guest of the Germans in several cases. My last visit as representative of the Department's work for the city came when I made a speech following Secretary Christian Herter and Willy Brandt, who dedicated the John-Foster-Dulles-Allee, at the Congress Hall, in July, 1959. Although my official participation in the formulation of policy was over, my interest continued.

It is because of the law of change and the need to look below the surface that I revisited Berlin in 1965. It is because changes are subtle and little publicized that they must be analyzed and proclaimed. A static policy, traditional opinions, often repeated slogans are not enough for the coming decade. The whole structure of friendship developed in the last twenty years can be torn asunder if the growing intent of the men born since the end of the war is overlooked. American policy, while keeping the central core of principle must reflect new realities as they occur. The demonstrations of the students against authority, the new and sometimes shocking statements of iconoclasts must be viewed as more than a psychological malaise. They are impressions of a growing force which will be healthy if it can be guided into the more constructive channels of a new Germany—a land which knows no Hitler, which seeks unlimited opportunity, and which feels the pulse of a new vitality in a world largely divorced from the wartime past.

Thus from 1952 until 1959, my main concern was the security and welfare of Berlin—the future of Germany and the American role in Europe. Even though I could only work on a small corner of the problem, the opportunity was extraordinary. It brought friendships and experiences which were of immense personal value.

In the Berlin work there were aspects of most of the postwar constructive developments as well as of the challenges of the cold war. New conditions, new people, new problems confronted the city of Berlin. I was not sure that there was a wide realization of how much the situation in 1965 differed from that in 1960 and earlier years. I went to Berlin in the summer of 1965, with some time in Bonn to get perspective from that angle. I had appointments from early morning until after midnight; talking with people singly, in little meetings of several persons, listening to debates between the students and among the experts over a number of current questions. Convinced that I had obtained a clear picture of present-day Berlin, I have sketched the outline in low relief in the chapters which follow. The change goes on—the conditions are not static, the future will be only partially a projection of the past. Then, and now, the changes in Europe are reflected in Berlin—in economics, politics, art, and education. No one who has become intimately connected with these developments since 1945 can forget the lessons of those years. To have had a part in the rebirth of Berlin and to share in its future hopes are privileges that any one could envy.

II. Historical Perspective on the Island City

Memories of the brief past encounters with the problems of Germany and Berlin [1] passed through my mind as I took over a new assignment in 1952. These earlier glimpses of the problems were, however, fragmentary and disconnected, the atmosphere rather than the history of the changing fate of Berlin and its significance from 1945 through 1965.

The evolution of the American policy in Europe has been complex and many-sided. It can only be understood if one reviews many elements including the early plans in 1943 and 1944, the decisions at Yalta in 1945, the conquest of Germany, early occupation days, the Blockade of 1948, the revolt of 1953, the recovery of the city, Khrushchev's ultimatum of 1958, the Vienna meeting of Khrushchev and Kennedy in 1961, and the Wall. Many other critical events in the city, and outside, bear on the present situation. The network of influences spreads in many directions. The documents continue to accumulate; scientific analysis continues. Not until there is a resolution of the problems of a divided Germany can a definitive history of Berlin be written. To attempt such a comprehensive statement now would leave many key questions unanswered.

One can regard the period from 1943 through 1946 as a period of planning and revision of plans. The dilemma of planning for the unknown is dramatically illustrated by the papers written on Berlin

1. In 1919, 1922, 1930, 1943, and 1947.

Historical Perspective on the Island City [23]

and Germany in Washington and other capitals between 1941 and 1945. The political assumptions regarding post-surrender Germany varied sharply at decisive points from those which were taken as basic in 1943 and 1944 in proposals for surrender, occupation, and the treatment of the conquered nation. The position papers and directives available in 1945 helped to prepare the United States for the unprecedented tasks that were to come with the end of the war, but the major decisions had to be altered soon thereafter. The price paid in this case for the inability to anticipate future conditions was high.

Neither Churchill, Roosevelt, nor Stalin was to determine the course of German-American relations in the twenty-year span from 1945 to 1965. The tide of history began to change in April with the death of Roosevelt and with the political defeat of Churchill in July, 1945, and later, in 1953, with the death of Stalin. Meanwhile, both the importance of holding Berlin and the problems that were entailed increased with the passing months. The issues that concerned Europe, the United States, and the Soviet Union took on new and unpredicted forms. The early mistakes with regard to military action and our failure to enter Berlin before the Soviets, while regrettable, cannot be considered to have been crucial.

While we in Washington were preparing for future contingencies, the men of the Third Reich had plans for conquering London, Paris, and other capitals. As the bombs fell on Berlin, the Germans must have wondered how well their plans would apply. When the battle lines broke in 1945, they must have anticipated in anguish what lay ahead, knowing the ferocity of the mood of the Russians as they advanced, and unable to assess American and British intentions.

The situation of the island city is the result not of one but of a number of fundamental errors, and it has been further complicated by a series of unpredictable events. Most of the major elements could not be forecast. Unquestionably, the illness of Franklin Roosevelt in 1944 and 1945 played an important part in the decisive concessions at Yalta. The behavior of the Soviet armies in Europe and the development and use of the atomic bomb were unknowns in 1943 and 1944. More important, the acquiescence of the German people to Western controls and the unpredicted lowering of the Iron Curtain over Europe were new realities in the world picture.

Thus, some of the errors in calculation were understandable although in retrospect many find them difficult to explain. Now, with a backward look, it is easy to take for granted that the winning of the war by the Allies was inevitable, and the fear of defeat chimerical. Thus, it appears to the critics that the position of postwar Berlin, deep in Eastern German territory, should have been more clearly visualized in 1945. These critics overlook the fact that there were only scattered signs of cold war maneuvers which were to dominate international relations.

To the American generals, considering logistic needs and the danger of large loss of life, the political instructions left considerable latitude. There were varying estimates in high quarters as to the capabilities of the German armies. There was wide speculation about the prospects of a last redoubt in the mountains, manned with suicidal determination, about the potential for resistance of the German people, and about the degree of destruction and chaos which would hinder the establishment of order. The only thing that emerged for the military was the uncertainty of the conditions that dominated the choices to be made. Their operations have been criticized after the fact, as responsible for the continuing Soviet presence in Berlin, but the record shows that there were agreements in the political councils in Yalta, in the European Advisory Commission, and elsewhere which made the location of the troops in Austria, Czechoslovakia, and in Germany in May, 1945, largely irrelevant for the later occupation arrangements. The political commitments were overriding.

The manner in which military and political action was frustrated for two years by the results of major errors in judgment, becomes increasingly apparent with time. The first and basic miscalculation that encompassed and modified the decisions and agreements of the postwar period was to assume that the greatest threat to future world peace would be the German people. There was a natural, if mistaken, fear that, as after the Versailles Treaty, they would burn with hate and plot revenge. This hate I had heard expressed in 1922. As I walked with a rucksack on my back, I met the young men on the mountaintops and in the youth shelters.

"We will see blood flow in the Paris streets," they said. "Heads will roll—we will be there."

At the end of World War II, there was little awareness in America of the meaning of the resistance movement, the popular response to defeat, and the psychological changes that had come with the vast devastation of the bombed cities and with the suffering in a war for which they realized responsibility could not lie with Hitler alone. There was no anticipation that America would extend help on a large scale or of the widening German appreciation of Allied efforts to restore order and bring food and fuel, first under the American Army administered Government Administration and Relief in Occupied Areas (GARIOA) and later through the Marshall Plan. The strange experience of a conquered nation welcoming, after a few weeks, those who were their masters by act of conquest was not a part of the advance thinking and planning.

The second major error in judgment came from the mistakes in judgment in 1944 and 1945. Official opinion was in many respects naïve and unmindful of what advantages of geographic position and political opportunity were conceded to the Soviet leaders. It was not recognized by the Western experts in 1945 that the USSR drive to protect the gains of the Soviet revolution and the fear of contamination from freedom would lead to the building of an almost impenetrable barrier between the world of the Communist East and the capitalist freedom beyond.

The first realization of the deep Soviet hostility and fear of democracy which led to the Iron Curtain came early in 1945 in the conquered nations of Poland, Hungary, Austria, and the Balkan lands, as the incoming "liberators" burned, looted, raped, and oppressed in the nations they professed to free from the remnants of Nazism. The Americans who were charged with occupation responsibilities saw the ominous signs, as refugees fled in thousands from the unrestrained passions of the oncoming army and told their stories to others in safer regions. Some believed only reluctantly the accounts of the terror and destruction wreaked by the Communist armies and of the oppressive measures employed. The raw brutality of those weeks was the prelude to the reshaping of political attitudes in the liberated areas and in the major capitals of Europe. The new policy did not become official for the United

States until 1946. The change from the Western policy of repression then came quickly.

The third major error in judgment was the anticipation of an early agreement on peace treaties to govern the future of the former enemies, and of Austria. This was expected within a period of one or at most two years.

The tentative draft documents and the scheduling of conferences in Paris in early 1946 were part of the optimistic plan first of Roosevelt and then of Truman to "bring the boys home" in a few months after the armistice. These plans were gradually revised in the face of evident danger to the future of democracy in Europe. Before the shift in policy many troops had already been demobilized, but the military occupation was to continue for years. Only five peace treaties (Finland, Rumania, Bulgaria, Hungary, and Italy) [2] were concluded in 1946. All served the Soviet interest and were acceptable to the Russians because they accorded them, in their view, a larger sphere of political influence. The controversial territorial, military, and political issues that prevented the agreements on a German peace treaty and the unification of Germany were regarded by the Soviets as limiting the sphere of influence; these issues were to cast their shadow over several decades of history. Thus Berlin remained a hostage of the opponents in the cold war and a victim of the misunderstandings and conflicts in the two world centers with regard to the manner in which power would be used to develop democratic systems or extend Communism in the center of Europe. This conflict was discernible, in retrospect, earlier, in the European Advisory Commission (ECA).

The fourth error of the years 1944 and 1945 was the hope and expectation that the United Nations Organization would develop rapidly and exert an effective authority to maintain the peace and assure the rights of men, in Germany as well as elsewhere. Winston Churchill, as well as President Roosevelt, was said to have spoken of the importance of the UN in their talks with Stalin about the future of Germany. The new security system that was to emerge from the charter adopted at San Francisco in April, 1945, was established only days before the German surrender. Since its exist-

---

2. Four of these treaties were ratified by the United States. The Finnish Treaty was not submitted to our Senate since we had not been at war with Finland.

ence was not tied to the peace settlement, as had been the League of Nations in 1919, the prospects seemed favorable for a long and significant role. Its prospective effectiveness in preventing war and furthering co-operative arrangements between nations offered a partial solution to the concerns of the Soviet leaders and the other wartime allies. It was anticipated that the more limited four-power agreements of early postwar months would end at a point where the United Nations would begin to safeguard security and adjust grievances. In this case, the United States need not carry such a heavy burden as would otherwise have been necessary.

Unfortunately, the views of the men in the Kremlin were different from those in Washington. These men were genuinely skeptical about co-operative international agencies. The direct and immediate use of power and the authority of the armies in the field seemed more important to Stalin as he looked to the future of Germany.

The reason these errors shaped war relations can best be understood after a reconsideration of the ideas and men in the early meetings in Moscow, Cairo, Malta, Teheran, and Yalta. In these meetings Berlin received scant attention. The talks at Potsdam, with Clement Attlee taking over from Churchill, Harry Truman succeeding Roosevelt, and Stalin in an intransigent mood, did not recover any of the ground lost earlier to the Communists.

Germany's Future—Teheran and Yalta

The stage on which the main actors appeared in the years 1941 to 1945 was shaken by the conflicting aims of the main personalities, notably Roosevelt and Churchill, who were pitted against Stalin. They sought to assure the continuance of the influence of their nations and to mold new systems of internationalism—Stalin, for his part, determined to perpetuate or to extend Communism. Each expected a degree of compromise and was tragically hampered by the physical, mental, and political preoccupations conditioning the decisions which they made. Of the three, Stalin, though worn by the bitter struggle of the war, appeared to have been in the best condition.

Much of the confusion in the explanations of the Morgenthau Plan—which, combined with the Yalta decisions, threatened the dismemberment of Germany, of the location of Soviet and American armies in Germany, and the zonal agreements isolating Berlin —is attributable to the disparity of views and to the clash between general views and specific facts. This lack of communication has been a frequent difficulty besetting the development of foreign policy.

New significant aspects of the tragic conferences of Teheran and Yalta continue to be revealed. The latest contribution to the account of concessions and compromises with regard to Germany, Poland, and the Mediterranean and Balkan areas has been published in Lord Moran's *Churchill*.[3] His reported recollections of Churchill's apprehension over Roosevelt's postwar intentions is thrown into sharp relief by his comments on the meetings of the three men. He describes Churchill's increasing worry at Teheran and Yalta over his failing heart, Roosevelt's marked physical deterioration, and the evidence of burning hatred of the Germans in Stalin's conversations. Thus he adds evidence to the views, expressed by other historians, that the bases for Communist gains and western losses in Europe are to be found before the war's end. After these several conferences, particularly Yalta, there was in fact little hope of convincing the leaders in the Kremlin that the United States would follow a policy of bringing a reconstructed Germany into the fraternity of nations. Berlin, East Germany, and the Balkans had been well nigh surrendered to the oncoming Russian armies before April, 1945.

In the light of earlier high level agreements, the detailed planning, while interesting and, in minor respects, significant, fails to assume the importance it would otherwise have had. The record shows that preparatory work was serious and competent. But a few major decisions contributed to the growing importance of Stalin's influence, and many of the position papers were formulated for an unreal world.

The mass of papers has been overshadowed by the Morgenthau Plan, which has remained the symbol of the American policy towards Germany in 1944 and 1945. The proposal, which had a unique history, was discussed between Winston Churchill and

3. Lord Charles Moran, *Churchill From My Diaries* (New York: Houghton-Mifflin, 1966), pp. 481–82.

Historical Perspective on the Island City [29]

President Roosevelt in Quebec in September, 1944. It was not the product of the established system of committees dealing with these issues but was prepared at the special request of President Roosevelt.

An understanding of how the errors occurred emerges partially from a consideration of early planning. During the years 1942 to 1945, a committee, under the late Leo Pasvolsky of the State Department's Division of Special Studies, was assigned the task of developing directives for the surrender and occupation of postwar Germany. This committee met frequently over a period of more than two years on the top floor of the old Walker-Johnson Building on New York Avenue, a crowded State Department annex. Other groups with similar responsibilities met at the Pentagon and elsewhere in Washington. A series of papers was prepared and transmitted through a co-ordinating interagency group (SWNC)[4] to the White House. These proposals were intended to lay the groundwork for the directives for postwar occupation of a defeated Germany and a liberated Austria.[5]

The twelve or fourteen members of the "German Committee" were economists, political scientists, and diplomats. A few had been in Germany, most of them read German, only one or two were old enough to remember the Paris Peace Conference of 1918–19. The members of the Committee, like their colleagues for the French, Belgian, Italian, Chinese, Japanese, and other committees, prepared studies on such subjects as surrender terms, reparation, finance, industry, education, political reconstruction, de-nazification, labor, wages, "displaced persons," standard of living, and a host of other subjects. When finished, these papers were put before higher co-ordinating committees, the President, and then in due course, if approved, forwarded to the European

---

4. This was a joint committee of State, War, and Navy.
5. Dwight D. Eisenhower, "My Views on Berlin," *Saturday Evening Post*, December 9, 1961. In this article General Eisenhower explains the nature of the relations between the committees, particularly the European Advisory Commission, the military generals, Roosevelt, Winant, Stalin, and Churchill. He gives his explanation of why the American Army did not take Berlin, comments on the political decisions as to the zones of occupation, and indicates regret that the zonal system of occupation was adopted instead of the joint and unified command that had been proposed. He speaks of the Yalta conference and some of the confusion and misunderstanding that affected decisions in early 1945 and says, "No occupation of Berlin by us could have been permanent."

Advisory Commission in London, where the late John G. Winant represented the United States as Ambassador to Great Britain. The Soviets were represented by Fedor Tarasovich Gusev and England by Sir William Strang.[6] General Charles de Gaulle was consulted occasionally, both directly and through his representatives.

In late 1943 and early 1944, the "German Committee" wrestled with the problem of the standards to be set for food rationing, levels of production, health, welfare, and the conditions to be established. The issues were hotly debated. There was general agreement that the food rations should be such as to prevent "disease and unrest," even though the financial cost to the occupying powers would be considerable. It was also agreed that the caloric consumption and conditions of living for the former enemies should be kept lower than for the "victims of Nazi aggression."

It was further a consensus that the conditions of surrender should minimize the danger that the German people would claim, as they had after 1918, that there had been a treacherous "stab in the back." This led to the much debated decision to require "unconditional surrender." The formula probably delayed the capitulation of the armies but brought home to the people generally the degree of their dependence on the Allies as their only hope for the future. It was costly, but it contributed toward later prospects of cooperation.

The Morgenthau Plan

The controversial and momentous American policy that has been called the Morgenthau Plan developed out of work done on labor conditions and wages in this Committee.

A paper was written which seemed to condone German atrocities as mere fortuitous expressions of typical human weakness and tendency to error. Its conclusions recommended a tolerant approach to the perpetrators of Nazi crimes. It became an "agreed" paper in spite of the objections of a small minority.[7] It was probably not the

---

6. *A Decade of American Foreign Policy*, prepared for the Senate Committee on Foreign Relations by the staff of the Department of State, U.S. Government Printing Office, 1950. See also Wolfgang Heidelmeyer and Guenter Hindrichs, *Documents on Berlin, 1943–1963* (Munich: R. Oldenbourg, 1963), pp. 8–20.

7. My memory is that there were two dissenting votes.

specific recommendations in the paper, but the confused thinking and hazy conceptions as to the causes of the war, of the extent of the political outrages, and of the nature of the tasks ahead that angered President Roosevelt.

It was said his response was immediate. He called in Henry Morgenthau, Jr., Secretary of the Treasury, and said, "Put your people to work on Germany." From that time on, early in 1944, as victory came nearer, the State Department did little work on German problems; other advisors spoke for the President. An informal group was formed which included several alleged Communists in the Treasury Department, and several outside of the Treasury, under the direction of Bernard Bernstein (whose loyalty has always been above reproach). They produced the well-known *Plan* and *Directive 1067*. This order restricted levels of production and trade and gave the outlines of a harsh "Carthaginian peace." It was thought by some that Germany could be reduced to a pastoral state. "Gil" Winant in London, an idealistic dreamer, full of hope for mankind, was bewildered by the changes. He was never able to reconcile the decisions at Teheran, Yalta, or Washington nor did he receive answers to his queries about them prior to the time of Roosevelt's death,[8] an event that introduced further uncertainties. The Soviets, in all probability, misconstrued the intent of American policy which was to be reversed a year later.

These aims and the prevailing attitudes are largely overlooked in discussions as to the lack of written agreements on access to Berlin, a query of major importance in considering conditions in later years. There was to be no continuing occupation of the four zones of Germany; there was to be no prolonged military occupation—an occupation which has in fact been continued for more than twenty years. In these circumstances there would have been no volume of traffic other than the military during a short period of foreign administration. The problems of access arose with the later phases of occupation and Allied responsibilities.

The chief officers who were responsible in 1945 for the administration of the city, particularly Frank Howley and Lucius D. Clay, like

---

8. Philip E. Mosely. *The Kremlin and World Politics* (New York: Knopf, 1960). He concludes that "Dismemberment, the Morgenthau Plan and similar war-time fevers had no firm footing in American psychology" (pp. 140–48).

Mark Clark in Vienna, were more conscious of the weakness of their isolated position than were the civilian authorities. The diplomats in many cases were concentrating on preparation for the treaties and on political and economic reconstruction.

The withdrawal of American and British troops from some of several areas in Czechoslovakia, Austria, and Germany, which they had conquered, began in July, 1945. This cession of territory, under pressure from the Soviet generals but in accord with earlier political agreements, was a warning to some of troubles to come. The possible cutting of access, if co-operation with the Communists failed, became a disturbing possibility.

The control agreement under which the four-power Kommandatura governed the city, further complicated the authority of the Western Allies since decisions were only effective when unanimous. The Kommandatura was thus paralyzed on most matters except those affecting the security of their forces, de-nazification, and the most elemental aspects of handling war devastation and public problems. Large-scale removals were permitted as valuable capital equipment was shipped eastward.

In February, Marshal Stalin delivered a major speech in which he said world revolution and Communism were marching forward. His officials showed no concern for the continued misery and economic deterioration in the city and the rest of Germany. But the dangers for all of Europe were becoming apparent to the Americans.

The New Policy

Many elements entered into the change of American policy towards Germany which was manifest in the speech of Secretary of State James F. Byrnes at Stuttgart on September 6, 1946. The statement came after the difficulties in dealing with the Soviets in both Germany and Austria troubled and exasperated the Western generals responsible for military government and others striving for a genuine peace in Europe. It was based on a new assessment of the behavior and aims of the German and the Austrian peoples. The change in policy was urged also by those who saw the great need for German coal and steel and other products that could help in the reconstruction of Europe. It was the result of the increasing authority of those who realized the advantages of bringing Germany back into the family of nations on a normal basis as compared with the weaker voices of those who wished to suppress the potential strength of the former enemy.

The new and unpredicted elements of occupation policy began to emerge first in Austria in 1945, and then in Germany. In Vienna, the time schedule for reconstruction was different for several reasons. The Austrian revulsion against Soviet actions and the suffering that came early with the Soviet occupation caused the people to turn for help and protection to the Western Allies, particularly to the United States. This need established, as early as July, 1945, a spirit of willing collaboration among the Austrians. It was some months later, in the spring of 1946, that the sharp distinction between the attitude of the Communists and the Western Allies was officially recognized in Germany as well.

The manner in which Secretary James Byrnes's speech was drafted and the care with which the stage was set were appropriate to its importance as a major turning point in our policy towards Europe. Without this change the Truman Doctrine, the Marshall Plan, and NATO would not have been possible. Similarly, the Economic Community of Europe has its roots in the decisions of 1946. By those who were working on occupation and reconstruction problems, the significance of this rejection of a Carthaginian peace and of ending the dominant attitudes represented by *Directive 1067*, was immediately recognized. By others, the speech was soon forgotten. Nevertheless, it was one of the earliest American statements about the dangers of the cold war. It indicated opposition to encroachment on German territory and stated for the first time that "security forces will probably have to remain in Germany for a long period. . . . We are not withdrawing. We are staying here."[9] It indicated that the practical problems, for example, with regard to displaced persons, de-nazification, relief, monetary reform, and local government had been foreseen and correctly outlined in advance.

9. U.S. Senate, Committee on Foreign Relations, *A Decade of American Foreign Policy* (1950), pp. 522–27.

Frustrating Struggle for Unity

The turn of the tide in German policy was followed by the futile two-year struggle in the Berlin Kommandatura and in Frankfurt for a common occupation policy and a stalemate between the Soviets and the West in efforts to achieve treaties to put both Germany and Austria on a peacetime footing. The Soviet leaders in the Kremlin and the Communist occupying forces had lost ground in Austria. Recovery was steady there, after they permitted both monetary reform and free elections in the autumn of 1945. Having seen the favorable results, they rejected both programs in Germany. Soon after the Byrnes speech, the first victory for freedom was won by the Berlin voters.

A crucial political decision was made in Berlin in October, 1946. There had been a widespread assumption in 1945 that the trade unions of the FDGB would exert sufficient influence to bring about a fusion of the Communist Party (KPD) and the Social Democratic Party (SPD) since their interests tended to coincide. A commission was established to examine the question of unification. At this time special pressure was brought on the Women's Organization by the Communists. Only the Christian Democratic Union (CDU) was in clear opposition to the unity movement. The study committee decided to create the Socialist Unity Party (SED) with the SPD agreeing on a contingency basis. The Socialists under Schumacher held that Berlin could not speak for the whole of Germany. This stand led to a dispute in the Kommandatura, and eventually the SPD and the SED were recognized inside Berlin. The SPD was not absorbed by the Communists, however, and the Soviet domination of the prospective election was thwarted.[10]

By October, 1946, the issues became clear. Partly as the result of various highhanded Soviet actions, the electorate saw the nature of the cold war contest. On October 20, the SED received less than 20 per cent of the votes, the SPD and the CDU, now known as the "Western" parties, gained a large majority in a new anti-Soviet alliance. Thus the rank and file rejected the agreement of some of

---

10. Philip Windsor, *City on Leave: A History of Berlin, 1945–1962* (London: Chatto & Windus, 1963), p. 131.

Historical Perspective on the Island City

the top officials for a merger. A turning point in Berlin's democratic reconstruction was passed.

It was evident then for the first time that the citizens would never choose Communism of their own free will. The moderate Socialist party, the SPD, predominated in the city's politics. The elected and appointed officials carried out their functions with increasing firmness of purpose. The persistence of the Western Allies and the prospects of reconstruction made the Communists fear that they would face a strong and united Germany, so they turned shortly to more drastic measures. These measures were intended to offset the Marshall Plan, already gaining momentum. In 1948, after sporadic harassment of traffic, they blockaded land access to Berlin. This toughening of policy came only a few weeks after the Communist takeover in Czechoslovakia in February, 1948.

The attempt to drive the Western Powers out of the city made real the serious weakness of the position of the city, that until then had been regarded as a relatively unimportant characteristic of its geographic position. These were the vulnerable corridors of access and the almost limitless possibilities of recurrent harassment.[11] It was no mere coincidence that Soviet rejection of American aid, the takeover of Czechoslovakia, and the hardening of policy in Hungary were timed with the action in Germany. Thus the Truman Doctrine of March, 1947, and the prospective reconstruction of Europe under the Marshall Plan had almost certainly convinced the leaders in the Kremlin of the need to consolidate their position and hold the East Zone as their sphere of control even if it meant considerable diplomatic and financial cost. It was not until later that the Warsaw Pact was signed.

Those who now condemn the inadequacy of American plans made in the early forties are for the most part overlooking this sequence of events and demanding retroactively a vision that would have penetrated the future—a foresight impossible for those living

---

11. The Yalta Agreements and the permitting of the Soviet Armies to take Berlin have been discussed at length. For example, see Robert Murphy, *Diplomat Among Warriors* (Garden City, N.Y.: Doubleday, 1964), pp. 226–44; Clay, *Decision in Germany*, pp. 51–53. See *supra*, p. 29, n. 5.

under the anxieties and tensions of war and the uncertainties of the pre-atomic age.

The end of four-power meetings, when the Soviet Commandant walked out of the Kommandatura in June, 1948, reduced the possibility of joint action and of continuing contacts. There remained the missions in Potsdam, just outside of Berlin, the Berlin Air Safety Center (BASC), and Spandau Prison where four war criminals were held. These continuing points of contact were not of use in dealing with policy matters.

The blockade marked a new phase not only in the Western responsibility to defend Berlin but also in the measures for the larger scope of internal German government in the Western zones of occupation. It hastened the attainment of sovereignty by the Federal Republic and led to a new attitude toward the administration of Berlin. In a few weeks, there were in effect two governments in the city. Ernst Reuter and Otto Suhr, given more leeway, took steps to consolidate the city government of West Berlin. These two officials, Ferdinand Friedensburg, and others continued to cross into the Soviet sector in an effort to demonstrate the Western insistence on the continued unity of the city, but the Communists set up the new *Magistrat*. They named Friedrich Ebert as "Oberbürgermeister of Greater Berlin."

In the West, the constitution of 1946 was amended, making West Berlin in the eyes of most Germans a *Land* of the German Federal Republic.

The stand of the Berliners with fortitude and courage has been a brilliant chapter of postwar Berlin's history. The details could fill volumes. The success of the Allies in 1949 was the failure of the Communists.

The New Nation, 1949–1954

On May 4, 1949, following the Jessup-Malik [12] talks of April 26, the Blockade was lifted. The Sixth Session of the Council of Foreign Ministers, meeting in Paris, decided to "continue their efforts to achieve the restoration of the economic and political unity of Germany . . . consult together in Berlin on a quadripartite basis."

---

12. Philip Jessup was United States delegate to the United Nations. Jacob Malik was his Soviet counterpart.

Historical Perspective on the Island City

The declared purposes included: (a) the expansion of trade, (b) facilitation of movement of persons and foods, and (c) administration of the four sectors "with a view to normalization as far as possible of the life of the city."

In spite of this four-power declaration, Communist harassment continued. The measures to strengthen the democratic position of the Federal Republic of Germany to increase its economic strength, and before long provide for rearming the FRG, were spurred on by this attitude of the USSR.

On May 8, 1949, the Basic Law was adopted by the Federal Republic of West Germany. On June 15, the electoral law for West Germany provided for eight non-voting delegates from Berlin in the Bundestag.

On May 14, 1949, the French, British, and Americans issued a "statement of Principles Governing the Relationship between the Allied Kommandatura and Greater Berlin." It indicated that they had granted wide legislative, executive, and judicial powers to the Federal Republic which would be "shortly established." They stated that they would not agree, at this time, that Berlin should be a *Land* . . . and reserved those powers necessary to ensure the good order and the financial and economic stability of the city.

On August 14 the first postwar elections were held in the Federal Republic. Konrad Adenauer was chosen as Chancellor with the support of the Western Allies. The new constitution of Berlin went into effect on October 1, 1950. The elections in the Western sectors, then separated from East Berlin, do not coincide in time with those in the FRG.

In the reformation of the political life and administrative development of the Federal Republic from 1949 to 1953, the German leaders were not in a position to do much about Berlin. Economic reconstruction and the place Germany would occupy in the Western Alliance was of prime importance to Adenauer and his associates. The European Defense Community (EDC) with German troops was a likely prospect from 1952 to 1954. Moreover, the city, unlike the FRG, was still occupied by Allied troops and under Western guarantee.[13]

13. "The security and welfare of Berlin and the maintenance of the position of the three powers there are regarded by the three powers as essential elements of the peace

Only gradually, as time moved on, did the full complexity of the postwar occupation emerge. After the new approach was adopted in 1946, it became apparent that even though the city was under protection, its status was not satisfactory. It was often referred to as "Land Berlin" and is held by the Germans to be a part of the Federal Republic, but the legal provisions for the city are not such as to create a typical structure of municipal or national rights and responsibilities. Even now, the status of the city is viewed in different ways by different authorities.

A brief statement of the situation has been outlined by one of the American legal authorities, Joachim von Elbe (in a personal letter), as follows:

The term "Land Berlin" signifies that Berlin has the status of a "Land" as distinguished from the status of a "municipality," or a "district," or a "province." Under German public law, a "Land" is a political entity which is not subject to supervision by another public authority.

Even though Berlin may be called a "Land" it does not follow that Berlin is a "Land of the Federal Republic," i.e. that it forms part of the Federal system as do the other German Laender (for instance cities like Hamburg and Bremen). In its decision of May 21, 1957, the Federal Constitutional Court declared that Berlin is a Land of Federal Republic. The Court added, however, that this is not the position of the three Allied Powers.

The position of the three Allied Powers that Berlin is not a Land of the Federal Republic is based on a reservation in the Letter of Approval of the Basic Law by the Military Governors of May 12, 1949. (The reservation, incidentally, was specifically maintained upon the signature of the so-called Bonn Conventions whereby the Federal Republic achieved sovereignty). The reservation concerned "the participation of Greater Berlin in the Federation." It says in essence that Berlin may not be accorded voting membership in the Federal Parliament (Bundestag and Bundesrat), and that Berlin may not be "governed by the Federation." Berlin, nevertheless, may designate a small number of representatives to attend the meetings of these legislative bodies. The Kommanda-

---

of the free world in the present international situation." This commitment was originally formulated in the tripartite declaration of Paris, May 27, 1952, and reiterated in 1954 in the Berlin Conference of Foreign Ministers. *Documents on Germany 1944–1961*, pp. 134, 155.

tura, without the Soviets, by letter of August 29, 1950 with respect to the Berlin Constitution, declared that during the transitional period envisaged in Article 87 of the Berlin Constitution (i.e., when the application of the Basic Law in Berlin is subject to restrictions) Berlin "shall possess none of the attributes of a twelfth Land."

Professor Plischke has also explored this question at some length in the *Journal of Politics*.[14]

The salient point is that the city is not only isolated geographically, as it lies 110 miles away from the Federal Republic, but it is also legally and politically apart. It still pays over 300 million DM in annual occupation costs, more than two-thirds to the Western Allies—and the rest to the Germans for support costs—and is subject to restrictions and controls with respect to measures of law and order, police, and various governmental activities. The restrictions are well adapted to changing conditions and are easily accepted by the Berliners, who are only generally aware of the limitations. Berlin's local political life is active, and its economy has not suffered even though the legal and political situation is unusual.

The limitations applied by the Western Powers to Berlin when the Federal Republic became sovereign demonstrate the peculiar legal situation that still prevails in the city. These required that a *Mantelgesetz* (covering law) be passed by the Berlin legislative assembly in order to make Federal Republic laws applicable in Berlin. Similar action was necessary to specify the manner in which treaty obligations entered into by the Bonn government affect Berlin. Thus Berlin has been brought under "the atoms for peace agreement," and the advantages and responsibilities deriving from German membership in the European Economic Community have been extended to it. A clear distinction between the Federal Republic and Berlin, imposed by the Western Allies, prevents the city from participating in rearming or producing arms and excludes Berlin residents from the West German army. Furthermore, no military personnel of the army of the Federal Republic may appear

14. For discussion of the legal status of Berlin, see Elmer Plischke, "Integrating Berlin and the Federal Republic," *The Journal of Politics* (February 1965), pp. 38–43; Heinz Kreutzer, "West Berlin: City and State," in Robson, *Berlin: Pivot of German Destiny*, pp. 67–99; and Charles B. Robson and Werner Zohlnhöfer, "Berlinproblem und 'Deutsche Frage' . . . Ein Literaturbericht" in *Jahrbuch für die Geschichte Mittel-und Ostdeutschlands* (Berlin: Walter de Gruyter, 1962).

in Berlin. Thus the relation of NATO is in a way one-sided in that the North Atlantic Treaty Organization extends its shield to Berlin, but neither the city nor its citizens are allowed to contribute in any way to its military potential.

All of these and other provisions merit consideration by those interested in the legal side of the situation, but the net effect, for the general reader, is that the city's relations with the Federal Republic were covered by various arrangements clearly spelled out, while the Federal Republic guaranteed aid and support of a significant nature.

Some leaders in West Berlin continued to press for *Land* status, and even for making the city the capital of the Federal Republic. They were not always aware of the fact that the continued Western occupation of the city and the assertion of the rights growing out of the surrender were the main bulwark against absorption by the Communists. If without a treaty this judicial chain of relations were to be abandoned, not only would the city be lost to the Communists but the division of Germany would become an uncontested fact.

During the months following the ending of the Blockade in mid-1949, there were, as before, frequent probes to test the firmness of the West and also the determination of the Berliners. Travel was limited rather than eased, as action was taken which contravened the Paris Agreements. On July 1, most of the crossing points between East and West were closed, limiting traffic to one autobahn. In 1950 there was a period of several weeks during which Soviet processing slowed down the military movements on the Helmstedt autobahn. In September barge traffic to West Berlin was interrupted, to be resumed in October after retaliation by the British, who held barges destined for the Zone. There was also an occasional threat to planes in the corridors.

The new constitution for Berlin went into effect on October 1, 1950. Later, in January, 1952, the number of delegates to the Bundestag was increased from eight to nineteen (it was later increased to twenty-two). Berlin also had delegates in the Bundesrat. At the same time, West Berlin was incorporated economically into the Federal Republic. The subsidies from the Federal treasury from these early days to the present have been essential to the remarkable economic development of the city.[15] It is not always recognized that American policy was consistently to bring pressure on Bonn to grant as much support and autonomy to the city of Berlin as was possible without weakening the occupation status.

The death of Reuter and the death of Stalin in 1953 marked a new stage of East-West relations in Berlin. The position of the city in the complex of German internal and external relations was set for the next decade. The failure of Stalin's policy to frighten, infiltrate, and starve the city—at the same time wearing down the patience of the West—became widely recognized. From then until the Wall, political conditions changed little, and the economy expanded without interruption.

The increasing unrest in the East Zone, marked by the large-scale exodus of refugees, exploded in violence in June, 1953. The bold attempt of the spontaneous revolt to improve conditions, and even to throw off the Communist regime, ended in failure. The Allies could not and would not support a rebellion with armed force, plunging Europe into war with the USSR. Many heroic youths were imprisoned and some killed. The result was only a slight improvement in working conditions in late 1953.

Political Stalemate, 1954–1958

The Berlin Conference of the Big Four Foreign Ministers in January, 1954, met to consider the broad problems of Germany in Europe. The discussion was interesting, but progress was nil. This meeting and the Geneva Conference of 1955 had little effect on the conditions in the city, in spite of the communiqué in 1955 reasserting the determination of the four occupying powers to reunite Germany after free elections. The moment of optimism, coming with the Soviet agreement to a State treaty for Austria in May, was not followed by any notable improvement of the status of Berlin. Meanwhile, arrangements for Germany's part in NATO had been effectuated on October 23, when the Paris protocol provided for the end of occupation which came into effect on May 5, 1955. Shortly thereafter, the Soviet Union accorded what it termed full

---

15. Wolfram Pohl, in an article "Berlin die teure Stadt," *Die Zeit*, April 26, 1966, gives estimates of the net subsidies since 1951 as 38.8 billion DM. The value of the deutsche mark (DM) is approximately $0.25.

"sovereignty" to East Germany, but they held their twenty-two divisions in the Zone in battle readiness.

The revolt in Hungary in 1956 shook Berlin as few events since the June 17 uprising. There were demonstrations that threatened to get out of hand but which were held in check by officials. The question of reunification seemed to be linked in Soviet strategy with plans for a neutralization of Central Europe along lines of the proposal of Rapacki, the Polish Foreign Minister. Such a solution was unacceptable to the West in view of the continuing aggressive actions of the USSR.[16] The United States had been forced to oppose Communist threats in many areas—Guatemala, Formosa, and the Middle East, as well as in Europe. The Soviets launched their Sputnik in October, 1957. There was talk in America of the missile gap. The emphasis in the Western alliance was on more strength rather than the weakening of Germany, and Berlin was recognized as a pivotal issue by NATO countries at their various meetings.

The most serious threat to Berlin since the Blockade came in November, 1958. Nikita Khrushchev issued his ultimatum in a bold attempt to force the Western Powers from the city. His plan was faintly disguised by talk of a "free city" and of the United Nations as a protector of the new status. The Berliners' reaction, after a few brief hours of panic, was defiant as they heard the immediate rejection of the proposal by Washington. The first rush to withdraw savings from the banks was reversed, and the elections of December 7 turned in a smashing rebuff to the Communists, whose party was legitimate but who polled less than an insignificant 2 per cent in spite of militant efforts to gain votes.[17]

In Washington and in the Paris meeting of NATO, Secretary Dulles hammered home the determination to hold the line, and in early 1959 he made his last visit to Europe. He knew that his speculative statements about methods of reunification and the possible acceptance of East Germans as agents of the Soviets had

16. The Warsaw Pact including satellites, but excluding the Soviet Zone, was signed in May, 1955, after the occupation of the Federal Republic officially ended. Even without the cold war the neutralization of Germany would be, in the minds of most politicians, unwise.

17. The SED-Communist unity party is legal in Berlin, but the Communist party KPD is not legal in the Federal Republic.

troubled leaders in Bonn and Berlin. He also thought it essential to demonstrate the continued unity of the Allies in their firm position in defense of Berlin. He found no rift in views among the other occupying powers.

It was on his return to Washington on February 11 that he had his last interviews in his office. The doctors had told him at noon that he must enter Walter Reed hospital at once. The two interviews were with the Socialist leader of Austria, Bruno Pitterman, and the Governing Mayor of Berlin, Willy Brandt. I sat in on the conference with Brandt in my capacity as "Berlin Desk Officer." Brandt and Foster sat on the leather couch opposite the portraits of my grandfather, John W. Foster, and my uncle, Robert Lansing, previous Secretaries of State. They talked of problems of access and the possibilities of invoking counter-measures to impress the Soviets. Perhaps it would be possible to restrict their trade, they queried, using economic measures to end the pressure on Berlin. Foster asked about the morale of Berlin, and Brandt assured him it was high and would not weaken.[18]

The death of the Secretary came during the Foreign Ministers Conference on Berlin and Germany which met in Geneva on May 11, 1959. The meeting adjourned abruptly to permit the ministers to attend the funeral in Washington on May 27. It resumed a few weeks later. The results were equivocal in that the Soviets may have thought our position was weakened, whereas the United States insisted there were no compromises.

The East Germans sat in the room with the conferees, as did delegates from Bonn. This, some regarded as a major Western concession. The general verdict is that the Western Powers were fortunate in that Soviet representative Andrei Gromyko rejected their proposals, which would have made the situation more precarious. The German leaders had been extremely nervous during these negotiations since the prospect of compromise loomed over the deliberations. The American position was saved for the West in part by the Soviet position because of Khrushchev's desire to visit the United States.

The Soviet leader's growing concern with world problems was

18. Eleanor Lansing Dulles, *John Foster Dulles: The Last Year* (New York: Harcourt, Brace and World, 1963), p. 227.

expressed in his talks with President Eisenhower at Camp David in September, 1959, and in his visit to the United Nations. The Berlin problem was pushed aside, temporarily, because of these wider preoccupations. In spite of rumors about the spirit of Camp David which have established certain myths, the records show that Eisenhower made no concesssions and that no change in position resulted on either side. Nevertheless, press stories gave ground for a conclusion that there was a relaxation of tension.

During these years, from 1949–1960, the political life in West Berlin was characterized by the vitality of its citizens, who were constantly aware of the threat of their security and freedom. Ernst Reuter was the outstanding figure of the postwar years. Immediately after the war, the SPD, which he headed in Berlin, emerged as the strongest element. After October, 1946, when its membership rejected the merger with the KPD, which formed the SED, there was no question as to the political orientation of the majority in the city.

The SPD held the position of governing Mayor, Regierender Bürgermeister, throughout the period, with the exception of the time between Reuter's death in September, 1953, and the installation of Otto Suhr after the elections of December 5, 1954, when Walter Schreiber of the CDU was in office as governing Mayor. During most of the postwar years, the SPD, although the dominant party, formed coalition governments with the CDU and in most instances FDP leaders were also included in the Senate, which in Berlin is in effect the executive cabinet or ministry. Thus there was no formal opposition in the Berlin House of Representatives but rather wholehearted co-operation among leaders of the three parties which, in every election held in the city, received more than 95 per cent of the votes cast. The SED was and remains a legal party in West Berlin (as well as in East Berlin and the Zone, where it is dominant), but it has never succeeded in winning as much as 3 per cent of the votes cast in any election. The co-operation of the major parties in West Berlin, like the restraint of the trade unions, was possible because of the general recognition of the common danger that called for a united position on all issues of importance. Within these limits, however, city elections were in every instance hotly contested among the major parties, and voter participation averaged more than 90 per cent of the eligible voters.

Historical Perspective on the Island City [45]

Reuter, as SPD leader in Berlin, was always supported fully by Kurt Schumacher, the Socialist leader in the Federal Republic. He worked with Adenauer on some if not all of the essentials of the reconstruction of political life. Bonn's official political concern for the German capital fluctuated over the years. The lack of manifest concern in the early fifties raised the question in the minds of some as to a possible conflict between Germany's membership in NATO and reunification. But, as time went on, there has been little discussion of this question. The subsidies of the Federal Republic to West Berlin's budget increased, and they now constitute an essential element in the financing of its programs. This is accepted in spite of the fact that Berlin's government is still dominated by the party (SPD) which is in opposition in Bonn, and in spite of the fact that in the last two elections in the Federal Republic (1961 and 1965), the governing Major of Berlin has been the SPD candidate for the Chancellorship. The Federal Republic's financial contributions to Berlin have averaged more than a half billion dollars annually in recent years.

The Bundestag met in the city from time to time in a symbolic gesture to Berlin, the capital of a reunited Germany. The most recent session was in the Spring of 1965. In the Bundeshaus of the Federal Republic in Berlin, a visible sign of federal representatives from Bonn, officials conduct business of mutual interest to the FRG and Berlin. Now the concern for reunification is in the forefront of political issues.

The New Society

After the Geneva Conference of Foreign Ministers in 1959, there was no major crisis again until 1961. The minor episodes in which the West came off moderately well in showing their will to hold to their rights, even though some were eroded as procedures, were modified and negotiated in small ways that seemed of little consequence to the outside world. In any case, nothing that happened in these years seriously interrupted the impressive economic progress.

The new city of 1966 could only have been created by new men. Democracy has its heroes in every land. In Berlin, the names of Ernst Reuter, the dynamic, dramatic Mayor, hated by the Communists because he had once been one of them and had later revolted against their tyrannical methods, is likely to stand at the head of the list as historians honor the courage of the citizens. He died of an exhausted heart, like many of his fellows, as the pressures of work and recurrent crises increased in the stirring weeks of 1953. Louisa Schroeder, frail, indomitable, the first to act as Mayor of the city, and the only woman, was tireless in her opposition to Soviet encroachment on Berlin's rights. Such men as Otto Suhr, Ferdinand Friedensburg, Paul Hertz, Otto Busack, Jacob Kaiser, Joachim Lipschitz, Günther Klein, and many others stand high on the roll of honor. Men who with their comrades defied the Communists and deliberately chose the side of democracy during the Blockade, risked privation, kidnapping, and assassination while they spent their strength and their short years to preserve essential freedoms. These are men now dead. The living carry on in the same tradition. There are still notable figures fighting for the freedom of Berlin—Brandt and Erler, Albertz, Amrehn, Lemmer, Gradl, Bahr, and hosts of others of various political persuasions, but all standing firm for the spirit of the new Berlin. How deep their faith in a rebirth of democracy is can only be appreciated by those who worked with them. There are others whose names could be mentioned, and there are still other hundreds of thousands of nameless fighters for the new Berlin with a will for democracy and a new philosophy. They have worked in the expanding factories, poured cement for the new roads and buildings, designed the garments, run the utilities, sheltered the refugees, and expressed their defiance of Communist pressures both in serious demonstrations and in gay festivals and sports, above all showing a determination to live life to the full in spite of stress and danger.

III. THE WALL

"The Wall," according to Baedeker, "consists partly of a concrete barrier 3 feet thick and partly of barbed wire entanglements, prefaced by a 'death strip' 10 metres wide and a closed zone of 100 metres. The houses situated immediately on the boundary were demolished or had their windows bricked up. No fewer than 55 streets connecting the two divisions of Berlin have been blocked, besides 129 roads formerly connecting West Berlin with the East Zone."

Troops, variously estimated, but probably 30,000 in number, man 193 watch towers, 208 bunkers, and other reinforced positions. The patrols on the sector border are always in pairs to lessen the likelihood of their own escapes, and they have orders to shoot unauthorized persons at sight. It is estimated that the wall within the city is more than twenty-eight miles long, and the barrier surrounding the Western sectors of Berlin is more than seventy miles long. At most places the wall is between nine and twelve feet high. At the wider crossing points there are staggered concrete implacements to prevent a car or truck from gaining momentum to crash the wall and permit a precarious attempt to escape.

The one main crossing point where tourists from abroad enter the prison state is Checkpoint Charlie on the Friedrichstrasse.[1] Here, in relative safety and for various purposes, several hundred curious or anxious persons are processed every day, buying their East marks for Ulbricht's profit and passing silently into the gray and almost empty streets. This is the new concentration camp of

---

1. It is near here that the U-Bahn crosses the line and where another checkpoint has been established.

the Communist dictators. Along the "green border" from the Baltic to Hof at the junction of the American Zone and Czechoslovakia, the land is mined.[2]

The building of the Wall could probably have been prevented in August, 1961, but only at grave risk. Walter Ulbricht had visited Moscow in the first days of August. He is believed to have urged that his economic system would collapse if the flow of refugees continued. It was thought afterwards that Nikita Khrushchev had given him full permission to build the Wall. The movement of Soviet troops and tanks toward Berlin in the week before the final step was taken indicates the serious intention on the part of the Communists. So does the declaration of the Warsaw Pact countries, on August 11, which was broadcast on the thirteenth, indicating their support of measures to assure Ulbricht an effective control of "all Berlin." The accumulation of barbed wire and concrete posts was so substantial as to permit quick Communist action.

In June, Ulbricht had said, in response to a reporter's question, that "no one would build a wall."[3] The month of July was characterized by the brutal propaganda and the tentative efforts to restrict movement. This only led to a rising tide of refugees. Then, in midsummer, Senator William Fulbright in a television interview on July 30 stated that he felt Ulbricht would be perfectly justified in sealing the sector boundary.[4] Because of the importance of his position, this declaration was held, in some quarters, to represent a considered Administration opinion. The effect of this interview shocked many of his hearers in the United States and in Germany. It may have been conclusive in Communist circles. Marshal Ivan Konev, touring the Zone and cognizant of coming events, assured the Western Allies that "their rights (meaning those of the occupying powers, not the Germans) would be respected."[5]

Putting all these signs together, it seems apparent that the lead-

---

2. I was told that the dead zone around Berlin and the Wall is not mined.
3. Pierre Galante, *The Berlin Wall* (Garden City, N.Y.: Doubleday, 1965), p. 9.
4. *The New York Times*, August 3, 1961; Jean Edward Smith, *The Defense of Berlin* (Baltimore: The Johns Hopkins Press, 1963), p. 259.
5. Professor Kurt L. Shell in his book *Bedrohung und Bewährung, Führung und Bevölkerung . . . in der Berlin-Krise* (Westdeutscher Verlag, Köln und Opladen, 1965), has made an intensive and useful study of the building of the Wall and its effects. His work is used here at many points. Reference is made particularly to pages 27–52 and 353–78.

ers in the Kremlin believed they could enforce this move without danger of war. At this time, the Foreign Ministers in Paris, including America's Dean Rusk, had considered the brutal statements and, mindful of the demand of Nikita Khrushchev for a separate peace treaty, had issued a communiqué. Probably for the first time in a formal statement they spoke of the defense of *West* Berlin. The classical wording of the Foreign Ministers' statement, which had been reiterated in 1952 and 1954, had given protection to Berlin—without distinction of the division of the city. This change of wording was noted undoubtedly not only in Germany but also in the Kremlin.

In spite of all the tension and the signs which were visible but which did not seem conclusive at the time, the German newspapers did not in fact forecast the coming events. As Kurt Shell says, "In no West Berlin newspaper was the possibility of a total control and eventual [counter]measures seriously discussed. . . . No one believed that the regime would go as far as to take the measures for a complete sealing off [of the Western sectors]." [6] The prevailing wishful thinking was based on assumptions that Ulbricht recognized the significance of a channel for escape which served to lessen the danger of a serious uprising as the more rebellious of his people fled to the West. It was also related to the credibility of the Allied guarantees, and to the assumed wish of Pankow to avoid the actions which might be considered provocative.

There had been a testing of Allied opinion as early as June and an exploration of less comprehensive ways of halting the refugee flow—but, by the first week in August, the lines to further action were almost certainly established. Khrushchev concluded that he should support Ulbricht's will and confront the West with a fact which would undoubtedly stir their ire—but still would be short of a cause of war.

The days of opportunity to deter this action were almost certainly in July, and the period of acute danger was in August. Only a reliable intelligence report quickly transmitted and correctly evaluated to indicate a complete closing of the border could have brought the Allies together in time for convincing and concerted action. Such "hard" intelligence was lacking even up to the zero

6. *Ibid.*, p. 30.

hour. The officials say that the exercise of patching together, weeks later, scattered items of rumors and information, does not give a reliable picture of how policy could have been developed. In July, 1961, the type of report which could have been the basis of Allied use of force in Berlin or for counter-measures elsewhere was not available. The substance of the Khrushchev-Ulbricht conference in Moscow was not revealed; the plan for the wall was a well-kept secret.

It is unlikely that the Germans who criticized the failure to act will ever be convinced that the coming events were at the time obscure. Those who have suffered directly are understandably bitter. There had been too many statements by Senators Fulbright, Mansfield, Morse, and others to make the American failure to act easily acceptable to the Germans. There had been disappointed comments on President Kennedy's July speech which, though sounding firm, promised *local reaction* and did not imply that the United States would consider illegal encroachment on Berlin as grounds for reaction elsewhere at selected points or on a world-wide basis or for the use of a nuclear deterrence in the final crisis.[7]

The widespread opinion in Berlin is still that, as Shell says, "The United States through weakness and uncertainty had allowed itself to be pushed back by Communism." The seeds for a growing distrust of Washington were sown in late July and early August.

Nevertheless, the feeling of panic in West Berlin, which came with the first conclusion that the Allies had been weak, gradually diminished in the months after the Wall went up. It is remarkable that there was no change in any of the economic indices for the second and third quarters of 1961. The token gestures and several measures, including the increasing of the British and American garrisons and refusal of the United States to sign an agreement for a direct Soviet-American airflight to New York, combined with measures aimed at increasing investment in West Berlin, led to a

---

7. See Eleanor Lansing Dulles and Robert Dickson Crane (eds.), *Détente: Cold War Strategies in Transition* (New York: Praeger, 1965), pp. 130–35; Dieter Hildebrandt, *Die Mauer ist Keine Grenze* (Düsseldorf: Eugene Diederichs Verlag, 1964), pp. 35–46; John Mander, *Berlin Unterpfand der Freiheit* (Frankfurt am Main: Athenaum, 1962); Wolfgang Paul, *Kampf um Berlin* (Munich: Langen-Muller, 1962), pp. 285–89; Jean Smith, *The Defense of Berlin*, for comment on Ulbricht's speech of June 15, p. 239; "Reflections on the Quarter," *Orbis* (Summer, 1961), p. 128.

surprisingly rapid restoration of confidence.[8] The much feared mass exodus from the city did not take place. The critical phase lasted only a few weeks.

The nine weeks between the Vienna conversations between Kennedy and Khrushchev of June first through the fourth, and the building of the Wall, had been disturbed and full of fear. It was inevitable that the dwellers in the East Zone should have thought that now, at last, there would be some kind of weakening of the Western position—that there would be some irreversible happening to shut them off from the free world. In these weeks there was a refugee flow of such large proportions that it threatened depopulation and the possible repeopling of the Zone with workers from Russia or the far east provinces. Walter Ulbricht was not the only one concerned. It was Ulbricht, however, who saw his economy in dire straits. He could not run his factories at normal levels, and the agricultural situation was deteriorating. The basic strength of the regime, built on technical skill, costly investment of resources, and German will-to-work was tottering.

As long as the flight continued, Ulbricht could not stabilize his labor force. There was always the chance to flee from exorbitant demands. The inducement to secure efficient work had to be increased continually to compete with the richer opportunities in the West. The men in the factories and mines were looking to the Federal Republic, excited by the prospects of seeking work in the West. Families considered their adjustment to local requirements to be temporary; there was little sense of permanence. Their "reunification" with relatives in the West was personal, not territorial or national, but the chance was always before them. They were not condemned to acceptance of Ulbricht.

After the Wall a degree of adaptation became inevitable, and, for this reason, we conclude that it was a success for Communism in spite of the damage to the reputation of the Ulbricht regime abroad.[9] There was a time when the Communist world would have liked to have created an attractive image in noncommitted countries, but they took the risk of condemnation. To some extent the

---

8. "Investing in West Berlin: A Special Report," *Foreign Commerce Weekly*, U.S. Department of Commerce, May 28, 1962, pp. 949, 992.

9. The long-range effect is likely to prove a defeat because of the demonstration of the Communist need to hold in their people by force.

gamble has been successful. For every ten visitors from Asia and Africa who have seen the Wall in Berlin, there have been hundreds of others who have looked on the growing production of the factories of the East Zone and who have seen that the material conditions were improving with more adequate food and equipment. Although the free world was at first outraged by the brutality of the cement barrier and barbed wire, the Wall has gradually become a kind of sadistic attraction for those who are themselves not confined. The drama of escape and the cruelty of the Volkspolizei leads to a morbid interest. The sympathy, which was real, has become somewhat dulled by the repetition of the stories. For, although many incidents reveal the repression and inhumanity, one cannot fully appreciate them except as they are made sharp and vivid in the intensity of personal experience. The pain diminishes as the months pass.

These conflicting aspects of the situation had not been unpredicted. For eight or ten years the students of East-West relations had speculated: Would the regime try to close the loophole that permitted thousands of its workers to pour into Berlin and settle in the West? Would Ulbricht risk the drastic measures needed to wall in his people? The possibility of sealing off the "workers' paradise" from the free world existed, but was recognized to be a difficult and costly endeavor. The houses in Berlin which bordered the demarcation line were many, and the cellars and sewers that straddled the border offered possibilities of passing back and forth even without the building of tunnels.

In 1953—when the June uprising led to the influx of Russian tanks, which were deployed along the sector border, and to the barring of the street crossings with armed soldiers, machine guns, and barbed wire—many hundreds swam the canals, jumped from roof tops, and stormed the barriers. They feared further obstructions that would make escape increasingly difficult.

At this time, temporary barriers failed to keep out escaping East Germans.[10] I talked to them at the Marienfelde reception center. They said that the crossing was difficult but that it could be done.

10. Rainer Hildebrandt, *Als die Fesseln fielen* . . . (Berlin: Arani Verlags GMBH, 1960).

In fact, the obstructions were taken down in a few days. At this time there was considerable talk of the possibility of sealing off West Berlin. It was discussed pro and con, and the consensus was that such an attempt would be difficult.

The cutting of the city in two at this time is interesting because of parallels and contrasts with the action in 1961. The earlier blocking of crossing points followed the outward flow of refugees and a time of speculation and unrest. In 1953, policy was considered uncertain after Stalin's death. In 1961, there had been a change of administration in the United States with questions as to new attitudes. In the later period, there are notable differences in conditions and motives related mainly to the expanding industry in the East Zone and in the even more serious loss of man power limiting a growing productive complex. In recognition of this economic situation in 1961, there was a general conviction that the determination to seal off West Berlin was a firmly developed Communist policy. In 1953, however, events were precipitated by the workers, and the regime in Pankow as well as leaders in the Kremlin were caught off guard. The response was improvised, whereas the later action had almost certainly been planned for several weeks. The frail strands of wire and wooden booms manned by soldiers in August 13 and 14, with only a few cement and stone obstructions, could have been breached. There were even a few crossing points open, but the separation probably could not have been thwarted except in terms of a major contest between the United States and the USSR.

As the successors to Stalin gained power after 1953 in the Soviet Union, the idea of Soviet economic strength began to take shape, along with the victories of the Soviets in both the atomic field and in space. The launching of Sputnik in 1957 changed the attitude of the Kremlin toward West Berlin. There is little doubt that the enhanced prestige of the Communists, whose economic and scientific achievements made them bolder, affected the situation in various ways. The Soviets were less afraid of reprisals for harassment of the city, and they perhaps felt that they even could afford the hostile reaction which came from their pressure on the people, to the point of building a "prison wall." Furthermore, the economic potential of the East Zone was substantial and needed to be exploited in order to keep the satellites moving in the direction of a strong Warsaw Pact, united for defense or for aggression.

By 1961, moreover, fundamental changes had occurred in East-West relations. Successive elections in the Federal Republic and in Berlin showed the repudiation of Communism and the strength of Konrad Adenauer, Willy Brandt, and other leaders of the several parties, all clinging to the Western security alliance. There was little hope of a German withdrawal from NATO.

After the Kennedy-Khrushchev Vienna meeting in early June, some found President Kennedy's attitude uncertain and the basis for doubt. The variety of pronouncements in June and July indicated confusion. Senator Mike Mansfield as well as Senator William Fulbright had speculated about Berlin in public statements. Professor Shell emphasizes the views expressed by the Chairman of the Senate Foreign Relations Committee, Senator Fulbright, in his television interview: "The Soviets could, if they wished, close their border without breaking treaty agreements. The West has no right to prevent them. . . ."[11] Herbert Wehner, a strong figure in the SPD, and Erich Mende, leader of the FDP, immediately reaffirmed the position, which the United States had always maintained, that the Germans on both sides of the line had full rights to cross each way.[12]

As suggested above, Western intelligence had many of the pieces to suggest the possible event, but hesitated to come out clearly in predicting specific acts at a definite time and place. In July, it became known in some quarters that large amounts of barbed wire and cement posts were being sent to Berlin. One of the officers in the United States mission in Berlin became so concerned over the prospects of the closing of the exit routes that he was thought by his colleagues to have an obsession. He was soon transferred, probably because of difficult relations with his fellows on this matter.

In early August, in the households of a number of American families, servants who had relatives in the East told of hurried preparations being made because of rumors that it would soon be

---

11. Shell, *Bedrohung und Bewährung*, p. 29, quotes the Berlin *Kurier* of August 1 on Senator Fulbright's television statement of July 30.
12. *Tagesspiegel*, August 1–3, 1961. This paper is one of the main Berlin dailies.

too late. I was told of several instances by Berlin friends. The feeling of tension was increasing.

In order to appraise the advance indications that a wall would be built, I questioned many people as to the extent of the knowledge of the facts and the ability to forecast the event. The variety of answers tended to cast doubt on the view that "we did know or should have known." One of the men I talked with—the chief of Radio in American Sector (RIAS), Robert Lochner—in July gave an opinion which carries unusual weight. He said:

It has become apparent that on that fateful day in August, 1961, when first barbed wire, then concrete blocks, were placed along the dividing line between East and West Berlin, that no one in the Allied missions in West Berlin had the slightest indication of what was happening. West Germans have frequently claimed since that the Americans knew all the time. This was not the case.

The rapid rise of refugees into West Berlin in preceding weeks had indicated something unusual was likely. But the consensus is that the Americans had not been able to figure out just what the end result might be. Even RIAS, usually the most reliable weather vane to reflect daily occurrences in East Berlin, had no indications of the extraordinary happenings to come.

Secrecy was such that *Neues Deutschland*, the leading East Berlin daily paper, was even able to come out with a special two-page edition to announce the event in the early morning hours of Sunday, August 13, simultaneously with the stringing of the first barbed wire.

The regular Sunday edition of *Neues Deutschland* was prepared as usual on Saturday night. On this particular occasion, however, a few hand-picked, hardcore Communist staff members remained after the regular crew had left, and, behind locked doors, put a second two-page edition together, announcing the wall.

The Western world knew that President Kennedy had been shocked by his meeting with Khrushchev. This conversation followed what his associates referred to as his anger and disappointment over the Bay of Pigs fiasco. Some were uncertain as to what the result of the Soviet challenge would be. The shadow of atomic war for the first time seemed to be looming. Threats like those in 1958, but somewhat more complicated in form, led to American voices raised to plead for a compromise solution—a negotiation that would yield minor Allied rights in the interest of avoiding a serious confrontation with the Soviets. In retrospect, it is now possible to see the effect on public opinion of the various conflicting statements and the seeming hesitation in Washington in June and July [13]—an effect that stimulated the outward rush of refugees and the subsequent raising of the almost impassable barrier.

The number of refugees in July had equaled, and then surpassed, the totals for corresponding time periods in February and March, 1953.[14] In that year, before the death of Stalin, the increasing harshness of Communist policy and the growing tension between East and West had led to panic in the Soviet Zone. A similar wave of fear gripped the East in this later period.

Official figures for the refugee flow after the Blockade in 1948, which made the new demarcation line of vital significance for the residents of the East Zone, were astonishingly high.

TABLE 1. THE FLOW OF REFUGEES FROM THE EAST ZONE [a]
(1950–1964)

Year	Number
1950	197,788
1951	165,648
1952	182,393
1953	331,390
1954	184,198
1955	252,870
1956	279,189
1957	261,622
1958	204,092
1959	143,917
1960	199,188
1961	207,026
1962	21,356
1963	42,632
1964	41,876

a. The fifteen-year total, 2,715,185, is less than the total number of refugees including those not registered and those not "accepted" at the refugee centers in Berlin, Ülzen, and Giessen. This is estimated to be at least 3,600,000. Not all of the refugees in 1962 to 1964 came over the Wall.

Source: Press and Information Office of the Land Berlin, Berlin (Impuls Verlag, 1962).

13. During an NBC television program in September, 1965, Ray Scherer said: "John Kennedy told me once in a personal conversation not one of his advisers here in Washington or on the spot advocated knocking down the Wall." American White Paper: United States Foreign Policy, National Broadcasting Company, September 7, 1965.

14. In 1953, on a few occasions the number surpassed three thousand from Friday to Sunday.

These figures were for those thousands who registered as refugees in order to receive the special privileges and opportunities for work, housing, and social insurance which would be theirs if they became regularly employed in the Federal Republic. Additional thousands came over but for various reasons did not register at the official center. The rate at which the refugees were coming into Berlin in late July, 1961, was unprecedented. It had exceeded a thousand a day and continued in August, thus reaching the highest rate so far. The causes were many, but, as suggested above, they were related to the two-fold influences—the several threats of the Soviets and the speculation of American political leaders (particularly some of the Senate leaders) about the need for new initiatives and possible compromise.[15]

The straws in the wind had been there to see, but intelligence data was put together and evaluated only slowly. The *Tagesspiegel*, on Tuesday, August 15 (there is no Monday issue), published a major article under the headline, "The Refugees from the Zone have known—their fears have now become reality." It stated that "those in the western hemisphere who were surprised in the action separating the Soviet occupied zone from free West Berlin must have kept their ears and eyes closed in recent times. . . . The thousands and thousands of refugees revealed their conviction that Pankow would take strong steps in the near future."

Appraisal of the prospects came too late to convince the top officials of the wisdom of Western counter-measures. Professor Shell gives a clear and objective account of the events and a moderate, even-handed analysis of both the Western reaction and failure to react. The various restrictions of early August against border-crossers and others were not actively countered by the Western Allies. After their Moscow meeting of August 3 and 4, the Warsaw Pact countries issued a communiqué with regard to "establishing order" on the borders of West Berlin. The discussion of Berlin problems by the Foreign Ministers, meeting in Paris, had struck observers as inconclusive and unconvincing. The willingness to take substantial risks to prevent greater danger in months to come was not evident as a characteristic of U.S. policy in the summer of 1961.

15. Philip Windsor, *City on Leave: A History of Berlin, 1945–1962* (London: Chatto & Windus, 1963), p. 238.

The Cuba stand of October 22, 1962, if it had occurred earlier, would probably have set a new tone with regard to the flaunting of Western rights in Berlin. It was not anticipated by the Soviets in 1961. The record of speeches, official pronouncements, and newspaper comments in America and elsewhere was confusing and went beyond the limits of useful free speech. Berlin was to suffer the consequences.

First Overt Acts

The menacing acts before the Wall included the new restrictions to halt the border crossings in both directions of the 80,000 workers in Berlin; border-crossers, or *Grenzgänger*, numbering 80,000 or more, had for many years crossed daily from homes in one side of Berlin to working places in the other. At this time troops were moving in to the outskirts of Berlin. On Thursday, August 10, Vopos (East German Peoples' Police) seized the Bahnhof Potsdam. This was the station on the S-Bahn which was heavily used by refugees and visitors. In the *Tagesspiegel* issue of Friday, August 11, which reported the seizing, there was a statement to the effect that "the Zone's *Volkskammer* reported that the Pankow government had a blanket authority to undertake comprehensive measures to secure a peace treaty and to prevent the 'dealings in human beings' as the SED called the flight of the refugees." It reported that the largest number of refugees registered at the Marienfelde receiving center in one day was 1,532, for that Friday. It also reported the decline of the value of the East mark. The Berlin government called a meeting led by the late Senator Lipschitz to consider this complex of problems.

Mayor Willy Brandt, who was on a campaign tour in West Germany for the election of the new Bundestag as the SPD candidate for chancellor, said the *Volkskammer* announcement put heavy responsibilities on the Soviet Union for the violation of existing agreements. Franz Amrehn, assistant Mayor of Berlin, spoke of the "naked terror" in the Zone that was causing the mass flight. Pankow authorities complained about the border-crossers and the number of refugees. In the next twenty-four hours, Friday and into Saturday, the numbers climbed to 2,400. The tension led to official pleas to remain calm in face of impending crisis.

The Critical Hour

The first specific report of the events to come was officially available from the crossing point at Duppel-Kleinmachow after five o'clock in the afternoon when a resident of the Soviet Zone confidentially told a friend that the entrance point would be closed on the night of August 12. A customs official relayed this information to the border police and said definitely that wooden barriers and booms would be placed at various points by the soldiers assigned to prevent transit. Later that evening a Pan Am night flight from Munich sighted troop concentrations moving on the border of East Berlin.[16] At 12:25, a customs official at Bernauer Strasse telephoned his Western headquarters a frantic message. By 12:30 a long line of trucks were parked with headlights blazing on the east side of Bernauer Strasse. At 12:37 both AP and UPI sent out a flash, "Vopos are unrolling barbed wire along the whole length of the frontier between East and West Berlin." By one o'clock the East Zone Press Agency had declared that the border was closed. Armored cars were stationed outside the Soviet Embassy —the alert against uprisings was far-reaching and the preparation carried to an effective completion. Thus the long, irregular 28-mile long line was manned with troops and barred by a variety of obstructions, wire, wood, and cement obstacles to cut the city in two. The troops were given the task of tightening the ring around Berlin.

The dreaded separation had taken place in the early morning while the guardians of Berlin's safety were asleep.

In East and West Berlin there had been dance music during the warm summer night. The Kudamm was crowded. The American soldiers were having a party. The American Minister in Dahlem was at home early. It was said that an early morning telephone call failed to wake him. The occupying forces apparently did not expect trouble. Willy Brandt was returning from Kiel; the Chancellor was on the train, after a vacation in Caddenabia. Macmillan was in Scotland for hunting, President Kennedy was vacationing at Hyannisport.

At three o'clock the music on the East German radio was inter-

16. Galante, *The Berlin Wall*, especially pp. 31–42.

rupted—a woman's voice announced that the border was closed. At 3:05 the West German police substation Berta announced large movements of Soviet troops and tanks on the road between Berlin and Hamburg. At 3:10 the Tiergarten police station reported that columns of workers between the Brandenburg Gate and Potsdamer Platz were tearing up the cobblestones and the streetcar tracks. By 3:27 reports from the region of Bernauer Strasse indicated that the Vopos were unrolling barbed wire and all the street crossings between the sectors were being closed off.[17] Armed soldiers and Vopos were standing guard while the work progressed. The German officials in Berlin and Bonn were alerted by four o'clock. There is no sign that the occupying troops were on special alert until morning.

On August 13, a hot Sunday morning, the city awoke slowly to the startling events of the previous night. By nine o'clock the people were beginning to stir. Mayor Brandt, informed of the crisis, boarded a British European Airways plane in Hanover. He had already written a statement as he flew into the city. Crowds began to gather at the main intersections, viewing in silent horror the rising barriers.

Meanwhile, in the Rhineland, one of Adenauer's aides joined Hans Globke, the chief of the cabinet, who hastened to bring the Chancellor the news. It was not complete or confirmed, so they put through a call to Berlin. The Chancellor had arrived at his house in Rhöndorf surrounded by rose gardens, at a little after nine. He urged the immediate exploration of the facts and set off for midmorning mass. He returned to hear more precise news at eleven. There was talk of an immediate trip to Berlin. "What can I do there?" he said. The moment of psychological opportunity was quickly passed. He took the view—echoed by Dean Rusk and the Ministers in Paris—we must not panic—the situation must not be exaggerated. The people of Berlin, who stood shocked and grieving by the barrier that was to become the Wall, wondered at the inaction. They conclude, as do many analysts, including Kurt Shell, that the crisis was underestimated by almost all of those outside the city.

By ten o'clock, the small group at Potsdamer Platz had grown

17. *Ibid.*, p. 42.

to more than five hundred. By eleven o'clock, the police estimated the crowd at the Brandenburg Gate to be more than two thousand. The news was spreading fast. By evening, more than ten thousand were gathered there. In the worker's quarters by the wire barrier, several hundred were preparing to stone the Vopos. At more than one point, West Berliners trampled down the wire and several persons crossed to safety.

The *Tagesspiegel* of August 13, set in type before the news came through, had given its main space to the harsh measures against the border-crossers. The paper appeared too early to reflect the dramatic events of the previous night. It was full of the "pre-Wall" story of the refugees crowding into the camps. The editorial discussion was concerned with the Khrushchev maneuver that had induced President Kennedy to consider that there were, according to Kennedy's speeches and recent interviews, few alternatives in the Berlin situation—either a standpat position or nuclear war. This was a bold and brutal tactic. It was, the editorial said, reducing in an unnecessary fashion the capacity to act. There were the usual stories on sports, on romance, and on petty crime.

Two items can be considered as forerunners of the many border incidents to come. On page twelve was the story of a young man who had driven a truck through the zonal border into Neukölln to seek refuge. He had been stopped at one point on the border by the Vopos in his attempt to return from a visit to the East sector. He had then broken through at another point. A second item told of a fifty-nine-year-old West Berliner who had strayed some thirty meters south of the Königsweg demarcation line and had been seized by the border police and taken in the direction of Eastern headquarters as a prisoner. Otherwise the paper gave no indication of the drastic measures that were developing. It would appear that the Germans on the twelfth and thirteenth were as little prepared for the critical moment as the Western Allies, and had no readily available contingency plan for counteraction.

Official Reactions

The hours following the closing of the border were full of confusion. The shock had been paralyzing. The show of Soviet force was impressive. Everyone looked to the Allies to take strong action. It was assumed that "something would be done." But nothing *was done*. The reasons were various and are colored by the particular political point of view of the different groups. The House of Representatives in Berlin, the *Abgeordnetenhaus*, met in special session on Sunday to condemn the Ulbricht action. Mayor Brandt in a strong speech made it clear that he considered prompt and vigorous Allied counter-measures essential. He said that if nothing were done, the people would feel betrayed.[18] Adenauer went, according to schedule, to Regensburg to make a campaign speech. He issued a statement that the Wall turned the Zone into a huge concentration camp. He recommended international counter-measures that would have put pressure on the Soviets somewhere else in the world. President Kennedy and Secretary Rusk seemed at the outset to take the same line. Neither the British nor the French made an immediate declaration.

In Berlin itself, nothing could be done. The demonstrations at the sector border were held in check on the Western side. On the Eastern side, Vopos under the menace of tanks and guns worked all day to build the Wall higher. The material obstacles to escape became rapidly more difficult and permitted the withdrawal of some of the soldiers from the closed streets after the first hours. It is probable that the firmness of the Communist intention is shown by the rapid construction and by the considerable military support which was a factor that fended off Allied action. There was a veritable state of shock and a waiting time that was later politically hard to comprehend.

It is clear that physically knocking down the Wall would have been entirely feasible on the fourteenth and fifteenth of August, 1961. It is also clear that the Western Allies could have sent their troops into the East Sector as a demonstration. What is not clear is the willingness of the U.S. policy-makers at that time to challenge the Communist position. If, as some say, Washington had determined to avoid a serious confrontation with the Russians in the summer of 1961, acts of defiance and a determined manifestation of our rights in the city would in all likelihood have been followed by some other form of harassment and other less dramatic means of keeping the refugees in the East Zone. The speeches of Fulbright,

18. *Tagesspiegel*, Tuesday, August 15, 1961.

Mansfield, Morse, and Kennedy as well as reported conversations by Secretary Rusk give ground for thinking that Washington did not wish to frustrate Communist intentions at this time.

In arriving at a judgment as to U.S. failure to act when the Wall went up—it is clearly not possible to do more than guess as to what would have happened if we had driven our tanks into the East Sector immediately and had challenged the guards at every crossing point. Maybe they would have withdrawn quietly—maybe there would have been much bloodshed. The answer would have depended in large measure on the attitude before the Wall and conditions elsewhere on the globe. What is clear, however, is that a policy which reacts quickly and positively to all encroachment on our rights is more likely to lead to the maintenance of our position and our aims at lower cost than is the more uncertain, hesitating inaction that gives grounds for doubting our firmness. Just as the missile crisis action partially restored the faith of the Berliners—so the Cuban crisis might never have occurred if the Soviets had faced a firm and determined stand or counter-measures in the case of Berlin in 1961.

In this time of uncertainty, it was remarkable that there was little disturbance to the normal life of the city. Accustomed to repeated attacks, those who were not vitally affected in their personal lives—and many, of course, were—returned on Monday and Tuesday to their business and household activities. The newspapers discussed the major political aspects but also reported the sports, vacation plans, affairs of financial and business concerns much as they would have after a destructive fire, once the blaze was brought under control, or after a flood, once the waters had receded.

On Wednesday, August 16, Chancellor Adenauer received Ambassador Smirnov at his request. The question of Berlin was uppermost in their minds. There are still resentful judgments of reports of this conversation in political quarters hostile to *Der Alte*. Partly because of his failure to go on Sunday to Berlin, as had Eugen Gerstenmaier, President of the Bundestag, his conversation with Smirnov was called "shameful." One of the leaders of the SPD stated that "not once in the course of the conversation had the Chancellor demanded that the Wall be taken down." There is no proof of the validity of this statement. In fact, the newspaper accounts do not bear out this accusation—but I heard it several times in conversations in the summer of 1965. The official release after the meeting of the sixteenth read, "The Chancellor of the Federal Republic took the occasion to state to Ambassador Smirnov his views on the Berlin situation." On the eighteenth, he made a long statement before the Bundestag denouncing the Wall. By this date, he knew Vice-President Lyndon Johnson was coming to Berlin. Whatever the criticism of his public position in those days, he was restrained by the occupation status of Berlin and the jurisdiction of the three Allies as occupying powers in Berlin. As the days passed without counteraction, there was a widespread feeling that the Western behavior of the moment reflected a false appraisal of the basic issues and that the Chancellor thought that the crisis over the German question would come to a decisive stage later and in another form. He thought then, it is said, that the maintenance of NATO ties furnished the only sure protection of Germany.

It is quite possible that Khrushchev also expected the move of Ulbricht to have other consequences. It is natural that, never having understood Berlin or its people, and having considered the Allied position incomprehensible, he would have calculated that the Wall would strike a mortal blow to the economy and the morale of West Berlin. If this was part of his thinking, he may have concluded that it would persuade a new and somewhat inexperienced President, surrounded by men who might perhaps consider that the Berlin policy had worn threadbare, to institute negotiations on the German question.

President Kennedy, disturbed and concerned as to what action should be taken, sent both Vice-President Johnson and General Clay to the city.[19] An additional component for the Berlin garrison, fifteen hundred American soldiers were dispatched from the West. Adenauer made his visit to Berlin on August 22. In this case, as in earlier instances, Khrushchev's estimation of the Allied reaction and of the endurance of the Berlin people was incorrect.

In Washington and in Germany there were various consultations which began almost at once and continued for some weeks as to

19. *Tagesspiegel*, Berlin, August 20, 1961, p. 1.

how to strengthen the Berlin economy. Measures were taken to give financial advantages to firms opening subsidiaries in the city.[20] The United States showed itself ready to aid if more assistance were required. General Clay stayed to see what kind of support might be needed. In fact, the scope of the new American help was limited to psychological support and the encouragement of American business to locate establishments there for patriotic as well as for financial and price advantages.

The period of general anxiety proved to be shorter than had been expected. With new financial encouragement, the production in Berlin increased with rapid strides. Unemployment vanished, and in the course of the next four years, a labor shortage developed while industry boomed. Few would have ventured to predict such developments in the summer of 1961.

Now in 1967, those who visit Berlin, from Africa, from Asia, from America, go to the Brandenburg Gate and climb the wooden platform—some twenty steps or more—to look over the concrete barrier into the empty streets that border the Wall. The space to the east of the barrier is forbidden territory. If one of the Zone residents wanders too far in that direction, the guns in the watch towers are turned on him. He risks his life. Vopos with binoculars look at the clusters of people on the west to see if perhaps some rescue operation for an escaping German is being planned.

At Bernauer Strasse, where so many have lost their lives in trying to escape, the platform is made of steel and one climbs thirty-five steps to look down on the dismal "death strip," the bricked-up windows, and the ugly guardposts where there is a long view of the empty streets. This is a place where there is a chance to communicate. Visitors stop to read in horror of the death of the sixty-year-old nurse Ida Sieckmann. They note the pitiful crosses and wreaths which lie as memorials under the windows where women leaped to their death in desperation, from windows now bricked and blind.

The Death of Peter Fechter

The tragedy of August 17, 1962, when Peter Fechter hung on the barbed wire with no one to help, marks a low point of despair and

20. See Chapter VII.

of disillusion for many. This episode has been referred to as marking a serious change in the Berlin attitude toward Americans which still influences current opinion.[21] Many of the accounts of this incident, which were repeated to me over and over by the younger residents of Berlin, have developed out of deep emotion more than out of a knowledge of all the facts. The legend that has gained credence and is often told, and which is even more shocking than the actual story, is that the boy hung bleeding for six hours while the American authorities consulted Washington as to what to do. They speak with bitterness of a cold indifference, of hesitating bureaucrats who do not understand the human suffering resulting from the division of Germany. This has now, for the rebellious, provided a focal point for criticism of foreign weakness and German irresolution which could be fanned into hostility.

Pierre Galante, in his book on the Berlin Wall,[22] vividly describes the attempt by Helmut Kulbeik and Peter Fechter to gain freedom in West Berlin. On August 17, the two young men started out for work in the morning, eating an early lunch of bacon and potatoes together. When the other men went back to work, they strolled over to a sawmill near the building site on Ernst-Thälmannplatz. "On the first floor they wrestled with the barbed wire and boards at the window, wrenched out the nails and staples, and pulled the barbed wire down. They took off their shoes and hid them among the rubble and bits of rubbish." Then they crossed the wasteland between the building and the barbed wire on the East side of the Wall.

They were near Checkpoint Charlie where newsmen and other observers are almost always gathered to watch the crossing into East Berlin and where a museum now stands to record the story of many dramatic escapes.

They slipped into the sandy roadway of the Zimmerstrasse. They did not know that above them at firing slits in bricked-up windows of the sawmill there were three Grepos (East Border police). The boys reached the Wall and climbed to where it was topped by barbed wire. There were two more feet of wire above them. Helmut

21. Shell, *Bedrohung und Bewährung*, pp. 360–62. Professor Shell in his discussion of the incident reflects the seriousness with which it was taken by the Berlin people.
22. Galante, *The Berlin Wall*, pp. 182–86.

was ahead. Looking back he saw Peter paralyzed by the fear of a Grepo standing a few feet away from him. Helmut was over the Wall in a moment, while Peter was felled by a burst of several shots from a tommy-gun. Wounded, he tried to climb but could not pull himself up to reach the top. The East Berlin police were close to him at the foot of the Wall as he fell back on the cement on the wrong side. He lay with his hand outstretched and bleeding.

The West Berliners had watched his desperate climb, and hundreds of them rushed to the Wall. There was no possibility of saving Peter. Newspaper reporters and photographers arrived in a matter of minutes. Some futilely tried to climb the Wall, but the police were there with guns poised. The Vopos threw a tear gas bomb over into West Berlin as American military police came up. It was almost forty minutes before steel-helmeted Grepos carried him away without waiting for a stretcher. Peter Fechter, only eighteen years old, was the fiftieth victim.

Although some aspects of this tragic event are obscure, it is not generally known that the action took place beyond the Wall and under the poised and smoking guns of the East Germans. The American military police, who came to the West side of the Wall within a few minutes after the fatal shots, were under orders not to cross the line into East Berlin while on duty. Because of the shocking nature of the event, however, they had immediately sent word to American authorities at Military Headquarters.

On this day, Charles Hulick, the Acting Head of the U.S. Mission in Berlin, was in conference with the U.S. Commandant in the General's office on Clay Allee. The first report that reached them during their morning conference on various matters was that a Vopo had been shot at the Berlin Wall near Checkpoint Charlie and was hanging bleeding on the wire. This report obviously raised problems, but it was still hearsay. They sent officers immediately to the scene to determine exactly what happened. It was approximately twenty minutes later that they learned that the man who was wounded on the East side of the Wall was an escaping East Berliner and that an angry crowd was gathered on the West side of the Wall. Before the American officers could reach the scene, some eight or ten miles from headquarters, the young man had been carried away. In a short time, a sign was held up at a window in the

East sector, "He is dead." Pictures of this event are grim reminders at the spot where Peter died.

There had been in the course of the brief few minutes between the time the boys reached the Wall and the mowing down of Peter by the several Grepos, no real chance for rescue. American soldiers could have shot the Grepos and Vopos, but they could not have scaled the Wall, even to save the bleeding body of the young man. While one cannot easily accept the fact that his death went unavenged, it is still difficult for those who know the precise facts of the situation to say what would have been the right course of action, but the indignation of the Berliners was outspoken.

The shots that were fired that day could have caused a serious revolt, many could have died at the Wall. Demonstrations of indignation and expressions of hatred for the brutality were what some hoped for and many feared. The crowd did not disperse for some hours. The people near the barricade threw stones at the Vopos and also at Americans until they were dispersed by force.

For several days after the slaying of Peter Fechter, the angry crowds continued to demonstrate their hostilities to the Soviets. They stormed the Russians' War Memorial that stands inside West Berlin near the Brandenburg Gate on Avenue 17th of June. As a result of the tension, the three Western Powers made two demands of the Soviets. One was that they cease bringing their guards to the War Memorial in armored carriers. The second was that they no longer use Checkpoint Charlie but take the shorter Sandkrug bridge. For some days it was not certain how this crisis between the East and West would be resolved. There was a time limit of a few days, and, before it expired, the Soviets backed down—the Western Allies had won their point.

In the Fechter case, there had been only two possibilities for action. One would have been the climbing of the Wall by American soldiers under the guns of the Grepos, a feat which would have been impractical without scaling equipment, not immediately at hand. If, however, the American soldiers *had* climbed the Wall carrying a Red Cross flag, the chances of their being involved in a shooting episode were admittedly serious. The other possibility—that of driving through one of the checkpoints with a military car—would have required more time than was available. It is the opinion of some Americans in Berlin that, if there had been another hour for the decision, there would have been a chance of a rescue attempt. This would have been, in any case, contrary to instructions, and would have meant grave risks of conflict. The view of officials, unofficially expressed, has been that rescue attempts should have been made, although clearly the men involved would have risked court martial, dismissal, or severe disciplinary consequences. As one man in a responsible position said, "It is not always possible to do the 'right thing' in circumstances of this sort, particularly in view of the uncertain information available in the first instance, and the misconstruction of facts by a public quickly aroused by the drama of escape attempts."

There had been several similar episodes in earlier months. In every case the first information reaching Headquarters had been confused and undependable. The issues involved in action clearly brought serious risks, whether action was taken or not.

An episode that received less publicity than the Fechter case but that partly reversed the prevailing cynicism of 1962 occurred in September, 1963. A German named Maier had been shot, but not so seriously as Fechter. As reported to me, "one of our Military Police—Hans Puhl—pulled the wounded man over the Wall." He was backed up by the West Berlin police who were returning the fire of the East German Vopos aimed at the refugee and Hans Puhl. This heroic action and the Kennedy visit of June, 1963, when taken together, served to refurbish our tarnished reputation in the eyes of our Berlin friends.

There are many known and also unreported tragedies. In December, 1961, before the death of Peter Fechter, a twenty-year-old student at the West Berlin Technical University, Dieter Wohlfahrt, had spirited his fiancée out of East Berlin on a fake passport.[23] Her mother subsequently indicated the desire to flee. Dieter arranged for her to meet him at a farmhouse on the sector border at Bergstrasse Ecke Haupstrasse in the British sector. Dieter cut his way through the first barbed wire fence and was crawling toward the second near the farmhouse when he was sighted and shot by a Vopo. There was every indication that the Vopos had been previously alerted because several more quickly appeared. A West

23. John Bainbridge, *The New Yorker*, October 27, 1962, pp. 57-144.

Berlin police patrol arrived a few minutes after the shooting and turned searchlights on the area but were driven back by the Vopos with submachine guns. British military police were also summoned. There was more shooting from the East, and no assistance was given the wounded man. Dieter died while the Allied soldiers and West Berlin police looked on. It was two hours before a truck arrived to remove the body. On the next day, the farmhouse was torn down.

Other stories that indicate an instinctive and immediate action deepened the dark shadows cast by events of August 17. It is not enough for the average Berliner to say that the circumstances are different. In one case where a fourteen-year-old boy swam across the Spree River in the center of the city, the shooting was countered by a Berlin policeman. As the boy lay bleeding on the bank of the river, shot by an East German guard on the opposite shore, the West Berliner did not wait for orders and, taking whatever risk there might be, without hesitation shot the Vopo who had been guilty of the attempted murder. The boy, wounded but still alive, was pulled to safety. This bold and impulsive act led to a general feeling that official orders meant a brutal indifference to the tragedies that were taking place.

For the occupying authorities, as well as for the responsible Berlin officials, shooting of citizens escaping from the Zone of occupation presents a cruel dilemma.

The Tunnels

The story of the tunnels is one of the most exciting and most disturbing of all. Many innocent people have fled through the dark passages, often crawling in muddy water to emerge to the warm and silent welcome of those who have dug these paths to freedom. Always they have been near the armed Vopos who were listening and waiting to shoot them or their helpers. Always they faced fear and danger to seek a new life in the free West.

Many tunnels were built and many were discovered and flooded or walled up. Students from the Free University were anxious to keep digging even after the technical methods for discovering the tunnels were perfected to a high degree. Many lost their lives in futile attempts when walls fell in and water mains broke. Many

The Wall

were shot in trying to gain the entrance to some escape route.

The best-known tunnel was the one that was begun in May, 1962. This was planned and financed in large measure by the Berlin staff of NBC. A beginning point was established in an unused but normal looking workshop on the Bernauer Strasse. Here small Volkswagen buses went in and out bringing electrical tools, lumber, and other things needed for the work. The dirt was stored in the cellar. Some fifty young men worked in shifts for a period of six months.

The greatest problem was of course secrecy. With so many working and over such a long period of time, the possibility of betrayal or of inadvertent acts that would give the undertaking away was alarming. The tunnel was not discovered, however, even after the first escapees crawled through the dark passage. The main threat to completion was flooding. At one point the workers broke into a cracked water main. They told the city authorities, who mended the leak without knowing how it had been found or why it was important to the informants.

The initial shaft that was driven down was fifteen feet deep and took three nights to build. The workers had to keep pumping and pulling the earth out in little containers for which they laid a track. In the digging, they crouched low, their feet in water. A stark electric bulb which they had wired themselves gave dim light to the workers who were in constant danger of cave-ins until they built a wooden frame with a supporting ceiling to lessen the risk. During the five months of construction there were two floods, one in June and another in July. Both threatened complete failure to the undertaking. Eventually the pumping succeeded and, with only a few inches of mud, the digging went on. The man at the far face of the 450 feet of excavation usually lay on his back with the shovel between his legs. Sometimes he had to use his hands to scoop out the sand and dirt. The tin basin, used when the hole was small, was dragged back by the men at the tunnel opening in the cellar. Space was limited because there must be no activity outside that could be noticed in either West or East Berlin. The Vopos were constantly patrolling above, as the tunnelers penetrated into the sector. They had always kept a careful watch at Bernauer Strasse, a frequent escape point. Their pacing could be heard by the men working far under the pavement. There was no talking in the tunnel because of fear that the East German police might hear.

The long task was not over until October, 1962. During those months dozens of shorter tunnels had been dug; some had been discovered and blocked up, some had caved in. There had been cases of shooting at the point of the reception centers. Some of the "passengers" had collapsed in the narrow tunnels, some, bleeding from shots before their escape, had died after they reached the West and safety. The methods of detecting the work of the tunnels constantly improved. The Vopos and Grepos drove stakes into the shafts when they found them. They probed likely points along the sector border. The tunnel-digging enterprise became constantly more perilous.

In mid-October a few people assembled, alerted by a youth with a West German passport who had been permitted to cross at Checkpoint Charlie, coming in twos and threes at spaced intervals. They gathered in a small cellar near the border. The Vopos walked up and down the streets not noting any special gathering and not interested in the silent couples in dark clothing with small packages or suitcases. In the tunnel from the West side the leader came out at the East and led the first of some twenty-eight persons through the long dark passageway to safety. These men and women had to crawl most of the way on hands and knees. They came out trembling, weeping but still silent, for the escape route must not be betrayed. They grouped in the dark cellar where they were embraced and given hot coffee. A few of the babies and children were dragged along in the tin basins that had been used for bringing out the earth. The mission was a success. The joy among the escapees was still mingled with a kind of nightmare of fright, but the reunion of the families was a reality that grew in its wonder.

A second, similar crossing and a third were carried out at short intervals, but with each episode and more people involved, the danger of discovery increased. Too many on both sides of the Wall knew of the operation. There was also the prospect of increasing water seepage as pumping became more difficult. The total who used the tunnel to come to the West was reported as fifty-nine. The tunnel was never discovered by the East Zone authorities, but the increasing risk, with repetition and spreading knowledge of

The Wall

what had been done, led the leaders to flood the shaft in late October to prevent loss of life. The story was out in *Newsweek* on October 22, in *Time* on October 28.

A controversy arose over the plan to show a television documentary on the tunnels. Both CBS and NBC were involved in the early stages of the plan. Then NBC secured control and, for a price, was permitted to film the construction and the escape. The State Department for days objected to the release of the film for television. Finally, they realized it could not be prevented. So it came about that this remarkable documentary of ninety minutes has been seen by millions—only after the possibility of using the tunnel was over and with the knowledge that the East German authorities had already perfected the listening devices and electronic equipment to aid in the detection of such activities. From the outset tunnels were not safe and they became ever more perilous.

The considerable cost of lumber, digging equipment, electricity, and wages paid to some of the excavators was met by NBC. Several of their top officers in Berlin worked over the blueprints and the plans and followed the digging in detail, advising and helping to administer the pumping that went on for several weeks during each of the two floodings. They agreed that, in the film, only the faces of those who gave their permission would be shown. Thus as one watches the dramatic moment when the first escapees climbed the ladder and were pulled up to the cellar by waiting West Berliners, many of their faces are blacked out in the picture. On some of the other faces the strain and emotion is deeply etched and the silence is broken only by low murmurs in the murky shadows of the small reception area in the cellar. The watcher, thinking of the hours of uncertainty, shares the tension as one person after another comes through, and the relief when the leader finally says, "They have all made it."

The Department of State had reason for its reluctance to have the film shown. They feared that in some way the workers, their families and friends, those who knew of the enterprise in the East and others who might be planning escape might be endangered. They also noted the inevitable commercial aspects of some of the escape measures. Money was involved. It took time and work to dig, it took hours off from regular jobs to make the complex arrangements for the meetings on the Eastern side. Meanwhile, equipment was needed and had to be carried to the right spot in secrecy. Considerable sums of money changed hands, and some disreputable characters became involved in a few of the more hazardous undertakings.

Many university students became excited by the adventure and deeply moved by the plight of Germans who wished to find freedom in the West. The life of the young people in Berlin was infused with a new heroism and zeal. This effort to help those imprisoned in the Zone seemed to them the one thing that they could do in the long years before reunification. Here was a political and psychological problem in which the American government was compelled to take a conservative position. The lives of hundreds of people were threatened. There was danger that emotions would get out of hand, that young men would throw caution to the winds. It was natural that there was bitterness on both sides as responsible officials tried to deal with this thorny problem. There had to be careful consideration of the major issues—Berlin must be held in orderly fashion without wild demonstration or adventurism. Berlin was the key to the future of Germany—of Europe—in many aspects of the free world. The problem for the State Department was real, even though their objection to the release of the film was criticized by the public.

The measures taken to prevent people from leaving the German Democratic Republic (GDR) are impressive. They include thousands of tons of concrete, millions of strands of barbed wire,[24] uncountable numbers of bricks to close windows and doors. They require approximately eighty thousand to a hundred thousand men in Berlin and from the Baltic to Czechoslovakia armed with machine guns, hundreds of hunting dogs, countless search lights, trip flares, and watch towers. They include border guards and agents, binoculars, cameras, police cars, tanks, and a series of road blocks arranged to prevent the cars of escaping persons from gaining speed and crashing barriers. They include threats, written and oral, explaining the horrors of the Western world, harsh voices that speak over the radio and from the lecture platforms. In this inten-

---

24. In 1966, at some points on the zonal border, concrete was being substituted for barbed wire.

The Wall

sive effort, no method is overlooked, no expense is spared, no efficiency is lacking. The doors of the prison are thick and the cost of failure to the escaping German is death.

The statistics of the Wall are grim. It is probable that more than thirty thousand have escaped. Many have been killed. It is not known how many are in prison for attempting to flee or for helping others to go as passengers to the West. These are unknown figures—the count against Communism which will never be totaled by those who live in freedom.

The escapes continue, but they are increasingly difficult and fewer in number. In August, 1965, two men slid down a wire attached to an East sector flag pole. A week before, two workers used official equipment to engineer an unexpected leap to freedom. The ingenuity of would-be refugees is unlimited. Recently two workers had been operating an inclined conveyor belt for some weeks. The movable assembly had a vertical height of some five meters in order to raise the sacks of coal into the storage bin. Suddenly the workers moved the machine to the Wall, hopped on the conveyer belt, and rode up the inclined chute over the Wall into West Berlin.

There is a long story of daring jumps, of stratagems and hopes—and of fears of being caught forever in the dull, oppressive system that is the expression of Communism. In Germany more than in Russia, the contrast between capitalism and the socialist state is sharply highlighted. The Russians have lived under the police state in poverty with a rigid class structure for centuries. The Germans have a pride and independence that make them feel they are potential masters. Even in spite of the years of dictatorship they had always an image of world power, of independence, of a creative capacity that is not being satisfied by the regime under which they live. Whether they will lose this spirit in a decade, in two decades, in a half century, no one can guess, but they have not yet lost their vision of freedom.

The number of Vopos who have left, singly and in pairs, has run to many hundreds. Since some of these men are stationed on the border to keep others from crossing, there is no system that can prevent them from going over if they decide to defect. There are also some from the East who pretend to be disgruntled with conditions and try to come to the Federal Republic with the idea of infiltrating or spying. Where unnatural barriers are imposed various psychological pressures develop. The administration of the system by the regime is not always easy to enforce.

It is not true, as the German pastor Martin Niemoeller has recently said, or at least implied, that the Germans have accepted the Wall.[25] Whether he was correctly interpreted or not is hard to say. Much of the Niemoeller statement quoted on August 14, 1965, by Omer Anderson, bears on the permanence of the Oder-Neisse line. The Wall has a more immediate interest to Berliners than the political settlement of the fate of the Eastern territories and the Oder-Neisse line.

How Our Position Has Emerged

In any case, acceptance is not the word to apply to the conditions that have come to exist in the half decade after concrete and barbed wire split the city. It is true that acute feelings have been dulled for many. For those whose families, jobs, and interests are not affected, life goes on. For all, however, there is a strong undercurrent of feeling. There is a will to change the situation. There is an explosive factor in Berlin and in West Germany which could mean a growing criticism of the Allies for weakness, of the Soviets for brutality, of the young condemning the old because so many mistakes have been made.

Judgment now on decisions made in 1961 is difficult. However, some facts stand out for those who, on the outside of official life, do not know all the reasons for the failure to act. Most of those who have read the speeches, the press, and accounts of those tragic summer days, particularly those who had contacts with border-crossers and refugees, think that the signs of the imminent erection of the Wall were clear. They believe that the rumors in July pointed to drastic and unprecedented action to bar the refugees from escape through Berlin. In the forty-eight hours before the Wall went up, there were many specific indications of the form the action would take.

For the three days or so after the thirteenth, the Germans and the Soviets expected some form of major action or counter-measure

25. See August 14, 1965 statement, *The Watertown* (New York) *Daily Times.*

from the Allies. They were bewildered and incredulous when nothing happened.

It can be deduced from the reaction in Washington, London, and Paris that the authorities in these capitals believed that, as in Hungary in 1956, the vital interests of the Soviets were at stake, that the plan to defend the Wall would be carried through with force. For reasons of global strategy, they did not wish to challenge the Soviets as they were to do later in Cuba.

The calm, which was advised, was viewed with cynicism in Germany. Since those days, serious questioning of Allied firmness has been expressed from time to time. The Germans had not then felt the impact of the Bay of Pigs. They did not know the increasing problems in NATO with Britain and France over nuclear arms. The time to prevent the Wall, if the will had been there, was July; the time to take counter-measures was August.

In consideration of worldwide problems, there was no will to knock down the Wall.

Wednesday, June 15, was one of the few warm days of 1965. Herman Dobler and a young woman in a bathing suit were sunning in a small motor boat on the Teltow Canal. Down the middle of the canal at that point, near Checkpoint Bravo, there was an imaginary unmarked line separating the free world from the Communist world. The boat drifted into Communist water. The guards in the unsightly wooden watch tower looking across the unmarked line, took aim as the man casually maneuvered close to the middle of the canal. Dobler realized his danger seconds before the shot was fired. The boat could not be turned so quickly. The man fell dead. The girl with a bullet through her brain lay beside her lifeless companion as the boat swung aimlessly in the quiet water. Western police rushed to the scene, holding the boat as they lifted the unconscious girl to the shore. She lived but perhaps will never know what the tragic end of the summer outing was. The guards stood silent by the sector border.

Another senseless attack had shattered a quiet sunlit day.

Some days later I was with Blythe Finke and William L. Allen, who were helping me gather information in Berlin. We were checking the Wall at the Brandenburg Gate. I saw some children coming down the steps from the crude observation platform. They had stopped in the wet grass by the Wall to pick wild flowers gaily blooming for the enjoyment of the casual passerby. I wondered what was in the minds of the children. They were shy but friendly as I asked them why the Wall was there. "I think the Communists built it," said the little girl in a blue sweater—with blond pigtails—while a little boy giggled at her boldness. "Why?" I asked. "I don't know," she said. And the group left quickly—running off under the trees to continue their holiday sightseeing.

The Germans and the foreigners are always coming to ask "why" the Wall. They are silent; they take photographs and talk quietly to one another. But they see few people on the other side. The wide death strip is constantly patrolled by foot police, and the grim watch towers are manned by two or three Grepos. Always there are the binoculars searching the viewers—alert for any signs of action, any movement that might suggest the intention to help an escaping German. There is little for any one to say. The stones and the wire are more articulate than words at this place.

On the last day of June, I was with five other Americans in the luxurious bar of the Hilton Hotel—some twelve stories up and about half a mile from the Brandenburg gate—and saw over the shining lights of the West Berlin streets the shadowy towers of the East. Bill Allen turned to me, pointing to a sudden flame of a star shell exploding near the line between brightness and dark. We knew there had been another desperate attempt to escape by some East resident. The flash against the blackness of the Communist world was to reveal another dash for freedom. Did the man escape? Did he live in safety across the line? Or did he die in the hands of the Vopos? The papers did not say. The men in the West did not know.

IV. The Relations of Divided Germany and Berlin

Many of us return to Berlin, we who have known it in its hour of trial and recovery, because of the immense interest it has politically, culturally, and humanly—because of the drama and because of the strangeness that we cannot fully explain. We return because of persistent questions to which we wish to find answers. Why do people want to live and work behind the Iron Curtain? Why is the city attractive to its own people and to visitors? How far does the Wall throw its shadow? What are conditions in the East Zone? How many want, expect, and demand reunification? What do the young men—leaders of the future—think of current policy? What lies ahead in the post-Adenauer era? What are the responsibilities for Berlin which fall on the United States in fulfilling its European security policy?

There are more questions than answers here—but I found in July, 1965, that the words of several hundred people from all walks of life, in easy, informal conversation helped to set at rest some doubts, and give a clearer sense of the direction in which events are moving. They reaffirmed for me the capacity to endure which has proved to be inherent in most Berliners in the postwar years. They give evidence of the significant contribution of American aid and support. They underscore the importance of NATO.

These conversations reminded me of the sobering fact that many of the more articulate Germans, rightly or wrongly, in considerable measure hold the United States responsible for the present division of Germany. Few doubt that the American troops could have taken

Berlin in April, 1945, and held a large part of Europe now under Soviet rule. Few accept the validity of judgment made as to the future of Germany at Yalta. While the views of the average person on military operations in 1945 may not be significant, a considerable number think that we could have liberated the Zone in 1953 and held it for the West. Some add that the uprising of June 17, 1953, brought a never repeated opportunity.[1] Their views are often more emotional than reasoned, but they influence public opinion. The fact that the revolt continued in the Eastern provinces for several weeks gives credence to the opinion held by at least a vocal minority that American armed support would have made liberation possible. In this matter the young men tend to hold the United States responsible and have not elaborated a logical analysis of the Soviet vital interests on this occasion. Some think that there may have been an opportunity to negotiate a settlement bringing reunification in 1955.[2]

Since America is the only nation with the power to challenge the Soviet Communists—our nation is in their opinion responsible for the continued enslavement of East Europe. They look on 1956 and Hungary with bitterness. This conclusion—ignoring our far-flung commitments in the Caribbean, in southeast Asia, in Africa, in the Middle East—is based on our fabled and frequently overrated military and economic reserves and places on us a psychological burden of political significance that must influence our public pronouncements as well as our long-run diplomacy. If now we were to abandon the hopes and aspirations of the German people, we would dash their confidence and bring a revulsion of feeling. We would, in the minds of many, not only desert all those vulnerable nations to which we have promised aid, but we would also turn our backs on world freedom; we would undermine the faith of those who have had the courage to resist tyranny.

This is the challenging lesson of present-day Berlin. It is not an easy truth to accept. It brings risks and sacrifice to leaders in more remote capitals, as well as in Washington, Paris, and London, to those who are reluctant to continue their efforts, to those who look

---

1. Alois Riklin in *Das Berlinproblem* (Cologne: Wissenschaft und Politik, 1964), pp. 161–64, discusses the meaning of the uprising and its failure.
2. *Ibid.*, pp. 181–84.

The Relations of Divided Germany and Berlin

for peace in the relaxation of tension. It promises no early solutions to present problems.

The Call for Reunification

I have never found preoccupation with reunification so marked nor the clamor so loud as it was at the time of my visit to Berlin in 1965. Certainly the talk on the subject has not been so universal since the conference in 1954, when there was widespread surprise at the degree of apathy and the hollow ring of government statements. Now political conversation is punctuated by comments on *kleine Schritte*, or "little steps," and contacts—on action now and not in the indefinite future. Rarely had a notion spread more quickly than the idea of *kleine Schritte*, the most recent approach to relations with the East Zone. The jokes, the cartoons, the newspaper editorials return almost daily to the question as to whether little steps lead anywhere—forward or backward, illusion or reality. Are *kleine Schritte* really *kleine Schnitte*—or "little cuts"?

The atmosphere of present-day Berlin and the persistent concern over reunification can be illustrated by a conversation held on Friday evening, July 2, 1965. Three professors (one a university official), a Berlin city administrator, and two Americans—all guests at a cold supper in my temporary home in Berlin-Dahlem—argued about reunification. This had been in recent months a main preoccupation. The core of the discussion was the degree to which hopes and expectations should be made to conform to the realities of the day as contrasted with the longer-run possibilities and policies.

One of the men denounced the political oratory that had characterized recurring statements. He decried the fact that none of the main political leaders could say what was a reasonable position to take with regard to the Eastern areas, the Oder-Neisse line, and the present Polish territories. "Perhaps," said one, "if we gave up all claims to East Prussia and the land now under Polish control, we would create a better impression of being reasonable."

"A better impression on whom?" the university official asked. "On the Americans, on the Russians, on the British."

"An impression of strength or of weakness?" asked another. There was no reply.

Another said: "Surely the constant reiteration of the possibilities of reunification have a hollow sound. We must do better than we have so far." A third volunteered: "But they are not linked with any time period—such a precision would make them absurd. We must keep up our determination."

One of the listeners added: "History is full of changes. These have been enormous in the past. Now there are major unknowns in Moscow, in Washington, in Paris, in Peking, and elsewhere. Since the future is fluid and uncertain, one is justified in looking beyond the present impasse to a new and unpredictable situation. At some future time the basic needs are almost certain to make their impression on leaders in many capitals. Then there may be action."

Three of the men stated at almost the same time: "Of course we expect reunification, but not now. What shall we do now?"

The conversation, typical of hundreds going on in Berlin in the year 1965, then turned to the question of current policy. The comments tumbled forth. "The little steps must be taken because no big steps are now possible. It is unthinkable to do nothing."

"But what are these little steps?" asked the visitor from the United States. "There have been few indications of feasible action to be taken."

The reply was immediate. "Contacts and more contacts. They can do no harm; they can keep alive the German spirit."

But a more tentative question followed: "Are there yet more contacts to be proposed by the West and accepted by the East than those varied contacts of the present time?" One of the professors urged, "Yes, many contacts—cultural and intellectual exchanges. We must invite East German scientists to lecture here, even though they do not invite our West Berlin scientists and artists to speak to them. No harm can come of it. If the Communists talk foolish propaganda, the audience will be disgusted. Then, after the third or fourth time, West Berliners won't go to the lectures any more. If they talk sense, there will be some interest, but it is most likely that the attention will hardly outlast the first few sessions. They have not enough to offer."

They were referring to exchanges that took place in the winter of 1964–1965. They said that there is a possibility that more will follow next year, but opinions in this friendly gathering differed widely as to the usefulness and as to the results good or bad.

On one further related subject—the re-establishment of telephone communications—doubts were raised. Now, in order to telephone the East Zone, it is necessary to call Frankfurt, and then Pankow, and then be connected with a point in the East Zone. This situation causes delay and expense. The first professor reflected, "Telephone communications should be proposed. It is a good gesture, but there is no real chance of the East Zone authorities' agreeing."

Another of the group suggested, "It would still be good to propose it, a good propaganda effect at the very least."

In spite of the wide-ranging discussion, they did not outline further little steps. There was general agreement among the four German guests that there must be an effort to manifest a will to act. The people must not be deceived by empty phrases. They must be given a reasonable time perspective for the larger changes. Meanwhile, the people across the line must be offered frequent and increasing opportunities to know what their brothers in the Federal Republic are thinking and doing. All four stressed the fact that the attitude of the Federal Republic officials should be strong enough to demonstrate confidence in the vital forces of democracy and freedom so that they do not fear to risk the exposure of all citizens to multiple contacts.

"What have we to fear from the efforts of the Communists to persuade us?" several asked. The conversation, lively but inconclusive, continued for several hours. Several ideas revealing the frustration and the profound discouragement which afflicts conscientious Berliners were gone over a number of times.

In another informal talk earlier in the day, in the same pleasant dwelling overlooking bright green corn fields and gardens with roses of many hues, another responsible Federal official of long experience stretching from the Weimar Republic to the present-day conflict, said, "Little steps are an illusion. I know the Communists. Little steps can be in the wrong direction. They can even become big steps and disastrous steps. We will be asked to pay a price as we always are—we can make big mistakes. There is no intention in the East Zone regime of yielding anything that will bring the two parts of a divided nation together. Even the passes of 1963—the *Passierscheine*—should be refused this year if they require a concession of official negotiation. Courage is needed."

He continued his argument with determination: "The *status quo plus* is not now possible. The *status quo minus* means defeat. In order to gain an eventual *status quo plus* we must defend the present situation. This will make possible gains at some later time. If we hold for ten years, we can expect gains in the following ten years. Change for the sake of a 'policy of movement' is likely to show dangerous weakness. In spite of considerable talks, the people of Berlin do not wish concessions. The barge situation of recent days shows that endurance, strength, a will to hold our rightful position, can be effective. We stopped seven East Zone barges in West Berlin because they would not present the Allied permits. After two days the point was won. We let the East barges through after they recognized the validity of the existing passes." He cited the helicopter incident of June 28 and 29 as another.

It was in late June, 1965, that for the first time the East Germans, not authorized under the Berlin agreements to fly in this area, intruded into the air space over West Berlin. There was much criticism in the cafés and in the press about the failure of the Western Allies to shoot down the helicopters. They did not accept the explanation that such an act would have been both difficult and dangerous to the crowded area over which the East Germans flew. They were partially satisfied by the announcement in the newspapers of the arming of the U.S. helicopters flying in the same air space. They thought that this act meant the possible shooting down of the East German planes. In any case there was an immediate halt to the illegal flights, which have not been resumed.

The official who criticized the U.S. reaction of the helicopter episode claimed that more could be done to frustrate Communist pressure, but he also stated that there was no clear thinking with regard to the proposal of little steps. He said there was evidence of impatience in a number of quarters which is not representative of the real intent of the people in the West German Republic.

He admitted, as do others, that the students of Berlin are restless. They want to break through the barriers, extend the field of their experience, travel in the East, explore the ideas and know the theories of the Communists. They find the accepted policies of the authorities too restrictive. They are unimpressed by legal precedent and by traditional reasons for watchfulness in regard to the avoiding of recognition of the Pankow officials in the conclusion of arrangements. They want a "policy of movement." They think change is good, almost irrespective of the success of old policies for more than a decade past.

Still another reliable authority expanded the general idea along these lines. Reunification has no meaning if there is loss of freedom. The freedom of Berlin is paramount, as is that of West Germany, but the meaning of the term reunification has never been held to be complete capitulation. Too great a degree of accommodation to Communist policy would inevitably change the significance for Berlin in the view of the Western Allies. Where this line of difference lies is not easy to define—but reunification is an issue of prime importance. The attitude of Germany towards arrangements and contacts in months to come, and of the United States in support of new proposals, will influence the attitude of the Germans toward the Soviet regime. Moreover, the youth are restless.

It is because of this attitude that Peter Bender's recent book, *Offensive Entspannung*,[3] with its recommendation for choosing a course that is synchronized with "the inner evolution of Communism" needs to be taken into account. The book discusses measures that might involve recognition. The GDR adopts an attitude which uses as its main standard the test of deciding what is likely to help the German population of the Zone. The route recommended, while long and arduous and requiring careful choice of steps to be taken, would be, in the opinion of some, a realistic approach to the essential goal. This program is still more of an attitude than a specific plan, but it is likely to become more concrete as time goes on. The view put forward is one which rejects the past and the possible future years of slow motion in the more conventional action and insists on an immediate change in direction from the line of the past.

3. Peter Bender, *Offensive Entspannung* (Cologne and Berlin, 1964), p. 165. Peter Bender has been, for more than ten years, a member of the political section of the radio station *Sender Freies Berlin*. He has written a number of articles for *Der Monat* and *Die Zeit*.

The analysis by Bender has found some fertile ground, although it has been rejected or ignored by many.

In fact, current opinion runs the spectrum from those who, going beyond Bender, think a confederation with *recognition* may be the only course which brings hope for "reunification in our time," to the more classical approach of those who say that the surrender of a single element of procedure, either for the Federal Republic or for the people in the East Zone, is not justified as a means of shortening the time of waiting. Many Germans reaffirm that the democracy of West Germany is a precious value that must not be sacrificed and that can be preserved only by the full and active co-operation with the Western Alliance. Any weakening of NATO, they say, threatens the future of Germany in freedom. Their lot is cast, their stand is taken, and the ties with the West must be strengthened rather than weakened.

In this time of ferment, which is likely to increase rather than diminish as the post-Adenauer era becomes the new factor in Europe, change is inevitable. Certainly every indication that can now be quoted—the literature, the polls, the speeches, the demands of the students, the expansion of interzonal trade, the concern with the holiday passes between West and East Berlin— indicate the likelihood of growing contacts, of modification in thinking, of altered policies. The changes to come will be controversial and perhaps shocking to the friends of Germany. They will be distorted and misconstrued by casual commentators. Some will find in the recent, more extreme writings of a few, signs that Germany has given up hope for reunification. Others will see signs of a realism as to action and conditions with which both East and West can live through a long and difficult period. Some will raise the alarm over a dangerous drift towards accommodation between Bonn and Moscow. Others will warn of a resurgent and belligerent Germany. The German question, which is central to the welfare and the political future of Europe, will stir fear in many, hopes in few.

One can count on the firmness of a solid core of experienced German leaders to watch the changing currents of opinion, but they cannot silence what is a legitimate concern for the fate of East Germany. They cannot ignore warnings that conditions in the Zone are changing and that time may be working against the present Western policy. In the Zone there are signs of an increasing tendency for the people to accept conditions that they are powerless to change. Along with acquiescence there is, paralleling the Communist propaganda, recurrent criticism of the Western Allies. As some have said in the East as well as in the West, the opportunity of 1953 was missed. So they say that Washington, Paris, and London have done little to help the Zone win its freedom.

What Has the West Done?

The price to be paid to the Communists for reunification has been high ever since the division became effective.[4] It has probably included concessions that were inadmissable in view of Communist aggressive policy—total disarmament, neutralization of all of Germany, and the maintenance of the Socialist economic system by rigid controls. These demands would have threatened the hard-won democratic freedoms of the Federal Republic. This fact is not always clear to the oncoming generation who do not understand why the might of the NATO alliance or even the capabilities of the United States alone could not break through the Iron Curtain, destroy the Wall, and force the release of German territory. "If the Allies cannot act, we Germans must, on our own, shape a more effective policy."[5] This is an opinion of many students, and of some of the younger politicians, of many of the intellectuals. This attitude is likely to be increasingly urged on the Bundestag and in the local elections. This issue, which was not brought into the open fully in the election struggle of 1965, will be sharpened in the debate with an increase in the tempo of demonstrations to show those who still doubt that there is an independence of spirit not perhaps characteristic of the German people in the first half of the century.

There are elements of strength and weakness in this changing environment. Both demand a deep appreciation of the stakes involved. For the United States the losses can be incalculable. This

---

4. See Willy Brandt, "Denke ich an Deutschland," July 15, 1963. Speech before the Political Club of the Evangelische Academie, Tutzing (mimeographed release of the Pressedienst, Berlin).

5. Karl Theodor, Freiherr von und zu Guttenberg, *Wenn der Westen will* (Stuttgart: Seewald, 1964), pp. 197-200.

government has founded its policy on an alliance for Europe and the West, in which Germany is a pivot. The economic strength, the military contribution, and the geographic location of the Federal Republic are of vital importance in this structure. If Berlin were to be lost, if the Federal Republic were to compromise its values in order to have a closer relationship with the Ulbricht regime, the threat to the fabric of NATO would be of grave proportions. If, then, the Soviets should see in this tactical change the possibility of weakened strategy in Europe, and should woo the Germans into acquiescence—the Allied measures to retain a strong "sword and shield" in Europe would be immeasurably compromised. So far, no ground has been lost. There is still a deep sense of gratitude for what the United States has done for the Federal Republic, and for Berlin, furnishing the economic essentials, restoring dignity and pride, sharing as an equal in most of the current problems. All the political parties are still committed to co-operation in the European Economic Community and NATO. There is a general strengthening of educational and cultural ties with America and other nations in the classical Greco-Roman tradition. There is a growing desire to assume some of the common burdens of helping the less developed nations. These are strong foundation stones on which to build a permanent structure of sound democratic society.

There is some reason to think, however, that these elements cannot be taken for granted. One of the issues—the economic relations between East and West in Europe—is being challenged both in Germany and elsewhere. Two converging influences of different strength and significance are eroding positions until recently firmly held. For one thing, many people talk about the relaxation of tension, believing, or at least hoping, that the Communist doctrine is being diluted by increased well-being and by the inevitable march of the new generations to positions of power. For another, the difficulties of holding a common front on the non-shipment of goods has led to an opportunistic approach that many substitute for a strategy based on the grimmer facts of life. The peace that prevails dulls the imagination to the gradual encroachment and almost invisible subversion which have been the result of Soviet strategy with respect to Berlin, as well as to parts of

Africa, the East, and Latin America. Many choose to ignore the Communist methods, which fall short of outright aggression.

Another area of doubt comes with the talk in Berlin of "NATO disarray." Some observers downgrade the current value of NATO and begin to develop a cynical attitude toward the alliance. A few forget that the destruction of NATO is a prime Communist objective and that without the concerted preparation fostered by the alliance, the Russians might already be entrenched on the Rhine—in which case Berlin would probably have been strangled.

There is no present voice raised to urge Germany to ignore NATO [6] or to edge away from the Western alliance, but there are questions usually attributed to others, not taking part in the discussion, which one can hear in Berlin, questions as to whether the price for reunification will not be the abandonment of NATO by Germany, or even the dissolution of the European alliance. If so, the conversation runs, would there not be many Germans who would take the risks prerequisite to reunification and a peace treaty as an answer to their deep-rooted desires? Who these people are and how many—one cannot now say—but they exist. The theoretical analysts admit their importance in reviewing all possible solutions.

With the passage of time, the number of persons who remember the past bitter years, and appreciate the unexpected aid from the conquering nations, is bound to diminish as the youth take over the responsibilities of political leadership and assume the burdens of middle age.

Berlin, thanks to help from several sources, has gained in prosperity and stability, even though divided since 1961 in a new and cruel way. The reasons for the war, the defeat, the Soviet occupation, the Allied presence have become dim. The explanations of the zones, the administrative purpose for these designations, the limitations on access, the inability to incorporate Berlin fully into the Federal Republic become unconvincing. The standoff with respect to dealings with fellow Germans in the Eastern part of the nation has become to the younger people unacceptable. A revulsion of feeling

6. Various official and unofficial comments attributed to political figures including Minister Schröder (July), Helmut Schmidt (August), the Bavarian FDP faction, and others suggest that membership in NATO might be negotiable if reunification in freedom could somehow be assured.

may come, next year, five years from now, perhaps later. The way in which this change will affect the Western world will depend in large measure on how well it is understood, how effectively it is anticipated.

What the more thoughtful political leaders expect of the United States varies from person to person. Few wish to see a reorientation of the basic security policy of Germany—only the very young, the highly experimental intellectuals, or a few tending to the far left. The worker, the businessman, the experienced politician, the dedicated anti-Communist follow the policy lines of Konrad Adenauer and Ludwig Erhard, of Willy Brandt and Fritz Erler, of Herbert Wehner and Franz-Josef Strauss. These well-known leaders, despite differences on other matters, all support the policies of mutual security and the community of interests of the Atlantic nations. While their backgrounds vary from ultraconservative to a history which shows a gradual edging away from Communist allegiance, they recognize the threat of aggressive power and the importance of the determination of the United States to stand with Germany in a contest in which either alone would appear to Moscow to be highly vulnerable.

For many, however, the years of the Blockade, the takeover of Czechoslovakia in 1948, the revolt of 1953, the brutal acts of Communists in Hungary in 1956, the Khrushchev ultimatum in 1958 are not realities with which most people have lived, but rather history in a book. For them, people with whom one can trade, debate, and carry on a normal social life exist on both sides of the Iron Curtain. Only the Wall is visible as evidence of something strange and forbidding. So the young men are restless and the intellectuals speculate about new situations. They even forget the gains of Western policy in the last years and are unaware of the misery which was overcome by that policy. The old policy, many students at the Free University in Berlin say, has brought no progress. The line between the two parts of Germany is viewed as a sign of complete failure. The German tie with NATO, membership in the European Common Market, the unprecedented prosperity of the country, and the high regard in which German political and economic life are held throughout the world are not recognized as enormous achievements. To these young men in a hurry, the one outstanding reality that dwarfs any alleged progress or gains in the past twenty years is the monstrosity of this cruel and unnatural separation of families and territories and populations "who must inevitably be reunited."

Freedom for Germans to Act

The preoccupation with the question of reunification came only after Germany emerged from poverty and confusion and when industry and trade had reached a brilliant stage of success. Only when the wealth of the nation, the firmness of the money, the reinstatement of armed forces, and the lively development of education and culture brought the nation to a level of the most advanced societies did this concern for reunification become vocal and widespread.

Now the increasing attention to the Zone, in the thinking of the more active and experimental minded, acts as a ferment that cannot be ignored. There are a number of commentators on German affairs in the United States who deny this interest.[7] These writers say that Germany would not be willing to pay the price for reunification and fear that any moves in this direction might diminish their own prosperity or alter the balance of political power in ways that they would not willingly accept. These men, some of whom visit Germany from time to time, do not usually sit in the students' coffee houses, or hear the debates in the clubs and cafés. They could, even without such experiences, take account of the fact that as the old men grow older, so do the young.

The State Department and the Department of Defense, the White House and the United Nations and NATO can count on moderation and patience on the part of their old friends and associates. The experts on Germany know where the major political leaders stand. But changes are brewing, and unless leadership is strong and clear and unless programs take account of new ideas, drastic and unrestrained tendencies will soon come to the fore.

For instance, understanding is necessary in regard to trade with the Zone. The German point of view, which must be amplified later, is that the Federal Republic, in the interest of Berlin and the

---

7. Note editorial in *New York Times*, European Edition, June 17, 1965, commenting on Eric Mende's statement in the United States.

future of the reconstituted nation, should be allowed a large amount of freedom and should not be deprived of leverage on the East Zone. Trade by the non-Germans with the Soviet Zone makes it difficult for them to use their exports or their credits to gain special advantages with respect to transport, travel, and other matters that concern them very dearly. If the East Zone can gain a large measure of independence by importing from England, France, Belgium, and perhaps from the United States, the offer of German goods, the denial of needed projects can have little or no effect on the political relations that are their primary concern. The Germans feel that the Western Powers should recognize the fact that trade with the East Zone is not international trade but rather trade across an artificial line within a nation which is fundamentally one people. They resent and are close to rejecting the classical Western view. They find the attitudes in Washington, Paris, and London irritating and hard to justify in their domestic politics. The officials insist, with some facts which they hold confidential, that in a number of circumstances they have used the threat of withdrawal of commerce as an instrument to gain concessions. The only such instance publicized was the proposed termination of the interzonal trade agreement in September, 1960. This act brought the renewal of the travel permits that had been cut off in August. Other cases are known but are treated with discretion so that the "tool will not be blunted" sooner than necessary. The trade authorities fear that the more commerce there is with non-German countries the greater the degree of independence for the Zone. If this independence grows, Bonn's maneuvers will become ineffective. It is the opinion of these officials that the Communist zonal authorities are striving with notable success to cut the percentage of trade they have with the Federal Republic.

Moreover, some, along with Peter Bender,[8] challenged the theory that one must always strive to weaken one's enemy. The case of the Zone, caught between Moscow and the Federal Republic, has unusual problems and characteristics.

With respect to other contacts, particularly travel between the Federal Republic and the Zone, the Germans assume that Americans appreciate the reasons why contacts are important to reassure

8. Bender, *Offensive Entspannung*, p. 109.

the millions of non-Communists in the Soviet-occupied territories that they have not been forgotten. It is estimated that the number of visits in both directions runs well over five million a year. Without these important manifestations of continuing interest and friendship, the atmosphere, which is undoubtedly changing in a number of respects, would breed hostility, suspicion, and alienation and thus render the future prospects dark indeed. There has been little tendency in the West to decry these crossings of the line. There has been only a careful watch of the negotiation for passes—particularly the *Passierscheine* in Berlin.

The Passierschein Agreements, 1963–1966

The *Passierscheine* and other special passes have played a significant role in the East-West relations in Berlin since the Wall. The fact that Willy Brandt in December, 1963, took the initiative, with a minimum of regard for the authority of Bonn, in negotiating the vacation passes that permitted more than a million to pass through the five check points on the Friedrichstrasse and at other crossing points, to visit their relatives in the Communist-ruled part of the city, was looked on with some anxiety in Allied quarters. The action was not condemned but was held to be in that legal no man's land which is a result of the long-delayed settlement of the German problem. It illustrated the frustrations and bewilderment of some, the will of others to act wherever uncertainty left a loophole for constructive arrangements. In any case, a plan was adopted, the people streamed through the barriers, and a new point of contact was established which will probably be renewed, now that the elections are over, if the concessions required are not too great. Yielding to Ulbricht is still too great a price for the average Berliner to pay. Many expressed to me, after the demands of the summer of 1965, a willingness to forgo this privilege or opportunity if the price is a whittling away of the established position of West Berlin. Thus, Bonn turned down the August proposal of Pankow.[9]

The *Passierscheine* are significant not only because of the human emotion of those who were at last able to see their relatives for a few hours, separated by the Wall and fearful of not living to know reunification, but because it shows a certain unsureness on the part

9. Later renewed and negotiated in 1965 but not in 1966.

of the East regime authorities and because it suggests that the pressures to breach the Wall are greater than some suppose. The idea that such visits might be arranged first developed in conversations in the interzonal trade group. It is generally assumed that Moscow wished some relaxation of tensions.

Willy Brandt assumed a political risk when he pushed forward with the conversations that led to the visits to East Berlin. He picked up the suggestion advanced in the interzonal trade conversations and permitted exploration of the plan to go forward urgently in both East and West Berlin where minor officials of both groups discussed the methods and arrangements for more than thirty hours of difficult debate. The record shows that he was in contact with the Bonn government and that he talked with Chancellor Erhard on December 9.[10] But it is true that both the Bonn officials and the occupying authorities feared he might go too far and compromise the Western policy of not negotiating with the East Zone regime. It is a sign of his courage and also an indication of the anomalies of the present situation that the agreement emerged on December 17, just in time for passes to be effective in the Christmas season.

The time for processing the applicants was short. The facilities arranged in West Berlin were not adequate to handle the large number of persons. Many stood in the snow and sleet for long hours in the day and night to secure the permissions. There was great anxiety on the part of whose who wished desperately to cross the Wall. Some failed to get passes because of the administrative delays. This first experience with knocking a temporary hole, which was to be followed by others, was both gratifying and heartbreaking.

In the eighteen days of crossings, more than a million persons, perhaps as many as 1,200,000, went over to East Berlin. Exact numbers cannot be given. Approximately 790,000 went in buses provided for the purpose. It is estimated that 400,000 went by subway. There were probably some repeaters, and no exact count was made on either side—the numbers moving through the five

10. See Presse-und Informationsamt des Landes Berlin, *Zur Passierscheinfrage: Erklärung des Regierenden Bürgermeisters Willy Brandt vom 9. Januar 1964 vor dem Abgeordnetenhaus von Berlin* (Berlin: 1964), p. 5. See also Vol. II, September 24, 1964.

entrance points were too great. Most of the people visiting their families took packages of food and clothing. These were "controlled" but few were confiscated. Some went in groups, some alone. No one who could not claim a relative was given permission to visit. There are, therefore, many in West Berlin who have never passed through the Wall.

The influence of this period of meetings was widespread. It was not only those who lived in East Berlin who benefited by the arrangements. Many thousands who lived in the Zone came to East Berlin to see relatives for the first time since 1961. The sense of having these personal reunions was multiplied many times as the exchange of messages and information spread throughout the restricted, Communist-held territory. The effect here and abroad of this mass movement was unforgettable.

This "eighteen-day experience"[11] marked the beginning of several similar holiday and "compassionate" agreements, reached after considerable negotiations and difficult sparring for position on both sides. The East Zone authorities used what they hoped was new leverage to gain increasing stature.[12] They maneuvered to have more processing stations in West Berlin. They demanded that officials of high rank deal with them. They attempted to break the traditional pattern of dealings which, by mutual understanding, had been played down as political actions and considered "technical."

In spite of the sensitive aspects of the arguments, under the anxious scrutiny of the Bonn government and of the Western Allies, the talks were reopened in early 1964 with a view to extending the plan to other holidays in addition to Christmas. Willi Stoph, the first deputy chairman of the GDR council,[13] had declared on January 4, 1964, that the Christmas pass arrangement was "a starting point for further efforts." In February, the Berlin *Senat*, reviewing the situation, withdrew its consent for a new agreement based on the December experience.

Willy Brandt, in March, anxious to widen the opening that seemed to have been broached in the Wall, proposed a joint meet-

11. *Ibid.*, pp. 35–46. Official Reports on the pass agreements of December 17, 1963, and September 24, 1964.
12. Shell, *Bedrohung und Bewährung*, 49, 79.
13. *Ibid.*, p. 30.

ing to reach an understanding by representatives of the Federal Government, the Berlin *Senat,* and the three main political parties. He felt the need for a unified position, since his efforts to push ahead alone had been subject to criticism. At this time, he also granted an interview calling for co-ordinated allied support.[14]

On this occasion he put forward an idea which is supported by some, but considered dangerous by others, that the various contacts including visits, trade, postal matters, telephone communication, railroad arrangements, and other affairs be put under a single commission to accomplish "humanitarian alleviations." It was obvious that the possibilities that such a group would achieve considerable status raised key problems. Mayor Brandt, in discussing the problem, praised the declaration of Chancellor Erhard in the previous October which set the framework and indicated the importance of reaching agreements consistent with the general policy of non-recognition. In April, Brandt was forced to concede that there were serious difficulties in the way of further progress. He was greatly disappointed that sharp differences of opinion as to the processing stations and the level of exchange between officials had prevented Easter and Whitsuntide visits in 1964. The GDR issued a complaint at the eight months' delay and expressed regret that the *Senat* "had raised new demands" preventing a reasonable solution.

The governing Mayor had made it plain in his announcement in the Berlin *Abgeordnetenhaus* that he had not, and would not, concede the point. He maintained that the Berliners' right to travel was unconditional and that the passes did not change the formal status or the Federal Republic's adherence to the allied legal doctrine. Nevertheless, he said it was important to take account of the "actual conditions and arrangements which exist between the GDR and West Berlin."[15] Thus, because the East was trying to raise the ante and because the position of the West was spelled out with considerable clarity, there were several weeks of silence after the failure in the spring.

Passes in the Future

The pause in negotiation was ended by the speech of Willy Brandt in Bochum on September 9, 1964. In this he was quoted

14. *Der Spiegel*, March 9, 1964.
15. State Department telegram of June, 1964, from the diplomatic mission (USBER).

in the press as urging more *Passierscheine* and little steps of other types. One should endeavor to secure small gains even if the larger objectives are presently unattainable.[16] Shortly thereafter, on September 15, Horst Korber, the Western representative, and Erich Wendt, representing the East German regime, met for new talks on the passes. On September 23, Ludwig Erhard, for the Federal Cabinet in Bonn, approved the new pass agreement, even though it was full of restrictions with regard to the categories of people and the circumstances of the visits.

The conclusion of these conversations prepared the way for the passes that were to be good for limited visits until June, 1965. These arrangements would apply particularly for Christmas, Easter, and Whitsuntide. The procedures had been better developed than in the previous year, and fewer people were turned away without the requisite piece of paper. There was also a special office for compassionate cases to help meet emergencies, illness, or death in the family.

The new agreement also provided for visits of retired pensioners from the East Zone and East Berlin—permitting some 240,000 to come to West Berlin by the end of the year for several weeks' visits. It was expected by the East Zone authorities that many of these older persons would not return. The policy in the East regime was to encourage the nonworking older people to leave; they were considered to be "dead wood." The Berlin *Senat*, aware of the financial burden of the visits from the East and also of the expenses for the stay and for gifts taken back, made financial allowances to the persons taking part in these two actions.

The visits went forward as scheduled, and on June 21, 1965, Korber, Kohl, and Wendt met again to consider the passes and also the future. The conversations encountered many difficulties as in the previous year. The East regime continued to try to make gains for their international status, even though, many think, they regretted the success of the renewal of friendly relations between those in the East and the West. The success for the Federal Republic was evident. It is generally agreed among hundreds of persons asked, and also in several opinion polls, that the operation had been a gain for the West. It underscored the popular feeling that Berlin was still *one city* and indicated that neither side could

16. This was the theme of his Tutzing speech of July, 1963.

turn against the other. Complete separation was not currently to be accepted in either the East or the West.

Agreements Over Passes

The efforts on both sides of the line to increase the number of contacts and visits must be viewed in relation to the long-run policy of the Soviets, and their talk of "peaceful coexistence." On the one hand, the Communists seem to have believed they could lull the free world into complaisance. In fact, they might have made some progress except for the frequent shooting of escaping Germans and the brutal attitude through the police controls and harsh conditions, even those that accompanied the special agreements as to passes. On the other hand, the West Germans believe that their goal of eventual reunification is furthered by keeping the family ties and by dissemination of information, so that the sense of Germanness in the East remains.

In spite of the uncertainty in the summer of 1965 as to whether the Ulbricht regime would demand new concessions in return for another series of passes, the Berlin authorities were able to reach agreement for 1966 which made no new concessions. During the year 1966 there were several periods of over a week during which those who received the proper identification at the screening point were allowed to visit relatives. Because of the fact that these crossings had occurred before little note was taken of them in the outside world, one can almost assume that the Communist East Germans have decided that they suffer relatively little from the contacts and may gain from this minor alleviation of the pressure and the adverse propaganda which is caused by the Wall.

In this respect the policy of the Berlin *Senat* and Willy Brandt seems to have been successful in a minor adjustment of the relations with the authorities across the line.

One formula used to ease negotiation of the many contacts between the two Germanys in this strange situation has been the use of special phraseology to designate the authority of the signers of documents. For example, under the signatures on the annual trade agreement renewals are the words "West German Currency District" and "East German Currency District"—the wording thus avoided the term "German Democratic Republic" on official documents. The formula was never palatable to Ulbricht. While the conversations on visitors passes were going on, in 1965 the East Zone Minister for Trade and Commerce again took exception to this formula, the Ulbricht was reported to have said that "the GDR is not a currency area, but a state."

The arguments over the passes demonstrate many of the varied aspects of the relations in a divided Germany—the politics of reunification, the pressure for status and for recognition of the GDR, the easing of the tensions caused by the Wall and, in the East Zone, the sense of common heritage, of continuing tradition, of sympathy, of understanding, and a knowledge of conditions on both sides of the Iron Curtain. The German arguments lay bare difficulties of the long delays and indicate a combination of patience in the face of reality and of impatience over a do-nothing attitude. They suggest sometimes indirectly, sometimes more pointedly, that the Allies do more on their own.

There are a number of persons who play upon the theme that since the occupying powers have made themselves exclusively responsible for the security of the city, they should use their power either in Moscow or elsewhere, as they can affect the Soviet interests, to gain concessions that are much more difficult for the Germans themselves to win. The concern for reunification has thus a negative aspect—as a source of criticism of the West—and a positive aspect as it has increased the effort to schedule specific action in Western dealings, however limited, with the East. This presents the United States with delicate problems. Germans have always recognized the heavy and complex commitments of the United States in the East, in Africa, in Latin America, and wherever freedom is challenged. It is not recognized that the NATO problems are increasingly troublesome, sensitive, and many-sided. It is not always remembered that for the Soviet Union and also the United States there are grave issues which, if precipitately handled, might trigger atomic warfare.

The problems here sketched out have a wide meaning. They are in the forefront of discussion now more than formerly. They are likely to become more sharply focused with the passage of time. They call for an unbiased view of the main points of view in

Germany today which can be summarized under four headings. The views, which vary widely, have evolved to a new stage in the past ten or fifteen years. They are argued with a multitude of explanations and variations as suggested below.

One, there are a few who say that reunification is, under present and foreseeable conditions, excluded. There is little to do but wait for the unexpected and be prepared to act in a constructive way when Moscow, Pankow, Peking, or some other political center shifts so as to permit a practical policy to be developed. While not many Germans express this view clearly, a large number seem to be thinking in these terms.

Two, a not inconsiderable group holds that the freedom of the Federal Republic and its government, laws, and privileges must be safeguarded and strengthened in an alliance with other democracies, even if it means the delay of reunification of Germany for many decades.

Three, there are others who hold that action of a very careful sort can so alter conditions in the East Zone that the separation of the two populations will become less—or at least not greater—and that eventually, with an "East" closely bound to the West through economic and cultural ties, steps towards reunification will be acceptable on both sides. This view is not clearly articulated but suggests that something must be done now and that later good results can be achieved, that recognition of Pankow as a sovereign or legitimate state should be strenuously avoided.

Four, a view—staunchly defended and held by a significant segment of intellectuals—is that the goal is clear and that measures toward this goal are desirable and necessary now. Some say that "since at some stage in negotiation for reunification there must be recognition," measures taken now which seem to move in that direction should not be feared. They assert that in relation to the Federal Republic, if the living standard of the Zone is raised, if the Pankow regime feels security rather than hostility, if the people have many and varied contacts, then there can be a confederation that will be equivalent to reunification in which the two Germanys can become integrated. The degree of accommodation with the West has not been clearly outlined, but the positive suggestions are based on what is alleged to be a large measure of independence

The Relations of Divided Germany and Berlin

from Moscow in Hungary, Poland, Rumania, and elsewhere. The manner of adjusting capitalism and communism is not spelled out.

In support of these various positions, there are gradations of emphasis on the humanitarian aspects of the question. Some favor contacts between people because of family relations and the desire to reduce the sense of isolation in the Zone. They also say that if there is improvement in the GDR, travel from the East will be permitted—since the desire to emigrate to the West will diminish. The Wall could then be pierced with many holes—the borders would become less significant.

In most of these arguments, stress is placed on the continued will of the three Western Powers to defend Berlin. Apparently, here is no thought that Western policy would be altered to weaken the Allied commitment, although Bender talks of new guarantees.[17] There is in some cases a hope that the Western alliance would not suffer and that NATO would remain. In other cases, it is assumed that there would be a virtual neutralization of all of Germany.

When the argument emphasizes the policy of little steps rather than a frank defense of accommodation and coexistence with Communism, it often contains some unanalyzed assumptions—for instance, that there can be a large number of contacts without a serious move towards recognition. Whether this is political salesmanship, or whether it is a belief in movement and change which might open new doors and present now unpredictable possibilities, is not at this time easy to say.

A Growing Problem for the West

Now more than at any time since the Wall went up it is important to review German attitudes towards the United States in particular and NATO in general. The threatened gap in understanding is bound to grow unless positive action is taken in the field of public relations, in negotiation, and in practical evidence of United States dependence on Germany as a partner in democracy. The Adenauer-Dulles friendship still has fabled significance. There has been no recent dramatic expression of accepted policy and mutual understanding to capture the minds and elicit a response among the newer men rising to positions of authority. The American stand in

17. Bender, *Offensive Entspannung*, p. 143.

the Cuban missile crisis, however, was for the Berliners a spectacular event, and the West gained back prestige that some thought had been severely damaged. The visit of President Kennedy in 1963 was the last important manifestation of understanding. Now the American attitude toward reunification efforts can have great importance for the European Alliance.

V. The East Zone—
Twenty Years After

The imagination and the fears of those in the Federal Republic who are coming into their first responsibilities in national life are stirred by thoughts of what goes on in the East Zone. The young people remember, if dimly, the misery and privations at the close of the war. They realize that the difficulties east of the Iron Curtain have been compounded by a harsh occupation and an oppressive government. They have known something of the poverty and the tyranny through the accounts of refugees, some of whom have been held as political prisoners for minor acts of rebellion. They know that now conditions are improving. The changes since the 1953 uprising have been substantial. The changes since the Wall are also notable. The West Berliners are convinced that there are beginnings of a national pride in the Zone which at times competes with the German loyalty to the Fatherland.

Many of the old people have stayed. The young left in large numbers.[1] More than three and a half million fled to the West. The economic conditions were for a time an element of some importance in the flow of refugees. Over the period from the Blockade to the Wall, the motives were mainly psychological. They fled from oppression to find a new climate of opinion as well as to seek economic opportunities.

1. Bundesministerium für gesamtdeutsche Fragen, *SBZ von A bis Z: Ein Taschen- und Nachschlagebuch über die Sowjetische Besatzungszone Deutschlands* (Bonn: 1965), p. 69. Actually, the population in 1963 was below that of 1954 and virtually the same for 1961, 1962, and 1963 (SBZ refers to Soviet Besatzungszone, or Soviet occupation Zone, hereafter cited as SBZ).

There were many temporary visitors. Before the Wall, on May first, there was each year a political cabaret in the open-air arena of the Waldbühne in Berlin. To this came several thousand East Berliners, showing their identity cards to get their admittance tickets. They were indistinguishable in the crowd of West Berliners. Their laugh was probably quicker, their enjoyment more keen. They always cheered loudly when told that an American woman had come to be with them on May Day.[2] The brief visit came as a breath of fresh air to those living in the police state. They could move back and forth freely then and could make small purchases to meet some of the scarcities they endured.

Conditions in the Zone are different now. More effort is made in inducing the young men to take a constructive part in the expansion of industry and to look for opportunities for advancement. At the same time, escape for those who feel oppressed is difficult and dangerous.

The observers in the Federal Republic are aware of these contrasting changes. Their respect for science and education in the East has increased. There are some who have said a few of the educational institutions are better than in the West. The more experienced are inclined to view the limitations on the humanities and the lack of broad philosophic studies as seriously restricting the universities even though they have achieved considerable progress in the field of training and scientific instruction.[3]

The new attitude of the zonal authorities should be taken as a sign that some progress has been made in economic and social reconstruction. Special importance attaches to the fact that non-Communists now have access to advanced schooling. The failure to insist on Party affiliation suggests a new Kremlin attitude toward the increasing strength and viability of the Ulbricht regime. Although the Soviet troops still remain—in 1966 some twenty or twenty-two divisions (more than 300,000)—the approach to the people is now more subtle and the presence of the Soviet occupiers is less in evidence. The willingness of officials to condone the

2. Eleanor Lansing Dulles, "The Soviet Occupied Zone of Germany: A Case Study in Communist Control," *The Department of State Bulletin*, XXXVI (April 15, 1957), 607.

3. Eleanor Lansing Dulles, "Education—Communist Style, American Style," *The Department of State Bulletin*, XXXVII (July 1, 1957), 25–29.

apparent neutrality of many of the people of the East Zone as a halfway station in the conversion to Communism is an element in current attempts to dilute the rebellious feelings of Germans who still wish to be united with their fellows in the West. In this "New Course," the acceptance of students without Party membership can, over the years, have a significant effect on the general attitude toward the regime and also bring satisfaction to those who receive valuable training.

The instances of new freedoms are still within rigid political and authoritative limits. The men and women who escape over the border testify to the unbearable sense of repression and for this reason risk their lives to throw off the bonds of Communism. There are, here and there, towns without traces of Communism. Some of the visitors from West Germany who stay with relatives in the Zone have said that in scattered small communities there are no party members and there is little political interference with the routine of daily life. Even in such places, however, where they feel the less specific surveillance and do not dread sudden intervention, they are aware of constant, if invisible, restraint.

It is in fact this element in the situation more than any specific aspect of the material life which leads to unrest. It attests to the human tendency to reject bondage and the continuing desire for independence which has not been extinguished. Those who know the German character forecast a will to resist which, however quiescent, will be prolonged indefinitely unless there are much more sweeping changes in the nature of the regime and the manner of administration. Nations with the tough fiber of the German people, like the Poles, Hungarians, and others who have been overrun and who have regained a degree of independence, are not easily assimilated into a unified monolithic or even a satellite system. This is all the more true in view of the traditional antagonism towards the Germans felt by the Poles, the Czechs, and the Russians. It will take more than food and education to win over the people either in the East Zone or in Berlin.

In spite of the persistence of hatred of the Soviets, the rejection of Communism, and the longing for independence, there is nonetheless a feeling of pride in the achievements of industry in the Zone. For the first time it is reported that many boast that the recovery of the economy to a condition roughly comparable to the levels reached by the Federal Republic in 1955 has been accomplished "without the help of a Marshall Plan." This idea gives a degree of satisfaction in the Zone, characterized to some extent by the Prussian spirit, which has a typical determination to overcome obstacles and gain a sense of efficiency. Thus conflicting emotions complicate a picture that is clearly discernible but not always comprehensible to outsiders.

As the years of divided rule continue, the relatives of the residents in the Zone of occupation recognize their common heritage and tend to sympathize both with their resistance and also with their industrious efforts to achieve a more tolerable situation. This change can have far-reaching political repercussions in the years ahead.

There is indeed a "New Course" with greater freedom of industrial planning and more stress on quality. The change came after the decision of September, 1958,[4] but the results were scarcely noticed until after the Wall. There is now an impetus which, though hard to measure, is impressing many observers, including those who visited the Leipzig Fair in September of 1965.[5] The statistics are illusive. Professor Karl C. Thalheim[6] cites the figures for increase in 1962 as compared with 1936, and also discusses the index of "Gross Production" as more than three-fold, or 365 per cent. He compares this figure with an adjusted index for the Federal Republic of 304, admitting that there are a number of uncertain factors that prevent strict comparability. He questions the resulting implication that production in the Zone has risen faster than in West Germany, saying that such a conclusion is in the "highest degree improbable." He notes the large increase in investment under the seven-year plan, but states that it is far below that in West Germany. He also notes that exports are low, as is the standard of living. He advises against attempts to adjust the indices coming from the Zone as an unproductive effort.

The most widely recognized facts have been the increase in heavy industry and the improvement in food standards. The changes since the erection of the Wall in 1961 are more notable

4. *SBZ*, p. 193.
5. *New York Times*, September 29, 1965.
6. Karl C. Thalheim, *Die Wirtschaft der Sowjetzone in Krise und Umbau* (Berlin: Duncker and Humblot, 1964), pp. 37–38.

than those just after 1958. They have influenced attitudes, political relations, and the over-all conditions; they have affected the young people more than the older generation.

Political Dilemma for Both Sides

As for the leaders in the Federal Republic, many fear that time is running against them. They conclude that the moment for showing their continuing concern with their fellows is at hand, and that theory as to dealings between East and West must not stand in the way of practical results. They even go so far, on rare occasions, as to imply that the Western Allies have developed an unreal and unconstructive doctrine with neglect for some genuine opportunities for loosening the bonds of their friends and relatives in the East.

Walter Ulbricht, too, is facing a dilemma. Although he has endeavored to exact a price for East-West contacts, this price tag changes as his appraisal of Western opinion changes.[7] He can never be sure as to whether the progress towards making his regime more respectable is worth risking the losses from infection by ideas of the democratic West. Perhaps there will be an increase in the number of those who conclude that the rules laid down for East-West relations are artificial and that a casual attitude toward *dealings* might be more fruitful in this strange and unprecedented situation. Many would agree with the suggestion that time and durability have done more toward making the Ulbricht regime seem real than any specific act by the Germans or the Allies in regard to negotiations and dealings.

In this connection, various episodes can be reviewed to advantage. One of the first hotly contested issues was the result of steps taken by the United States in June, 1958, to free the American crew of a helicopter that had been downed in the East Zone. Here two military officers from the American Army and the Ulbricht administration conferred over the conditions under which the fliers would be returned.[8] Few now remember the episode which at the time aroused fear in official Washington circles that our action would add significantly to Ulbricht's prestige. Even the presence of East Zone representatives at Geneva in 1959, in the same room as

---

7. See the above discussion of the *Passierscheine*, pp. 93–96.
8. U.S. Department of State, *American Foreign Policy, Current Documents*, 1958 (Washington: U.S. Government Printing Office, 1962), documents numbers 272–77, pp. 875–65.

representatives of the four major powers and the officials from Bonn, does not, in retrospect, seem to have altered the status or acceptability of Ulbricht to any considerable extent. Willy Brandt's negotiations in 1963 over the passes for West Berliners [9] have been much debated because of the importance attaching to these joint conversations. Such modifications of relations between Bonn and Pankow as have occurred are difficult for either side to appraise exactly. Who has won and who has lost in this shrewd contest of political strategy?

There is no doubt that the East Zone as well as Berlin presents serious problems to the Communists in Pankow and in Moscow. Virtually every anxiety in the West has its counterpart for the East. Any increase in pressure on the population in the Zone breeds danger for the authorities.

There is always the question whether there has been a significant relaxation of controls since 1961. If so, what have been the motives? The free world wishes more interchange of ideas but recognizes that trade can make a considerable contribution to military strength that can be used in case of aggression. They feel, as do the more intuitive of the Communists, that rigidity of policy can create extremes of opinion that endanger stability in both the West and in the East.

While the free world does not fear the contagion of Communism, there are many who fear that a carefree attitude toward the alien system can lead to mental confusion on the part of the less experienced. To some extent any modification in the commitment of the leaders of the democracies can be interpreted as a partial surrender by those who search for signs of weakness. The conflict of views on both sides of the Iron Curtain over trade, travel, passes, and the increasing intellectual debate are expressions of this dilemma and a widespread divergence of opinion as to both aims and means.

The report of the travels of three journalists in the Zone in recent months are significant in this regard.[10] They speak of the sixteen different controls to which they were subjected in the Berlin area in a single day—senseless delays and long waits at the barriers while

9. *Zur Passierscheinfrage*, pp. 66–78.
10. Marion Gräfin Dönhoff, Rudolf Walter Leonhardt, Theo Sommer, *Reise in ein fernes Land* (Hamburg: Nannen, 1965), hereafter cited as *Reise*.

baggage was searched, identity papers examined and discussed. The journalist were surprised at such precautions; their papers were in order and they did not reside in West Berlin. They were not, as are West Berliners, under strict restrictions in the rare cases of travel in the GDR.

The approaches to the city are always the ones most carefully watched and hemmed in by thousands of guards. Many Saxons who reputedly do not like the West Germans are chosen as Vopos and put at the barriers, and some of the police are thought to be ardent party members.

Throughout their journey, after leaving Berlin, the three were relatively free to go as they pleased. They did not try to explore sensitive areas, they moved inconspicuously or so they said, from town to town. They found living conditions tolerable, but not usually comfortable.

In their book they report a factual and convincing account of what they found on their journey. In many conversations they explored some of the reasons why the economic system had changed in the last three or four years. In spite of stable conditions and improvements in some respects, the travelers found an inefficiency that made them feel at times as if they were several decades back in terms of hotels, automobiles, telephones, and various means of communication as well as in respect to the familiar luxuries of life.[11] They learned of the changed attitude toward production methods and planning which has been a major factor in bringing the Zone at least statistically up to a new high level.

These travelers, in talking with residents of the Zone, were told that the flight of the refugees, before the Wall, had made the attempt to adopt new methods pointless. Some spoke of the estimates of large financial drain on the regime by the flight of technicians and skilled workers, in each of whom they had invested training valued approximately at ten thousand East marks—with a consequent loss in the neighborhood of thirty billion marks worth of the national wealth as more than "three million useful persons" fled to the West.[12] In contrast to this limit on resources, since the building of the Wall, the uncertainty as to the labor force has

---

11. *Ibid.*, p. 22.
12. *Ibid.*, p. 33. Thirty billion marks would be equivalent to two or three billion dollars.

ceased and the stability of the industries could be assured. There seems to be no doubt that Walter Ulbricht considers his Wall a success, as do economists on both sides. They reason that the industrial progress that has been accomplished and the political stability gained more than outweigh the propaganda elements that make this a "wall of shame" and an outrage against mankind.

The changes that have been noted include not only the amounts produced and the attitudes of the workers who find there is no longer an easy escape but also a new attitude toward prices and profits.

In East Germany, more than elsewhere in the Communist world, the profit system was being incorporated in a comprehensive planning system. The combination of German workers with Teutonic traditions and the urge to gain in the competition with the Federal Republic has led to a substantial modification of the planned Communist control of production. The system has probably undergone a greater modification than the economies of neighboring Poland and Czechoslovakia. The changes over the last ten years which have taken place here are of special interest, not only in connection with reunification but also because of the conclusions that may arise out of this experience which bear on methods in other Communist-dominated lands. In the Zone, the Communist party exercises firm control with respect to leadership and management—but does not now demand either membership in, nor sympathy with, Communist aims as a requirement for a high position. The new economic policy does not mean any general abandonment of the Lenin-Marxist dogma but rather a special practical adjustment.[13] The system of control continues to be institutionally complicated and personally oppressive. So far, success has come mainly in the heavy goods industries, and there are serious shortages of light goods, household wares, and quality items.

All of these and other aspects of production have been studied in the Gradl-Mende [14] report. This is a research project published by

13. *SBZ*, pp. 191–93. Thalheim, *Die Wirtschaft der Sowjetzone in Krise und Umbau*, p. 37. The "New Course" of 1953 was modified in September, 1958, by the "New Economic System of Planning," which was in some measure responsible for the increase in production after the Wall.

14. See also *Vierter Tätigkeitsbericht*, 1961–1965, des Forschungsbeirat für Fragen der Wiedervereinigung Deutschlands beim Bundesminister für Gesamtdeutsche Fragen (Bonn; Bundesministerium für gesamtdeutsche Fragen, 1965). Hereafter cited as *Bericht*.

TABLE 2. PRODUCTION OF SELECTED INDUSTRIAL GOODS[a]
(Per Capita)

	East Zone	Federal Republic
Washing machines		
1963	15.0 per 1,000	17.5 per 1,000
1965	16.9 per 1,000	25.7 per 1,000
Vacuum cleaners		
1963	20.2 per 1,000	20.3 per 1,000
1965	19.0 per 1,000	26.3 per 1,000
Radios		
1963	45.4 per 1,000	61.0 per 1,000
1965	47.5 per 1,000	65.1 per 1,000
Television		
1963	34.7 per 1,000	33.3 per 1,000
1965	31.5 per 1,000	47.0 per 1,000
Binoculars		
1963	7.6 per 1,000	4.2 per 1,000
1965	4.8 per 1,000	4.0 per 1,000
Bicycles		
1963	24.9 per 1,000	17.1 per 1,000
1965	26.1 per 1,000	18.3 per 1,000
Household sewing machines		
1963	13.7 per 1,000	8.2 per 1,000
1965	11.7 per 1,000	9.4 per 1,000

a. Data calculated by dividing production by population.
Source: *Statistical Yearbook, GDR*, 1965, p. 168–70; *Statistical Yearbook, GDR*, 1966, pp. 3, 171; and *Statistical Yearbook, FRG*, 1966, p. 254.

the Ministry of All German Affairs and designed to lay a basis for economic planning to be made ready for the demanding requirements at the time of reunification. Although it is recognized that the period when adjustments of the economic systems will be needed is at present unpredictable, it has been thought useful to explore now the elements of the problem. There is constant concern for what changes take place now and what can be expected later.

This four-hundred-page volume will continue to be a useful work for those interested in reunification. It serves to refute some arguments which impute to the Germans a fear that the bringing together of the two economies might seriously slow down or even reverse the upward movement of the economy of the Federal Republic. This is a view that I never heard in the course of my conversations in Germany. Although it might be inferred it would not be likely that the Germans, in talks with an American, would express the more materialistic approach to the political question, it can be stated that in the heat of discussion of these questions the presence of one foreigner among a dozen or more Germans was largely forgotten.

The general outlines of the Gradl-Mende report are of considerable interest and present the dimensions of the recent economic improvement. They reflect the lag in transportation and the weak spots which result from the limitations on consumer demand in an economy that has been for almost twenty years adapted to the requirements of Soviet defense, and that had to meet the basic reconstruction needs that resulted from the large-scale Russian reparation removals and war devastation. It is a bipartisan and expert study and serves to guide policy both in current times and in the more distant future.

The report discusses the social and economic institutions and their operations with comparative statistical data from 1950 through 1963.[15] It emphasizes the significance of the seven-year plan. It describes the currency reforms, the price level, and the banking, investment, and the "plow back" of earnings, and related economic matters.

A comparison is made of the volume of commerce between the regions of Germany now divided by the Iron Curtain. Whereas in 1936 this approximated eight billion Reichsmarks (the pre-1948 currency), in 1964 it amounted to two billion DM although the production of West Germany and West Berlin was substantially higher. This amount is estimated to be a likely amount under normal conditions. The most significant shortcoming from the point of view of zonal production is in the field of metals, notably special steels. Hard coal deliveries remain important to the Zone.

15. *Ibid.*, pp. 83–234, especially p. 222.

The external trade of the Zone is increasing in relation to the shipments to the Federal Republic, as the efforts of the regime to attain independence intensify.[16] In spite of this policy, the industry of the Soviet Zone of Occupation remains closely related to and in continuing need of the products of the machine, electric, and steel products of the Federal Republic.

The gap between receipts and deliveries of the Federal Republic, leading to a "swing" or credit from the Federal Republic for the Zone, is mainly attributable to the increase in the deliveries of fertilizers. The report concludes its section on trade by underscoring the aim of the Federal Republic to maintain a strong bond between the two parts of Germany. It forecasts an increasing exchange of products through 1965.

The discussion turns to the important point of whether reunification would bring serious disturbances to industrial patterns. Problems of automation, reorganization, and new investment would have to be faced. The extent of the needs would depend on production levels at the time of the integration. The new demands are assumed to call for increased buildup and investment of varied natures.

It would not be appropriate here to summarize the work of the various commissions. It is sufficient to indicate the scope of the work, its stress on preparedness, and the general conclusion that a job must be done unhampered by doubts and fears that the economy of the West might suffer.

What Germans Think about the Zone

The detailed factual material in the report is known only to a few, but the general knowledge of conditions corresponds to these findings. Certainly the view, sometimes expressed outside of Germany, that reunification would present almost unsurmountable difficulties, has no currency.

Conversations in the evening—and the Germans in Berlin like to talk far into the night over beer or wine—almost always turned to questions of what was happening in the East Zone. Although few Berliners ever reach there, many from West Germany do. As a result, we know about the feelings, hopes, and fears. The problem

16. *Ibid.*, pp. 223–24, 243.

of development of policy does not depend on intelligence agents. The many visitors have reported consistently what the situation is; scores of books have been written and are publicly available, as are statistics of a wide variety and considerable accuracy.

One of the most useful general guides to conditions, issued yearly by the Ministry of All German Affairs, is the *SBZ von A–Z*. It presents the more recent figures on trade, production, population, agriculture, and brief summaries of critical issues. It comments on such subjects as youth, religion, Marxism-Leninism, the "new course" in economic life, labor policy, military forces and programs, culture, and education. With this book in hand and the analytical studies of Ludz [17] and Thalheim and others of the Ost Europa Institut in Berlin, one can gain a clear knowledge of the actual situation and measure the material changes in the Zone.

Much more difficult, of course, is the judgment of the mental and moral changes which are of major concern.

Of interest in appraising trends are the views of Dr. Kurt Leopold, who was for many years the West German negotiator of the interzonal trade agreements. His frequent conversations with the commercial officials of the Ulbricht regime gave him a realistic understanding of the tone and attitudes of some of the minor officials with whom he had to deal. Now that he no longer has this responsibility, he looks back on his experiences and summarizes them in an article in *Quick* magazine.[18]

It is his view that restrictions in export from the West to the Zone have not altered the policy or strategy of the Soviets in their handling of East Germany. The Communist authorities have always had complete control in the Zone, he states, and the restrictions on trade have hurt the people and held back economic progress, thus depressing the standard of living.

Leopold considers that the error in this policy has been the result of considering the residents of the Zone more as Communists than as Germans, a view he finds destructive and harmful to the long range objective of reunification.

He reinforces his point by drawing a distinction between the

---

17. Peter Christian Ludz and associates, *Studien und Materialien zur Soziologie der DDR* (Cologne: Westdeutscher Verlag, 1964).
18. *Quick*, Munich, July 11, 1963.

old-style East German negotiators and the new. He recounts an incident four years ago during the negotiations over repairs of the Rothensee ship locks. At that time, some five or six years ago, the East Germans were making no effort to put this vital trade artery into passable condition, and negotiations were achieving nothing. Finally, Dr. Leopold gave Herr Orlopp, his East Zone counterpart, an ultimatum that if the repairs were not made, West German deliveries of iron and steel to the East would cease. He says this caused a violent reaction on the part of the older man who hammered the table with his fist and broke off the meeting. Today, he said, these "old guard" Communists have been replaced by a new breed of technicians.

When a similar impasse was reached in the dealings over the Saale-Autobahn bridge at Hof, the reaction of Leopold's negotiating partner was very different from the earlier case in dealing with the Communist-indoctrinated Orlopp. The new man was young, confident, well-trained, and definitely of a different generation. For him the stories of war and concentration camps were mere hearsay; his interests were economic and he was little concerned with party doctrine.

Leopold concludes that the East Germans are developing a new "GDR consciousness," leading to a sense of permanent separation from the Federal Republic. The West Germans have been misled by the nature of the regime and their preoccupation with the unacceptability of Zone leaders and a failure to distinguish between the regime and the people. He criticizes his West German colleagues who "have done little to prevent the growing feeling of separation."

"We have failed to take many steps," Leopold writes, "for fear of helping Pankow or Moscow." However, what West Germany does cannot influence the Kremlin's attitude toward the GDR, or self-styled "German Democratic Republic." Thus we have left the East German people in limbo. Twenty divisions are there and cannot be forced to leave by economic or political pressure. The power situation and capabilities in East Europe are not affected by our trade. He queries, "When we see the East German officials as Communists, and not as Germans, are we not forcing them to be that way?"

He recommends that everything possible be done to promote the German consciousness. Personal visits, gift packages, and economic contacts are all important in order to develop an awareness of the bonds between the two areas of "West and Middle Germany" in the East sector.

By means of interzonal trade, West Germany can provide investment resources and industrial equipment, and for this purpose long-term credits would be necessary. Now, laborers in the East work harder and live less well. The improvement in the living standard is a worthwhile goal.

If some sacrifices were to be made in such industries as glassware, optics, and precision machinery, which would face new competition, "the West Germans are willing to make these sacrifices." The question of reunification transcends the interests of individuals.

Leopold's argument is interesting both because of his intimate contacts with the Zone authorities, with whom he has had more dealings than any other West German, but also because other Berlin observers have suggested the same evaluation of conditions in the East Zone. On the one hand, there is no reason to doubt his assertion that a new generation of technicians has appeared. On the other hand, Leopold's logic in declaring that the withholding of certain goods from trade has in no way affected Communist policy, or the power situation, is far from proven and would require further evidence.

It is not possible now to see what the tactics with regard to Berlin would have been, if steel and other important raw materials had been available in larger amounts. Leopold's voice is, however, not the only one of those now heard; he is joined by others at this time of transition.

A recent statement by Rudi Georgi in Leipzig (GDR) gave much the same impression as the Leopold article. He said, "I'm the boss, not the politicians. I direct everything from market research and sales and services, and my main objective is to produce top quality goods at low prices." [19] In the not-too-distant past, such comments by Red managers would have been sufficient cause for prompt and permanent "retirement." Thus, in this part of the Eastern bloc there are indications of criticism of "rigid central

19. *The Wall Street Journal*, Vol. CLXVI, No. 66, October 4, 1965.

planning," a sense of accounting and workings of price economies and a loosening of party control. The evidence of change is of significance in any attempt to forecast trends in the Zone and elsewhere.

The situation in the Zone, however, remains complex and contradictory. If one is to understand it, one must observe that in the Federal Republic as well as in the Zone, years of dictatorship did not suppress the desire for freedom. Now that the youth in the West, raised in freedom, are seeking more power, they assume that one of their responsibilities is to break the fetters of the East.

In 1965, for the first time, there was a consensus that the East Zone population would not rise in revolt against the Ulbricht regime if the Soviet armed forces were removed from the occupied Zone. When I inquired in former years, it had always been stated that once the troops were no more in evidence the dangers of a political conflagration would become serious, that a spark could set ablaze an uprising of serious proportions which would be likely to succeed with or without West German help. This view seems no longer prevalent. One can ask, however, if this is a fact, why the Soviets keep men under arms in the Zone. Speculation on this point is interesting, but the current views cannot be considered to be conclusive. In any case, West German estimates are cautious and hold the probability of a significant demonstration against the regime to be remote. The stability that has been much talked about is not entirely an illusion.

There is a tendency on both sides of the Iron Curtain for some Germans to blame the Allies for a failure to accomplish more while there was an American atomic monopoly, and little comprehension of the obstacles to action. But they do not always realize the extent to which the German question is a central issue for the Soviets on which they have no present intention of yielding. The young men are in the mood to seize the initiative, and, at least in theory, many are willing to challenge both the Allies and the Soviets in this matter.

They see the Zone becoming less dependent on the Federal Republic for trade,[20] with only 8.7 per cent of its total trade in 1964

20. SBZ, p. 44. I discussed this at some length in an interview with Alfred Pollak, Chief of Interzonal Trade Affairs, on July 2, 1965.

going to West Germany as compared with 16.0 per cent in 1950. They see education improving rapidly in what are called the "neutral subjects"—those with little political content such as mathematics and chemistry with 9 per cent of the students receiving scholarships, even those who are not committed Communists. They find that food is adequate in the Zone and industry improving. They have reason to think that the accommodation of the men and women born since the war to the Eastern regime lies in developing habits of mind, not limited by the religion or world culture to which they still hold. They find that travel to the East from the Zone is increasing while the barriers to the West are still insurmountable. In Berlin, more than in the Federal Republic, where many visit the Zone, there is a growing concern with the political doctrine which, in their view, makes the contacts fewer and actually builds a Western wall of policy against interchange of ideas. This separation, which they find increasingly dangerous and a threat to eventual reunification, they blame in part on the Western Allies, and they could make it into a serious issue if the thinking of the pro-Western leaders fails to be acceptable.

The answer to the question which seems to them of prime urgency is to overlook the technical aspects of dealings with the Ulbricht regime and to do whatever is necessary, whenever opportunity offers, to bring about exchanges of ideas, of persons, and of goods. It is generally admitted that the population of the occupied area is anti-Communist. It is also generally concluded that it tends to be anti-Western. The East Germans have little basis for understanding Western democracy and no experience with its tolerance and its constructive impulse. They believe a part of the propaganda and find the looser methods of government and the more casual approach of Americans, British, French, and the West generally unconvincing. *Planning* seems to them reasonable, and the free price system impractical. Their view is bolstered by the visible improvement in the standard of living and by the expansion of industry. They forget at times the misery that prevailed through the first years of the occupation, and they find that living conditions have improved in the past three or four years since the new course. Those who reside in the Federal Republic tend to underestimate the vast difference between production in the West and in the East, and they do not think that this difference is enough to act as a magnet to turn the interest of the younger men in the Zone towards the West. They take a conservative, and at times pessimistic, view of the relations between the two areas.

What is not realized by the less expert is that the new course has not taken full account of the difficulty of moving from the phase of heavy production and basic construction to the more subtle interrelations that come with the attempt to expand consumer goods industries and the products that make life not only bearable but attractive. This stage has arrived for the planners in the Soviet Zone. Until they solve these problems, they cannot expect to gain the ground that is lost in comparison with the West—the estimates of output of consumer goods which place this category several hundred per cent behind the Federal Republic are not known to the general public and have been masked by the recent substantial growth of a number of the key industries.

Moreover, the direct advantage to the workers of an expanding economy that characterizes a responsive wage system in an individualistic society are not evident under the Communist system. A high degree of governmental restraint and a lack of ability to choose one's trade have led to a discontent that is likely to affect many workers in the future as it has in the past. During the years when laborers could defect to the West, this fact was blamed for a certain laxness that amounted in some cases to sabotage and that slowed down production. Now that the option has been virtually eliminated, there has been a notable spurt ahead.

How long and how far this will go cannot be estimated. To bid for more intensive economic effort, it has been necessary to introduce capitalistic kinds of incentives and to permit non-party members to share in the special rewards and promotions, even to open up new opportunities for the unconvinced Germans. These changes, foreshadowed in 1962 and incorporated in public statements on July, 1963,[21] were intended to keep the operation of the system within the outlines earlier laid down and centrally planned. The need for far-reaching price changes can be considered indications that the arbitrary system did not in fact bring a dependable relation between cost and selling price. Returns on production did

21. Thalheim, *Die Wirtschaft der Sowjetzone in Krise und Umbau*, p. 72.

not assure the proper financial balance needed to bring the most effective results. We see in the attempts, the changes, and the failure to accelerate in many cases the contradictions implicit in a highly controlled system, and we can identify the German restiveness, East and West, which is likely to continue as long as the comparison with West Germany has a special meaning for the workers in the Zone.

Agricultural Conditions

Agriculture since the war has been the weakest element in the Eastern economic complex, but it has made some strides in recent months.[22] The difficulties were the result of reorganization and collectivization. Now there is considerable use of fertilizer and grain; milk and potatoes are slightly above what they averaged a few years ago.[23] Pigs are more numerous, but sheep and fowl are fewer than a year ago. The figures for 1963 show slight changes in the past four years. The caloric consumption was said to be 2,560 in 1955 and 2,623 in 1961. A few other figures illustrate the general situation.

Agricultural comparisons between the East and West are meaningless unless one takes account of the very great differences between the two regions before the war. There had been a division of labor in the various types of production which had suited the nation at that time but which does not work so well in a divided country. In every important type of agricultural production, the Zone formerly had more land under cultivation. With respect to cattle, however, the situation was the opposite, with the Western territories raising more animals. For example, in pigs, the East had six million in 1935–38 as compared with thirteen million in the West; cows were 1 to 3, fowl less than 1 to 2. The improvement in agriculture reported for the last two or three years has been limited by the lack of incentive in a system that has imposed an alien type of production on what used to be the family type of farm. Until recently, the shortage of fertilizer adversely affected the yield for farmers, who were also reluctant to produce for the occupying Soviet troops when they themselves were on short rations. The

22. *Bericht*, pp. 87 ff.
23. SBZ, p. 253.

TABLE 3. AGRICULTURAL STATISTICS

Growing Area (in 1,000 hectares)

	1935–38	1959	1963	1965
East Zone				
Grains	3,124	2,414	2,239	2,304
Potatoes	791	771	747	725
Federal Republic				
Grains	5,152	4,900	4,930	4,924
Potatoes	1,162	960	925	783

Selected Comparisons of Agricultural Production (in kilogram/hectare)

	1935–38	1955–59	1960–64
East Zone			
Grains	23.9	21.5	25.5
Potatoes	194.3	153.4	169.0
Federal Republic			
Grains	22.4	27.3	30.5
Potatoes	185.0	220.7	247.6

Livestock (in thousands)

	1935–38	1959	1964	1965
East Zone				
Pigs	5,812	8,283	8,759	8,878
Sheep	1,628	2,115	1,972	1,963
Fowl[a]	21,690	38,604	38,210	37,988
Cows	1,947	2,158	2,132	2,169
Federal Republic				
Pigs	12,622	14,876	18,146	17,723
Sheep	1,900	1,084	1,124	1,027
Fowl[a]	55,054	64,083	80,616	82,295
Cows	6,049	5,670	5,816	59,108

a. Only 1938 figures.
Sources: For "Growing Area," SBZ 1962/63/66; for "Selected Comparisons" and "Livestock," SBZ 1962/63/65.

smaller acreage of the privately held land has regressed steadily from over 94 per cent in 1950 to less than 8 per cent in 1960. In view of this development, it is remarkable that food production has improved at all.

Nevertheless, there are indications that efficiency in agriculture has improved and that the attitude of the farmers has changed slightly. Rationing of food ceased in 1958, although shortages still require standing in line and long waits for such scarce items as meat, butter, fruit, and other products long plentiful in West Germany. A factor easing the demand for basic foods has been the decline of population. Some 3.5 million refugees fleeing to the West more than outweighed the natural increase of the population, and there were also some reductions in the number of Soviet soldiers living on the land.

The estimate most often heard is that the living standard in the East is 60 per cent of that in the Federal Republic, though even this difference does not take account of the degree of choice and the many luxuries available in West Germany. Only in housing space—largely because of the outflow of refugees and the influx into the FRG—have there been comparisons favorable to the East; but many buildings are falling rapidly into disrepair. In transportation, particularly automobiles, the comparison is about 1 to 7. There is no desire to encourage travel within the Zone for the average man—he is supposed to stay on his assigned job and not to move freely from place to place, upsetting the control of a managed economy.

There may be a closing of the economic gap in the years ahead, although most economists doubt this, but the political differences between East and West largely remain. The education, though excellent for training for specific jobs, is sterile and unsatisfying to those with wider interests. There is no stimulus for speculation outside the limits of prescribed doctrine. In the field of religion, the effort to stamp out independence has been directed mainly at the youth. The atheist oath of loyalty to the regime—the *Jugendweihe*—has long been a problem for the church. At first the official church doctrine was that those who took the oath could not be baptized, married, or buried "in the church." Then, as the hold of the Communists in the area became so comprehensive that it was clear that no young man could hope to hold a tolerable job or seek an advanced education unless he took the oath, in 1959 and 1960 the church began to relax its attitude and permitted the religious rites to those who had accepted this oath for practical and not for ideological reasons. The duality of the situation has been recognized by the Communists also, who appear now to count on gradual erosion rather than outright suppression. They have directed their attack rather against the religious leaders, making their lives intolerable and, with rare exceptions, preventing the travel of the bishops.

A hero of these years has been Bishop Otto Dibelius. His regular sermons in East Berlin and his frequent travels in the Zone were manifestations of a courage that gave new will to endure to those who knew that their religion would cost them preferment and even safety in the face of the hostile regime. This tough-fibered man of small stature, bearded and with bright, flashing eyes, had stood up to the Soviets when they came into Berlin in 1945. He told me of a dinner with Marshall Zhukov in the early weeks of the occupation. He had insisted that food be taken to his chauffeur who had not eaten a proper meal for many days. This demand surprised the Russian general, who said that chauffeurs "are only people," and the Bishop for his part was surprised when the chauffeur told him that the Russian had demanded the few marks in his pocket as payment for the privilege of eating.

His trips into the East had continued long after he was threatened with harsh treatment. At eighty-two years, beginning to grow old, in 1965 he said that his trips would still be undertaken if they were physically possible. Now, very few of the churchmen are allowed in the area. Although Ulbricht in 1960 announced that the members of church and synagogue could attend services, the basic conflict between religious faith and dialectical materialism lies at the root of the over-all policy. In 1962, in the "interests of order and security," the police administration forbade the meeting in the Zone of the all-German *Kirchentag*; and "radio GDR" announced February 6, 1962, the separation of the church in the Zone from the church in the West. These acts deprived the religious communities—the majority Lutheran, the minority Catholic, and the small group of Jews—from help from the West and made them largely dependent financially on the Eastern regime, with a sense of isolation tending to weaken the spirit of even the most staunch and devoted believers. In the face of difficulties, it is a tribute to the people that the church has survived.

The outlook for the Eastern part of Germany at the present time is bleak—with hate rather than loyalty, with natural science rather than culture, with little sense of local pride, with no outlook for political freedom. No one denies that a degree of economic progress has taken place but the products of industry do not flow in any considerable amount in consumer goods. Moreover, the atmosphere continues to be oppressive and frightening to those who have democratic ideas. It is the brilliant achievement of the Federal Republic, nourishing a varied life, with freedom of travel and a world outlook, that attracts the interests and arouses the fears of those who rule the Zone.

The Eastern part of Germany has been called the largest prison in the world.[24] It requires almost 100,000 border guards to keep the people in. It is estimated that there are 30,000 or more Vopos and Grepos in Berlin alone. Stationed along the "green border" with its mine fields, its watch towers, its machine guns, and its police dogs, are some 70,000 more armed men. These are told to shoot to kill and have already murdered some unnumbered victims who have attempted escape. The exact number will never be known; wounded men have been dragged from the barbed wire. Some, even though shot, have managed to reach asylum in the West. They bear witness to a partially articulated philosophy of freedom and a sense that the restrictions under which they live are an outrage to their human dignity. The number who have come over since the Wall was built is estimated to be many thousand. Although almost all the ways of escape have been denied by preventive measure, some few continue to work out ingenious methods of crossing the barrier. East Berlin, and the crossing points into West Berlin which were open at most streets until the Wall, provided an escape hatch from the Zone of Communist restrictions and oppressions. Those who were discontented could move easily to the West as refugees or could become border-crossers with jobs in the West while still living in the East.

Here, too, was the dramatic contrast in method and in style. The varied buildings in West Berlin, many constructed with private capital, were stimulating to the imagination and even excited the admiration of those who liked their bright appearance. In East Berlin there is a central complex of buildings which has been newly

24. *Ost-West Kurier*, special edition, Frankfurt, May 5, 1965.

The East Zone—Twenty Years After

built or partially restored. There are several large apartment buildings faced with blue tile which impress the casual visitor as does the partially restored area of Unter den Linden, near the Soviet Embassy and the Opera House. The new apartments border the area that, before the change in doctrine, was called Stalinallee—now Karl-Marx-Allee—and which surrounds the plaza and bus station where tourists are permitted to buy postal cards with the East marks that they were forced to buy at the point of entry at the rate of one to one, as contrasted with the black market rate of one to four or five, as they cross into the East sector. What some do not see is that, in the rear, many of the buildings are in bad repair and that a few blocks from the favored areas the houses and shops are falling apart. The guides on the bus tours take these differences into account, and the tourists are often impressed with recent progress.

In connection with a tour by bus to East Berlin in 1965, the final stop was at the Berolina Hotel. This hotel is the headquarters of a new "Interhotel" setup initiated by the regime to try to attract more foreign travelers and to capture the tourist trade to East Berlin and East Germany. Under "Interhotel" are a group of new hotels in the Berolina style—in Leipzig, Dresden, and already planned in other cities. Presumably these new buildings, not unattractive in appearance, are being built along international standards with comfortable beds, baths with each room, television or radio piped in, shops, restaurants, and bars. Someone told me that with this ambitious system East Germany hopes to attract 750,000 visitors by 1970.

The soft drinks on sale and the pleasant waiting room in the bus station impress the casual visitor who has been told that conditions in the East are shockingly low. He even finds the sparse traffic restful and the streets clean as compared with the hurlyburly of busy thoroughfares in West Berlin. Because of the limited exploration of the sector and the superficial basis of comparison of the few streets traveled, the desolate nature of the remote parts of the city are not seen by those making a short trip to the East. The lack of flowers, the absence of bright, small shops, the dingy street cars, the silent people are not always noted by Americans in tourist buses driving to the impressive Garden of Remembrance, where the statue of Mother Russia broods over the graves of fallen Soviet soldiers.

The pudgy guide who shouted praise of Ulbricht to us on a hot July afternoon would have been a buffoon on any stage, but he amused rather than annoyed the curious foreign visitors who had been told of restrictions and who were now being invited to visit the East Sector "every day, all day, without interference, but not without amenities."

The Berliners, East and West, as well as the more sophisticated of those who come from the outside, know that the contrast between the two parts of the city is enormous. In West Berlin, the varied buildings—churches, apartments, business buildings, factories, hospitals, schools, theaters, museums, auditoriums, and concert halls manifest the interest of the Federal Republic and of the American government in the future of the city. These buildings are not concentrated in any one location but are scattered and connected with a well-planned system of streets and thoroughfares. In East Berlin, the new buildings are grouped in those parts of the city which tourists visit. Why has Ulbricht restored only this small central portion? One reason may be that the flight of the refugees rendered the demand for housing less pressing than it might otherwise have been. Perhaps also it may now be thought that the workers who would use construction machines could find ways of escape over the Wall.

The Eastern part of the city still has the magnificent Pergamon and Bode Museums with their priceless treasures. In 1965, when I drove to them in a rickety taxi from Friedrichstrasse, I was struck with the dismal atmosphere of the area. The buildings were still scarred from wartime artillery action. There is relatively little traffic. Inside the museum, several busloads of visitors, presumably from the Zone, were wandering in silence through the large halls, pausing to look at the ancient statues and tombs. The collections are in good condition, but the oppressive air of delapidation is emphasized by the long grayish curtains covering the windows like dirty bed sheets with many a patch and darn. It seems strange to see these relics of ancient culture in a place where the present is miserable and the future uncertain.

As I came out into the street and searched in vain for a taxi, I wondered why the Communists had not yet devoted a major effort to the restoration of the area. Elsewhere, the impressive ruins of Unter den Linden have been emphasized by the building of the new opera house, the Soviet Embassy, and by restoration in the region of the partly destroyed Humboldt University. The large ruins near the Wall have not been completely cleared away. Even if the work now said to be in progress clears away the rubble and the broken walls, the newly reconstructed building of the Reichstag in the British sector will look down on a sad and deserted area. To a certain extent, according to one's expectations, one sees either the new buildings with their conventional but still impressive structure, or the wreckage which rises behind them in this part of Berlin which once knew grandeur.[25]

Whatever the Communists think, the reasons for this policy are hard to understand. Surely they could build more and better. Perhaps the drabness of the city streets does not strike the imagination of those who were schooled in Moscow.

There has been considerable discussion about the return of refugees to the East. There have been several thousand—a tiny fraction of the millions who have made their new homes in the West. The reasons for these returns are various. Some of the refugees were not "accepted" at the refugee screening centers, since their motives for crossing over led to uncertainty as to their loyalty and their desire to strengthen the democracy in the West. Thus, deprived of special job opportunities and housing privileges, these returnees were ready to bid for advantages in the Soviet Zone which were granted to them almost automatically for propaganda reasons. Others, because of their dependence on the controls and the socialistic systems of the East, found the independence and the realm of choice in the West confusing. The fact that there have been a few defections has been disturbing to Western observers, but is understandable in a people who have been subject to dictatorship for more than thirty years and who distrust the easier ways and less regimented approach of the West.

   25. There is a useful symposium on East sector conditions which also bears on the Zone conditions. There are also, for instance, several articles on economic conditions by Professor Thalheim, an article on youth by Hans-Peter Herz, and an article on building by Dr. Gerhard Abeken. *Berlin Sowjet Sektor* (Berlin: Colloquium Verlag, 1965).

There is no doubt that the building of the Wall drastically changed the situation in the East. It led to resignation and psychological adjustment that is the cause of concern in the Federal Republic, and changed the time schedule that had seemed to permit indefinite delay in the movement towards reunification.

VI. The Vulnerability of BERLIN

The erection of the Wall, and the hesitation of the Western Powers to exert their legal rights on this and other occasions, indicates in dramatic fashion the vulnerable position of Berlin in this atomic age. The fact that there is no easy way to protect the freedom of the city, when the United States is endeavoring to avoid a clash and at the same time protect our vital interests there and elsewhere, augments the difficulties of the day-to-day protection of the city. In some instances, the issue seems too slight to invoke the protective shield of NATO or to use the armed might of Western nations. The imbalance of the significance of a delay of traffic on the autobahn and the threat of world war, shock many to inaction in a situation where swift and decisive response would be the best answer to Communist harassment. Varied geographic, economic, political, and psychological elements of the situation plague those who would protect the city.

How does this city, with its wall of division and its narrow corridors to the outside world, differ from other cities of the world? One could stay there a month, even a year, and if not politically minded, could think of it much as one would think of any city. In spite of both economic and political strength, the city is vulnerable from many points of view.

Berlin has more cultural life than today's Washington, more theaters, concerts, art students—a new Art Academy and interesting churches and educational institutions—and a more vital air. It will soon have one of the best hospitals in the world. Many conference halls, museums, and sports arenas are available. It has an atomic research reactor. Its shopping centers are attractive. Its restaurants are good. Its night clubs are gay. Some 100,000 to 200,000 tourists visit the city every month.

This city of two and a quarter million is one of the major industrial centers of the world. Few metropolitan areas, none if the comparison is with the central city areas, not taking the suburbs into account, produce as much in value as Berlin. This is a city without a hinterland. For years the barbed wire has been strong around the outer limits of the city. It is a workshop that must get all its raw materials [1] from miles away, usually 150 to 200 miles or farther.[2] It is a city dependent on three main roads and three air corridors for its material and psychological support. It is a city surrounded by hostility. It is a living center that powerful forces are determined to destroy.

It is recognized that in the developed countries there are few cities more tortured, more beset with difficulties, and, from a purely strategic point of view, more vulnerable. Here, where the shooting war stopped more than twenty years ago, there is a city still occupied, still paying millions of dollars in occupation costs to the visitors, still without full constitutional and legal rights. Here is one of the main battlegrounds of the cold war. A place where innocent men, wishing to visit friends, relatives, children, are shot on sight—by men of the same nationality, in broad daylight—because they step into a cleared strip of the city's streets to cross an unlawful political boundary, set by hate and force. Here is perhaps the most critical dilemma of the free world, and one of the most puzzling and frustrating problems for the Communist world. Here the aggressive Soviet march was halted and remains stalled for the foreseeable future.

The people of Berlin are as confident as an expert on the tight

---

1. The "GNP" of West Berlin is 14, 805 million DM ($3,701 million), an amount equal to 3.9 per cent of the GNP of the German Federal Republic. West Berlin also produces 3.4 per cent of the total industrial production of the Federal Republic. "It Pays to Invest and Produce in Berlin," *Der Senator für Wirtschaft*, Berlin (November, 1964), p. 4. (A senator in Berlin is equivalent to a minister and is appointed.) Karl Schiller succeeded the late Paul Hertz in this position.

2. West Berlin receives 9,250 million DM ($2,312.5 million) in shipments annually. The city receives 88.1 per cent of its trade from the Federal Republic and ships out 9,400 million DM ($2,350 million). See "Die Industrie in Berlin (West)," *Der Senator für Wirtschaft*, Berlin (1964).

wire. They, like such a man, expect the sense of balance to keep them suspended in their precarious position with no disaster for the time they need to reach security. They think they can withstand the disturbing efforts of Communist bullies to shake their poise. They know that in a split second all can be lost. They depend on the Western Allies for the support that is the very essence of their safety.

They think we will stand by them because we have promised and because we have stood by them in the past. They are accustomed to our commitment; they like to see our soldiers marching on their streets on the Fourth of July with fifty state flags waving. The military reviews are attended by large crowds. They are happy when our tanks rumble down Clay-Allee on a Saturday morning. They like our visitors, they are tolerant of American ways, and they think of the GI's as friends and protectors.

The more sophisticated are sure that the entire German position, as it now exists, is an essential element of NATO. They conclude that if the keystone of Berlin is pulled out of the structure, and if the Americans acquiesce in weakness, the credibility of the alliance will crumble. In spite of their casual behavior, there is always beneath the surface of their faith a gnawing fear that some day the whole intricate structure will seem to be too troublesome for the United States.

In this special psychological and political sensitivity is rooted the unique situation of a city which seems in most respects so normal. Not even the Wall is so great a threat to the future of Berlin as would be the misstatement of a President in Washington, an unwitting declaration in Congress, or the inept remark of a responsible official. In fact, any act or word that might throw doubt on the continued maintenance of the Western position could have serious results. The life of the city hangs on a phrase, on a promise.

It is easy to hypothesize a series of events which would lead to panic. It almost happened in 1948, in 1958, in 1961. The consequences of disillusion in Berlin and Bonn would mean an outflow of people, a flight of funds, a blow to industry, a collapse of the standard of living, a sudden increase in unemployment, a loss of morale, a downfall of the whole brilliant structure. As of today, the Berliners shrug their shoulders. We can hear them say again, as they have for a dozen years, "We have stood harassment, we have faced danger, we have laughed at threats, we have built and traded, improved our plants and increased productivity. We have drunk and danced and sung. We have pride and expectations for the future. Surely the Americans who sent their boys to fly the airlift, who gave us millions, who have waited in convoys at the barriers, who have lived with us for twenty years—surely they will not desert us."

The reasons for this sensitivity and this trust are obvious. They lie in the geography of Berlin, in the zig and zag of Communist action, sometimes in the fluctuating Allied reactions.

The overwhelming importance of the American commitment to defend Berlin along with that of the French, the British, and the other NATO Allies, results not from the failure to make proper agreements about the city,[3] but in the refusal of the Soviets to honor the letter or the spirit of the agreements that have been made from the time of the European Advisory Committee in 1944, Yalta in 1945, the Paris meeting of 1949, and the Geneva summit statement of 1955. In all of these, the method of handling Germany —and the goal for a postwar Germany, implied or stated—was that there should be economic unification of the area, leaving for later decisions on the Eastern territories, with normal traffic in and out of Berlin. The fact that traffic has not been completely normal since the 1945 surrender and that it became increasingly circumscribed over the years was a matter that was politically disregarded at times. In other times, as during the Blockade or periods of intense harassment, it brought the world close to atomic war.

The statesmen on both sides of the Iron Curtain, in spite of Soviet deviations, recognize the interconnections of the series of treaties and arrangements. These commitments are firm and not subject to unilateral modification.[4]

It is because the Soviets have a duality of views and have broken their own agreements that there is no basis for the citizens of Berlin to put their faith in future promises of the Kremlin. They are convinced that their lives and destinies cannot be made secure by a treaty with no visible American support. The memories of the old men and the experience of the young have joined their security with the American soldier. The stars and stripes mean more to them

---

3. See above, Chapter II.
4. *Documents on Germany, 1944–1961*, p. 364.

The Vulnerability of Berlin

than diplomatic protocols. They have concluded that Berlin represents for America a vital interest.

Land Access to Berlin

In this battle for survival the access problem is a sign more than a cause. Berlin can flourish with the existing roads and canals, "train paths," and air corridors. There is no problem apart from the deliberate effort to use the legal and geographic situation to wring concessions from the Allies. It is true that many things would be easier and that the situation would take a different form if there were a comprehensive written statement as to the manner in which the military and civilians would enter and leave the city. The best of such statements, and one which should suffice if honored by all four parties, is the agreement that terminated the Blockade in May, 1949.[5] Agreements have been broken by the Soviets and will continue to be broken as long as their intentions diverge sharply from those of the United States.

The aggressive acts, the holding of Americans, the shooting of Germans, the absurd pretexts for delaying convoys and maneuvering in air corridors, the threats, kidnappings, and blackmail on canal and road, are sufficiently blatant to reveal the assumptions in Moscow. When the Soviets gave more leeway to Walter Ulbricht and, as in 1965, permitted him to send his helicopters illegally over West Berlin, and when now they carry out provocative acts which endanger the peace and push the Allies to the borders of retaliation by force, they are expressing two concepts—acting with two assumptions: one, it is unacceptable that Germany be allowed to increase its strength through normal interchange, and, two, that the United States is committed to avoiding war, short of the ultimate threat to the survival of Berlin.

Their tactics have varied over the last twenty years, but their goals are the same. A recent study of the USSR states:

After assuring the West German Government that Soviet policy toward Germany would remain unchanged following the removal of Khrushchev, the new Soviet leaders have swung toward a harder policy, accom-

---

5. *Ibid.*, p. 90. Art Buchwald, in his column of October 24, 1965, in *The Washington Post*, in a humorous discussion of relations with Canada, suggests that they could interfere with access to Alaska. Clearly, the failure to obstruct or harass is the result of friendly relations and not of any specific written agreements.

panied by a rapprochement with France and other efforts to exploit the existing strains in the NATO alliance. . . . Actions by the East Germans [in Berlin] cannot be construed as representing their own policy, resulting, as it is alleged, from growing tendencies on the part of the East European states to seek independence from Soviet leadership, but are clearly also a part of the Soviet policy of aggravating relations with West Germany.[6]

The Soviet hope had been through 1958-59, perhaps into 1962, that Berlin "would wither on the vine." They underestimated the ingenuity, the imagination, and the endurance of the people. They were surprised when they seemed to flourish on danger. They had heard some Western commentators say that the situation could not continue long, and thought perhaps that when the early heroes died, the younger men might grow restive. How could a city so isolated survive, particularly with the knowledge of the slender chain of legal statements, the changing but consistent tenor of political attitudes. They were blinded by a typical Communist error. The error is to assume that what is logical and rational is the only important reality with which they have to deal. They have believed their own propaganda about the "abnormality of the situation," and their hopes have become their expectations.

So the intangibles of the Berlin spirit, the American understanding, the Bonn support became the foundation stones on which the city was rebuilt, rededicated, and revitalized. The spirit of freedom is indeed real in this city. The goods flow in and out, the people travel, and they face each new access episode with fortitude.

When one looks beyond the psychological factors to the material elements, one recognizes that the *access problem* does create a vulnerability that could have been fatal but that has proved not to be. The daily conditions of flow of goods are vital; the economic life constantly nourished from the outside. This is the reason every change in permits, in road conditions, in harassment, in interference with men and goods, is of immediate concern to the occupying powers as well as to the Germans. While the Soviets have in recent years indicated their willingness to assure military transit, at least as far as official statements are concerned, they have continued

6. Albertine Aubrey, *The New Turn in Soviet Policy Toward Germany*, (July, 1965), No. 374, Institute for the Study of the USSR (Munich), pp. 1, 6.

The Vulnerability of Berlin

to ignore the more significant aspects of civilian traffic.[7]

Clearly the flow of raw materials into the city played a vital part in this expansion. The main industries—steel, electrical, chemical, and machine tools—all required materials from beyond the city limits. They and another of the principal industries, the garment trade, were dependent not only on imports but also on the ability to deliver promptly and reliably to consumers in West Germany and abroad.

The Inland Waterways

In the heavy-goods imports, the canal system of Germany has long been important to economic life. The network radiates from Berlin. The visitor is surprised to find the many canals, rivers, and lakes with a multitude of bridges crisscrossing the city—one of my friends told me there were more bridges than in Venice. The Havel leading into the Wannsee is heavily used by barges. The Spree is an important feature of Berlin's life. Some of the smaller lakes are mainly recreational. The canal network radiates from Berlin. The Communists, recognizing that they could not carry on their own traffic without Berlin waterways, had a program for establishing their independence of the main arteries passing through the Havel. They built a canal around the city. This project, to which considerable work was devoted, proved to be relatively ineffective. The result is that there is a curious situation with the East dependent on West Berlin canals for a considerable volume of water traffic and on western freight which moves into the East Zone through these waterways.

Between August 14, 1961, to the beginning of November, 1963, no East German or Soviet Bloc barges passed through West Berlin. Since November, 1963, there has been a steady build-up of this traffic. In 1965, some 2,872 barges carried 765,000 tons of freight, almost a doubling of the traffic over the previous year, but the tonnage was still small in comparison with the year before the construction of the Wall. In 1960, some 17,600 East-registered barges carried over 3,500,000 tons of freight through West Berlin.

It is because of the intricate interconnections with the Federal Republic that as a provisional, indefinite arrangement, much of the

7. See Khrushchev's assurance of Allied rights, Riklin, *Das Berlinproblem*, p. 275.

responsibility for East-West conditions of barge traffic was delegated to the Hamburg Waterways Directorate. This practical method of meeting current needs does not alter the "rights and responsibilities arising out of the joint occupation of Germany," which cannot be affected by any unilateral actions.[8]

Recently, even more than in the first reconstruction period, more than 30 per cent of the traffic is by barge over the interzonal canal system to Hamburg and Bremen and various points in the Zone. The brown coal comes into the city by canal from the East under the interzonal trade agreement. The problems of the ship pilots' licenses and barge permits, though less dramatized abroad than the road traffic, because the pilots are civilian and are not involved in allied military traffic, are in fact of the utmost importance.

A recent crisis came on June 25, 1965, when the Communist East regime endeavored to enforce new conditions for documentation of vessels on inland waterways in the Zone. Here again efforts to enhance the standing of Ulbricht's men were involved. For a few days, the use of the canals was imperiled with a threat to the economy of the Zone, and to a lesser extent, of the Federal German Republic. But the concern over the new demands by the Ulbricht regime was limited mainly to official and industrial circles. No one in Berlin expected a long interruption of this essential traffic. Even the uninitiated knew that the East Zone needed the trade as well as the West. The issue was resolved swiftly. The economic life of the city was undisturbed.

The problem was not new.[9] A few years earlier the barge permits had been refused for a year, and the result had been extremely disturbing as the licenses of one pilot after another lapsed. Both sides suffered, until suddenly it was agreed by the East to allow traffic under the previous conditions to be fully resumed. Undoubtedly, the importance of the materials in trade between the zones accounts for the reluctance of the East Zone to interfere with barge transit for any considerable time.

8. U.S. Ambassador McGhee's statement, *The Berlin Bulletin*, July 6, 1965. The Hamburg Waterways Directorate is responsible for issuing navigation permits to West German barge operators for movement on the waterways connecting Berlin with the West.

9. Eleanor Lansing Dulles, "Berlin and Soviet Methods in Germany," *The Department of State Bulletin*, XXXVI (June 17, 1957), p. 982.

New barge permits were agreed to in the summer of 1965. They are said to pose no serious threat to the conditions of transit. The documents themselves are in German only, rather than in the four languages [10] according to established occupation procedures. The present papers are signed by the barge captains who pay a fee of 200 DM per year. Bonn agreed, not in writing, to permit the shipowners to sign, on the assumption that this implies no recognition by the Bonn government. There are presently no delays in the shipping and no hindrance of the access, which is the real concern. A part of the East German desires were met, however, as the barge captains now accept the East German passes.

At the same time, the July, 1965, incident of holding the East barges in the Havel was considered a victory for the West. The East Germans had claimed that the old four-power passes were no longer valid and issued their own passes. When West German authorities refused to recognize the new passes, and insisted on the signing of the old passes, the barge captains then said they would sign the papers, but only under protest. The West Germans remained firm. The East German captains could either sign the papers without protest or turn their barges around. They signed.

The outcome of these exchanges in July, which the Americans called "a stand-off," indicates the importance of maintaining the flow, including the passage of East Zone barges through the Havel in West Berlin. The maneuvers in this connection included the acceptance by the East Zone authorities of the existing pilots' licenses. To the industrialists on both sides of the Iron Curtain, the accommodation that this settlement represented brought great relief; to the politicians in the West, the nagging question was whether a stronger stand would have impressed the Soviets and thus the East Germans with our firmness. The riddle is not easy to solve because it is impossible to read the minds of the antagonists in this strange struggle. The main point is that after seven barges from the East had been held by the West Germans in the Havel during the first few days in July, and dickering over the various papers had gone on for about a week, the crisis appeared to be over. Few outside the official circles in Washington or New York realized what fundamental issues were at stake. Surprising though it may

10. English, French, Russian, German. See also Chapter IX.

seem, there was no ripple to disturb German economic circles, although the political aspects were actively discussed.

The Germans have the theory that the access problem for the civilian economy on canal and road is largely dependent upon the interzonal trade. It is for this reason that they have been reluctant to accept our view that they should cut trade, even though they know that the regime is making a significant contribution to Soviet arms production; but they think there are important offsetting considerations. They have a complex set of motives, which include their interest in continued contacts, their feeling that the Zone, or Middle Germany as they call it, is part of the homeland, and their estimate of the importance to the industry in the Zone of having goods flow without interruption.[11]

Air Traffic

Ever since the Blockade of 1948, the attention of the world has been focused mainly on the trucks and trains. The air corridors have been taken largely for granted. And yet the travel of persons to the West from Berlin and also into the city from Bonn and elsewhere is in the air corridors. The Soviets cannot check the individuals on the French, British, and American planes that fly the corridors to the West. Many commentators are worried about the danger of aircraft being buzzed or shot down. The physical capability of the Soviets to interfere with air access to Berlin is almost unlimited. The fact is that the Soviets have always possessed the technical means to interrupt or halt flights into the city. They could have stopped the airlift of 1948, if they dared to take the risk, and they still have the capacity to stop any future commercial traffic or a new airlift. The issue is not one of practical capabilities but of the political risks.

It is generally assumed that the Soviets recognize the extreme danger of even a hint of interference with the planes.[12] The possibility of minor annoyance to the commercial and military flights is

11. West Berlin receives 0.5 per cent in trade shipments from the Soviet Zone and ships 2.1 per cent of its total trade to that Zone. "It Pays to Invest and Produce in Berlin," *Senator für Wirtschaft*, p. 4. The trade between the Federal Republic and the Zone is much greater. Later figures show that West Berlin receives 2.1 per cent in trade shipments from the Soviet Zone and ships 0.5 per cent of its total trade to that Zone. Annual Report of the *Senator für Wirtschaft*, Karl Schiller, "Daten zur Entwicklung der Berliner Wirtschaft (West)," p. 4.

12. A British plane was shot down in 1953.

The Vulnerability of Berlin

less feasible than in the case of cars and trucks. An air disaster would be more shocking and the danger greater if they undertook hostile action in the corridors. In the minds of the Berliner, as well as to the outsider, the risks involved in Communist interference with allied planes is too serious to contemplate. Here the stakes are generally considered to be world peace or war.

It is important to note that the Berlin Air Safety Center (BASC) has continued to operate and that it constitutes, along with the policing of the Spandau Prison, one of the few signs of the four-power occupation still in evidence. It is an indication of the importance with which air travel to and from the beleaguered city is regarded everywhere. Although the Soviets have occasionally objected to civilian use of the air and have condemned the flying out of refugees, they are convinced that the Western world would retaliate in forceful manner to any interference.[13] The difference between land and air traffic [14] lies not so much in the nature of the agreements—the definition in November, 1945, of the air corridors to Berlin was more specific than some of the other agreements—as in the nature of the risks. Interference with air access would presumably be by shooting down planes, acts so provocative as to be likely forerunners of war. Thus the agreements have not been seriously strained, although the shadow of threats has been extended in that direction on an exploratory basis on several occasions.

Because of the crucial importance of the free use of the air corridors, the Western Allies have scrupulously observed the original agreements and have not permitted any flights into Berlin except those of the occupying powers. The fact that the Soviets permitted foreign flights into East Berlin has not fallen within the agreements but has not been treated as a matter for serious protest. The flights of the Eastern regime helicopters over West Berlin in July, 1965, were clearly provocative and were in violation of the four-power agreements. They led, according to reports, to the arming of American helicopters with machine guns. There were hours in July when it was thought that the dangerous situation might lead to a physical clash in the air with grave repercussions in Soviet-Allied relations.

The existence of stockpiles of food, fuel, and raw materials in

13. Riklin, *Das Berlinproblem*, p. 271.
14. Shell, *Bedrohung und Bewährung*, pp. 2–3.

Berlin has not been interpreted by observers as indicating any intention of the Allies to tolerate interference with flights. A normal precaution after the airlift seemed to be to bring into the city those materials that were difficult to fly in—thus allowing a breathing space in time of crisis, while rearming, negotiation, or counter-measures could be prepared—with Berlin adequately fed and with raw materials sufficient to keep industry and public works going for a time. Once the plan for the Berlin stockpile was developed, it was natural that the supplies should be built up to quantities that in fact exceeded the minimum for a period of preparation and emergency. How much the Berliners are aware of these stores is hard to say. The fact that they are warehoused in many sections of the city and constantly renewed to assure fresh and usable rations and appropriate raw materials is known to thousands. Neither the Germans nor the Allies think of the defense of Berlin in terms of a new blockade. The Communists know after Korea, Cuba, Vietnam, and the other crises of the past seventeen years that aggressive action would bring reaction and a defense of wider scope than an airlift.

A review of the technical aspects of access to Berlin would be of little significance here. Both legal and practical problems of access are thoroughly explored by Alois Riklin in his book on the Berlin problem. He reminds the reader that the agreement of Paris, May 20, 1949, assured the normalization of the rights of access to Berlin—both civilian and military. The agreement was to establish the previous rights and increase and expand those rights with a view to free access. The wording is explicit and leaves no room for misinterpretation.

In 1955, after the end of the Geneva conference,[15] Khrushchev[16] visited East Berlin with a view to action which he considered appropriate after his failure to achieve his aims in the recent conference. The result of his visit is embodied in the Bolz-Zorin correspondence[17] and the declaration that East Germany was a sover-

---

15. The communiqué of the four powers promised reunification and free elections leading to a single German Government. *Documents on Germany, 1944–1961*, pp. 192–93.

16. See Riklin, *Das Berlinproblem*, p. 179, and Windsor, *City on Leave*, pp. 189–92.

17. See Smith, *The Defense of Berlin*, pp. 186–87, 252, for more complete discussion of this note.

The Vulnerability of Berlin

eign state. The Soviet interpretation of the meaning of this action for the improving status of the Federal Republic was that the agreements in Paris in 1949 with regard to access were no longer in force. They claimed that civilian traffic was under the control of the GDR. With respect to military traffic, they have varied in their statements but have endeavored to substitute East German controls wherever the substitution seemed feasible.

How vulnerable to the blockade of surface access is present-day Berlin? Now that the standard of living of Berlin has risen to a high level, I was told, the return to austerity conditions would create serious political and sociological difficulties. Some even went so far as to say that the people of present-day Berlin would not support the resulting restrictions on living standards. Others said that the fortitude of the Berliners would, in an emergency, be no less dependable than before, with the proviso that action by the Allied Powers in time of harassment or cutting off of access must be sufficiently convincing to hold out hopes of early rescue. No one expects a new blockade.

Clearly, the contingency planning of the Allies cannot be known to the public nor can the plans for Berlin in an emergency be understood by any but a small group. The technical possibilities of supporting the city can never be a complete answer to the needs for protecting two and a quarter million people. The answer to any attack on the city's freedom, or the Allied position there, must be in terms of over-all Western power and the will to use that power.

It is interesting to note, however, that if there were need of defending the city from Communist attack—economic, psychological, military—the adjustment of the city to special emergency conditions would be adequate to meet all the physical needs for many weeks. Even the prevention of shipments of heavy products out of the city for a short period would seriously affect only certain segments of the heavy goods industry. Inevitably the readjustment of production after a short period of weeks would lead to a change in the nature of production in about one-third of the manufacturing concerns.

All speculation regarding interruption to access is subject to a wide margin of error, but clearly a complete stoppage of production is not to be anticipated. A leading industrialist in West Berlin said that, in the event of a new blockade, it would be possible to continue operations for a considerable period of months. The Allied intention is, of course, to maintain adequate access, free of crippling restrictions, according to international agreements.

The conviction remains among Allied authorities in West Berlin that the only way to protect freedom there is to keep all traffic routes—air, land, and water—open. Since the Blockade, and despite periodic harassment, the Allies have been successful in accomplishing this objective.

The maintenance of access has been related to the policy on East-West Trade by Alfred Pollack, Chief of Interzonal Affairs of the Berlin government, in a conversation on July 2, 1965, and by others in Berlin. They have indicated that the flow of goods to and from the Zone gives a degree of protection to the traffic in and out of West Berlin. It is interesting to examine the figures of 1964 and 1965 and to discover that in 1964 the tonnage of trade between West Germany and the Zone (11.78 million metric tons), and between West Berlin and the FRG (12.4 million metric tons), were approximately equal. The amount of commerce means that an interruption of trade with Berlin, if it led to a cut-off of interzonal trade, would harm the Zone to a substantial degree. The following unofficial statement from American experts in Berlin confirms impressions with regard to the access problems above:

> There is no doubt, we believe, that the East Germans would suffer some disadvantages if water, rail, and highway connections to international markets were not open to them through West Germany. We believe the chances are good that with the current economic build-up of East Germany, the East Germans will become even more dependent in the future on West German routes for the movement of their goods. This can also be said to a lesser extent of the Czechoslovakians, who have apparently put pressure on the East Germans to make improvements on the Elbe river to enable smoother access to Hamburg. Although it is clear that the impact of interruption of traffic on West Berlin would be much more serious, it is nonetheless of significance that for the Zone the tonnage is substantial.

Soviet Inconsistency

Soviet policy has been changeable through the years. The on-again, off-again tactics of the Communists were evident in the 1960 August cancellation of the permits for West German visitors.

TABLE 4. TRADE BETWEEN THE FEDERAL REPUBLIC, BERLIN, AND THE EAST ZONE, 1965
(in metric tons)

From Berlin to FRG

Total	2,152,000
By water	414,000
rail	282,000
road	1,456,000

From FRG to Berlin

Total	10,223,000
By water	4,147,000
rail	2,570,000
road	3,506,000

From Berlin to SBZ

Total	7,000
By water	—
rail	5,000
road	2,000

From SBZ to Berlin

Total	2,909,000
By water	1,078,000
rail	1,669,000
road	162,000

From FRG to SBZ

Total	2,792,000
By water	752,000 inland craft
	96,000 seagoing vessels
rail	1,859,000
road	85,000

From SBZ to FRG

Total	6,061,000
By water	380,000 inland craft
	22,000 seagoing vessels
rail	5,508,000
road	151,000

Source: *Statistisches Bundesamt, Senat Verkehr und Betriebe.*

These were promptly renewed after the Federal Republic threatened to cut off interzonal trade. In his speeches in that year, Khrushchev made a clear distinction between civilian access and the rights of the three Western occupying powers to enter and leave Berlin.[18] Nevertheless, there was in October, 1963, what was then termed the "little blockade." The officers at the control points requested that the soldiers in an American convoy at the Helmstedt control point dismount to be counted and checked. The Americans refused according to the Allied agreement as to procedure. The result of the temporary stalemate was that the soldiers remained on the vehicles for forty-eight hours. Then, for no obvious reason, the boom was lifted and the convoy proceeded. There was a short delay a few days later, but the incident was ended as the Communists recognized that they were on dangerous ground and that the Americans did not intend to back down. This soon forgotten episode demonstrated to those who follow these matters closely in the Western capitals and in the Kremlin that determination, even stubbornness, has an important part to play in this strange game—with the stakes the future of Germany and more.

In general in the more recent period, access delays and probes have been directed against German travel and trade and not against the Allies. The episodes are too numerous to recount. Those who are sensitive to the changing climate of Communist intentions are puzzled by the current situation and some forget that the manufacturer who has contracted to deliver merchandise in West Germany risks a considerable loss if a shipment is delayed. He may fail to write new contracts and lack sufficient orders if his performance seems unreliable. For the politicians there are unpredictable humiliations when they are made to wait long hours at the checkpoints. In April, 1965, for example, Willy Brandt, returning to Berlin from Hanover, was turned back and forced to leave his car and fly into Berlin.

This occurred in April, 1965, when the Bundestag met, as it had on nine or ten occasions, in Berlin. In addition to the usual Communist protests that their decision to meet in Berlin—which they call the capital of the German Democratic Republic—was an

---

18. See also Konev statement of August, 1965. Shell, *Bedrohung und Bewährung*, p. 31.

insult to the regime, the Soviets buzzed the Congress Hall where the deputies were meeting. While their low flights were hazardous for the hundreds underneath, the Berliners treated these flights as a joke and called them "the Communist salute to the Bundestag."

No End to Harassment

It is important always to remember, as Berlin experts point out, that Ulbricht will go as far as he thinks he can to attain his ultimate goal, Western recognition of the GDR. The Allies always must make it clear what will or will not be tolerated. "Strong words and no action" is the worst possible combination, my Berlin friends told me.

There is no possibility of preventing the nerve-fraying pressures that are put on those who have low thresholds of reaction. There have been kidnappings, shootings at the Wall, threats to individuals, searching of trucks and cars,[19] breaking through the sound barriers by Soviet planes, tin foil in the air corridors, military maneuvers on the roads, delays to the trains, stoppage of the barges, seizure of people at the checkpoints, goose stepping Nazi-like soldiers on parade, libelous assaults on individuals, and inflammatory broadcasts to excite the people.

This situation constitutes the vulnerability of the city; this is its weakness. It cannot have tranquility, but it can have strength. This strength lies in the combination of American assistance and in the inherent characteristics of the Berlin people themselves. Their resilience, their wit, the capacity for amusing themselves even in times of difficulty have made it possible to shrug the shoulders, and say, "Where can we go, we are here, here we stay." Of the story of American aid, more needs to be said, for its crucial importance should not be forgotten. The support of Berlin is a joint enterprise and depends on local resistance and help from distant capitals.

The Communist efforts to exert pressure through the denial of normal access has been one of the major instruments in the strengthening of the Eastern regime.[20] Their leverage has been considerable but their permanent success infinitesimal—a nuisance rather than a defeat for the West.

19. A friend told me that the Communist guards at the border drove a sharp stake into the baggage compartments of cars, to wound anyone hidden under the luggage.
20. Riklin, *Das Berlinproblem*, p. 179, and Windsor, *City on Leave*, pp. 189, 192.

VII. The Strength of BERLIN

The Use of Initiative

The toughness of the city is evidenced by its resistance, its growth, and the intangibles which make up morale. In this creative effort there have been many ingredients. Not the least important has been American aid. Most essential has been Western political support. These two elements—internal vitality and external aid—merit comment.

Here the frequent statement by critics that America reacts but does not take the initiative is proven false. The treatment of Germany has been a positive policy. The reconstruction of Berlin has been imaginative, vigorous, and successful. After the first months of miscalculation and error in 1944 and 1945, the policy was reversed, and the joint action of various European nations, with strong American leadership and a wholehearted German effort, has halted the westward march of Communism, has built a fine new city on the ruins of old Berlin, and has restored to the German nation pride, dignity, and hope.[1]

The extent of America's commitment, and its significance to the future of Europe, has been impressive. Politically, financially, and militarily, our involvement has been consistent and extensive. Neither the nature of our support nor the reasons we have extended aid have been adequately reflected in the literature on Berlin. The omission of this important part of our program is striking, particu-

---
1. Eleanor Lansing Dulles, "Concerted Efforts Against Tyranny," *The State Department Bulletin*, XXXIII (September 12, 1955), 422–26.

larly in view of the threat implicit in the large unemployment. Western observers avoid discussion of our helpful role in some cases perhaps because of a continuing revulsion against past Nazism. Some distrust our postwar program—they fear potential German strength. This view leads to deprecating Germany's development and at times a derogation of American effort in restoring membership in the community of free nations to Germany. It is high time to redress the balance.

The rebirth of Germany, its part in NATO, its financial stability, its economic contribution to the underdeveloped world, is a success story. In these developments Berlin's strength is important even though the free world is the poorer for the division of Germany. As Professor Schiller writes, "The German phoenix' . . . has actually been paralyzed in one wing."[2] Bitterness and a sense of loss will cloud the vision of those who feel, with considerable justification, that failure to achieve early reunification is an indication that the price of attaining this goal is beyond the possibility of current payment. Since only communization of West Germany would be consistent with the mid-century goals of Moscow, more time must pass, more changes must occur, before the disparity of aims can be bridged.

American Aid

The co-operative reconstruction program in West Germany and Berlin represents one of the great achievements under the Marshall Plan and perhaps the most efficient and effective aid program the United States has undertaken. The economic facts speak for themselves. Germany and Berlin have had the most rapid and enduring increase in production of any nation since the war. Germany is today a leading financial power. The Federal Republic is contributing more to science, investment, and defense than other European nations. The standard of living has risen in twenty years from below subsistence levels to the highest of any nation outside the United States. The recovery of Berlin is all the more spectacular because of the political and access difficulties that have been described. Extraordinary measures have been required because the

2. Karl Schiller, "Germany's Economic Requirements," *Foreign Affairs*, XLIII (July, 1965), p. 671.

city is not viable as it stands alone. Only with the help of American funds and programs, only with large-scale support from Bonn, has its prosperity been achieved. Since, however, experience shows that this support can be forthcoming to the extent needed, this dependence does not impede the achievement of prosperity in extraordinary circumstances.

The city at the end of the Blockade was still close to the subsistence levels of 1946 and 1947. The unemployment, probably more than 30 per cent of the labor force, was reported as well above 300,000. Housing was short. Confidence was at a low ebb. The young people were leaving the city, the old people were weakened by the stress of war, by defeat, Soviet removals, and the Blockade. One can name a long list of those who died prematurely, aged by the suffering and privation. For the first months after the war, there was little concern on the part of the victors for the misery. The conditions were, admittedly, the result of the evil policy of the old Berlin, but although the survivors were not, for the most part, responsible, those who remained in the city bore a feeling of guilt.

The need for special attention to the Berlin problem became glaringly apparent in Washington as the attempt to restore normal economic life after the Blockade met almost insuperable difficulties. There was little optimism in those days. A complex of issues, with the need for confidence at the core, hampered efficiency—the shortage of capital, the urgent need for housing, and dependence on purchase orders from outside. A strong effort was needed to stimulate economic activity. This was the time when I heard people say, as they looked at the rubble in the residential quarters, that "they are not rebuilding"—"people do not like to order goods from Berlin because of uncertainty"—"the people are aging," and "the young men are going to West Germany in search of opportunity."

This was also the time when the United States was just beginning an ambitious aid program; when millions of dollars in counterpart marks, and millions more in new dollar grants, were made available for the rebuilding of the city that had courageously cast its lot with the Western world.

During the blockade and airlift—which cost the United States upwards of $300 million—food, fuel, and other supplies to the

The Strength of Berlin [149]

people of Berlin had totaled more than an estimated $220 million. Before the Blockade the share in the total aid to Germany under GARIOA—Government Administration and Relief in Occupied Areas—had been more than $240 million. Thus before 1950 the American government had begun to assume its role in the support of the city, in response to a policy co-ordinated with the French and the British but which, because of the large grants and active role, set the United States apart as the special guardian of the city's welfare.[3]

The period during which substantial dollar funds flowed into the city—in newly generated counterpart marks and, to a small extent, as dollar payments—was roughly between 1947, when the survival of the population was at stake, and 1959 when the Federal Republic was capable of making sizable grants and concessions to keep the city prosperous. From 1960 on, the funds from U.S. sources were small compared with the budget support and special assistance from the Bonn government.

Varied Programs

The variety of the help granted in co-operation with the Berlin and Bonn officials has not been matched by any other aid program. A detailed recapitulation of the methods and techniques would throw the story of present-day Berlin out of balance with the other issues.

The extraordinary scope of the effort to revitalize Berlin can be indicated by a cursory look at the list of topics I covered on one of my trips to Berlin. In the Bureau—later Office—of German Affairs, I was occupied with the whole complex of aid and support. Early in 1957, after five years and a dozen trips to the city, I was again in Berlin. There, I had meetings with the economic and political officers along lines agreed in meetings with my Washington colleagues. I had taken a checklist of matters to deal with in Germany. These included such problems as the condition of the Berlin stockpile and a program for additional purchases, plans for the financing and construction of a Student Village to house some seven hundred men and women attending the Free University,

---

3. 235,000 tons a month in April, 1949, alone. Davison, *The Berlin Blockade: A Study in Cold War Politics* (Princeton: The Princeton University Press, 1958), p. 261.

arrangements for the construction and fueling of an atomic research reactor. Plans for a business institute, a study of interzonal trade, recent problems affecting military convoys going into the city, and counter-measures to induce the Zonal authorities to cease harassing the traffic.

A number of meetings were held to expedite the construction and the opening ceremonies for the Congress Hall, which was to be dedicated in September with a series of photographic exhibits, one-act plays, concerts, and symposia.

Other questions of interest to me on the Berlin desk included the housing and interviewing of refugees, the Pan American air fares for flights in the access corridors, and relief projects for the inhabitants of the East Zone, our contribution to "social housing," the Berlin Film Festival, the forecasts of prospective elections, and visits to the United States of German leaders, including Bundestag members, Franz-Josef Strauss, and other notables. These and other matters were of concern to the Department. Some dozen other topics for discussion and negotiation were in our program to support a growing economy and stable society.

Stages of Reconstruction

The work in the difficult early years from 1947 through 1949 had consisted mainly of relief and help in the programs of rubble removal, bomb detonation, and the heavy work of clearing roads, re-establishing sewers, power lines, and the basic utilities of the devastated city. Food was needed to make this arduous task possible. Much of the brick and concrete was heaped in park areas where the "rubble mountains" now stand, memorials to the tragedy of war and misery of the first postwar years, where men and women, often with bare hands, gathered the bricks and stone and pieces of marble which were the broken remnants of ambition and aggression. Fifteen years later, in 1965, pines, birches, and rhododendrons grew thickly to make recreation areas of these hills. Only after dismantling and clearing was done, could construction begin to create the city of which the Berliners and the Americans are justly proud.

The cost of reconstruction, financed by extraordinary means, runs into several billion dollars. The amount cannot be exactly

The Strength of Berlin

reported.[4] American governmental aid has exceeded a billion dollars. The manner in which it was given, however, was such that not only did it act as a lever on larger amounts of aid by the Federal Republic, but, since some was loaned and reloaned at special rates to stimulate production, the revolving funds for industry amounted to considerably more than the original face value. It is estimated that the amounts were equivalent to several thousand dollars for each man, woman, and child. Moreover, the co-operation engendered in the process of programming and spending the money was an ever visible sign of America's continued concern for the fate of the city. It is surprising that this part of the defense of Berlin has received so little attention.

Our aid fell into several successive phases. Once the public utilities had been partially restored, by 1952, major attention was turned to the heavy industries that had been the backbone of Berlin's prewar productivity and that could employ hundreds of thousands of men. In particular, such firms as Siemens, Allgemeine Elektrizitäts Gesellschaft (AEG), Telefunken, and Borsig, were given loans and grants.[5] After these came a number of large concerns and machine tool industries, notably Fritz Werner; Flohr-Otis, the elevator concern; Schering, the chemical and drug firm; and other of the lighter industries. Then a special effort was turned to rehabilitating the garment industry and consumer goods enterprises such as food, beverages, and printing. These stages of support illustrate the manner in which the urgent necessity to cut down unemployment shaped the aid programs.

One main tool for helping manufacturing was the Industrie-Bank, through which hundreds of thousands of counterpart marks [6] were fed to industry, always with a view to a multiplier effect. This led, in the closed, or nearly closed, economy of Berlin, to vigorously expanding production. The city can be considered by the econo-

4. Only a rough estimate can be made on the percentage of American aid to Germany which was allocated to Berlin in the early years. *Western German Economic Recovery, 1945–1952* (Cologne: Office of the U.S. High Commissioner for Germany), pp. 74–75. (Reprinted from *Report on Germany, September 21, 1949–July 31, 1952.*)

5. See *Senator für Wirtschaft* for exact distribution of industry in West Berlin as of 1963.

6. When aid was sent in the form of commodities sold by the Federal Government for marks, these marks were called *counterpart*, and spent, as agreed, for aid and investment.

mist to be a large-scale laboratory operation in which interaction between financial injections and a sense of security led to increasing prosperity.

The two main economic programs, initiated by the Office of the U.S. High Commissioner and the Berlin city government, were the industrial investment program and the work relief program designed to create 250,000 to 300,000 new jobs between 1951 and 1955, with an expenditure of approximately 400 million dollars.[7] Thus aid went beyond relief and became a program for remaking a city in the years of the 1950's.

Impact Programs

Overlapping the continuing industrial help were the special projects which the United States initiated and in which joint effort led to notable results. These included a wide variety of housing construction—for refugees, for workers, large apartment complexes such as Mehring Platz for more than twelve hundred families, smaller dwelling units to which the Berlin *Notstands Programm*[8] contributed, the two groups of American-financed, prefabricated Finnish houses for some twelve hundred families, the high dormitory building for some eight hundred Technical University students, and the twenty-nine or thirty-building "Student Village" for the Free University.

Emphasis on buildings as the most impressive impact projects was determined in some measure because the structures were visible evidence that the occupation and the protection of the rights of the people had a time span, very different from the tents pitched by an army on the move. Moreover, their meaning is much clearer than that of the sterile Soviet war memorials. The idea must occur to the Communists that there would be no point in building hundreds of thousands of dwelling units and imposing structures with American and German funds if the Western powers intended to leave.

The America Memorial Library is a large modern building, with unusually easy access to books and a special children's wing. It is heavily used at all times. The Henry-Ford-Bau, financed personally

7. Margaret Woodward, "Berlin Rebuilds: Economic Reconstruction of West Berlin, 1948–1953," *The Department of State Bulletin*, XXX (April 19, 1954), 584–88.
8. Welfare program.

by Henry Ford II, has fine assembly halls, classrooms, and large library and reading rooms. The Congress Hall, built near the sector border and the burned-out Reichstag, has a bold cantilevered roof; it was designed by the American architect Hugh Stubbins. It is one of the fine new buildings of Europe. It has seven conference rooms and an auditorium with a capacity for twelve hundred people. There is an exhibition hall, a post office, and a large restaurant overlooking the Spree. The Otto-Suhr-Bau, also financed from American aid, is exerting a constructive role as it provides facilities for the political science institute.

Of these impact projects the Klinikum, the medical teaching center still under construction, is the most ambitious and spectacular. According to the 1965 specification and contracts, it will cost more than $82 million in DM equivalent. Some of the funds come from dollar aid. It was planned under the guidance of the Benjamin Franklin Foundation, with Arthur Davis serving as American architect and Franz Mochen as his German colleague. The program was developed when the Soviets were hurling threats in their efforts to expell the Western occupying forces from the city. Thus the timing of this impressive building and educational project was not a coincidence—it was one form of answer to Khrushchev. The willingness of Washington to program aid for a building to serve the city for many decades was intended as a message to the Kremlin, a practical answer to parallel the official statements of the Western Powers that there could be no concessions on Berlin. The huge structure, with more than eighteen hundred nursing beds and ample surgical space, one of the largest buildings to rise in Europe since the war, includes facilities for scientific research, teaching, and hospital care for many thousands. The shining structure of concrete and glass was intended to evidence an enduring policy to keep Berlin free.

The aid in these years also included the continuing support of Radio in American Sector (RIAS), which broadcasts hard news and cultural and political items to a loyal, numerous audience in East Germany and beyond, and which serves as an impressive witness of unchanging Western concern for the future of the German people.

Aid included participation in some fifteen or more fairs and exhibits—always planned with a view to the political implications, permitting the usual commercial considerations to fall to a minor position.

Washington linked with our aid program and with our diplomatic efforts dozens of visits—one by President Kennedy, several by Secretaries of State and by many other high officials. It is recognized that the Berlin response to the visit of President John F. Kennedy in June, 1963, was spectacular.

Everything that was done for the youth of Berlin—in the universities, in the libraries, in the housing, in the Amerika Haus, in the festivals and fairs, in the Kinderlift [9]—was designed for an enduring future. The atomic reactor was placed in West Berlin as an aid project to expand the research of the Max-Planck-Institute für Forschungen auf dem Gebiet des Bildungswesen. This is a part of the Max Planck complex that carries on work along the lines developed by the former Kaiser Wilhelm Research Institute located in what is now East Berlin. The Otto-Suhr-Bau was intended to underscore the importance of sound political analysis and teaching. These were reminders of our American commitment and of our faith in what the Berlin people could do, if given the facilities.

The many-sided approach can be exemplified by several programs in 1953. In an endeavor to show to the residents of the East Zone our understanding of the bravery and the desperation that lay behind the uprising in June, 1953, the food package program was devised. For a brief period, this provided a way of communicating our hopes for the future and our awareness of oppression through gifts of food to those who wished to demonstrate their friendliness by coming to West Berlin. Their travel at some risk evidenced their feeling of unity with the Western Powers.

This American program of action was disturbing to the Communist authorities. They saw the response as a sign of defiance. After a few weeks, they pulled some of the travelers from the trains, and the danger and reprisals for those who took the parcels increased. When this Communist response became apparent, distribution in

---

9. This was an American army operation to fly children out of Berlin for vacations.

West Berlin was halted by the Americans, and instead there came a series of other programs in co-operation with the Ministry of All German Affairs and Berlin officials to maintain contacts with the residents in the Zone. These affected the lives of millions of Germans over a period of approximately ten years before the American funds ceased to flow.

Another type of support took the form of the stockpiling of food, fuel, and raw materials already referred to. The exact amount of these large accumulations is not published. These stocks are intended to supplement contingency plans for swift reaction if the Communists break their agreements and ignore legal rights.

It has been known to the Berliners that the stocks exist since Ernst Reuter discussed them over the radio in 1953. They have been financed to a considerable degree by the Germans, although our financial share and planning activities have given us a major say in the composition of the stores and responsibility for their maintenance. They are rotated to prevent deterioration and have been supplemented in recent years to include modern medicines, baby foods, and various raw materials.

On a number of occasions, without directly referring to the stockpiles, policy-makers have indicated that they have no intention of tolerating a condition such as the Blockade of 1948. Unacceptable Soviet offers have been rejected on various occasions, and this response, combined with aid, has made possible the achievement of a brilliant level of prosperity.

A key factor of Berlin's general progress and economic prosperity has been the support by the Federal Republic. The tax concessions and special efforts to stimulate industry have been referred to. The budget support in the years 1951 through 1965 came to a total estimated as 38,840 DM (or approximately $9.7 billion). This sum includes direct payments to the Berlin budget, special help in connection with occupation costs and war compensation, and a net contribution in social insurance. The need arises because the city cannot be permitted to suffer a deflation of industry and production and because normal investment flow is not sufficient. Berlin is, as Wolfram Pohl says, "an expensive city." [10]

10. *Die Zeit*, April, 26 1966. Wolfram Pohl has written a valuable article discussing the economic dependence of Berlin on the Federal Republic.

The Success of Aid

The American aid programs in their varied manifestations, usually involve co-operation with the FRG, including the welfare, housing, industry, education, science, cultural events, RIAS, the visits of high officials, speeches and declarations in Washington, Paris, London, and elsewhere, and add up to a continuing and consistent policy. Rarely has the United States made evident an engagement outside its territories as serious as that for Berlin.

Figures for the American aid granted to Berlin vary with the inclusion of cultural, military, and private contributions to the city. The sixteen-year total exceeded a billion dollars. The aid took the form of grants; dollar loans were not a part of the program since repayment by the city was considered to be undesirable.

TABLE 5. UNITED STATES AID TO BERLIN, 1945–1961[a]

Total	$1,094,010[a]
	(in thousands)
Pre-Blockade (1945–1948)	$ 240,000
Blockade (1949)	220,000
Post-Blockade (1949–1953)	265,637
1953–1961 (including stockpile)	368,373

a. The above totals are figures that have been approved by persons responsible for these programs. It is believed, however, that the figures for pre-Blockade aid fall short of the total by a little more than $100 million, since these figures do not include UNRRA aid, private charity, or all aspects of military aid. Moreover, the cost of the Blockade is difficult to calculate.

The programs included in aid figures are Regular Investment Loans, Risk Investment, Working Capital Guaranty Fund, Productivity, Working Capital Credits, Order Financing, Reconstruction, Miscellaneous Economic, General Construction, and other programs.

Sources: *Handbook of Economic Statistics*, Federal Republic of Germany and Western Sectors of Berlin (March, 1965), pp. 56, 60; Margaret Woodward, "Berlin Rebuilds: Economic Reconstruction of West Berlin, 1948–1953," *The Department of State Bulletin*, XXX (April 19, 1954), 584–88.

The estimated amounts gain added significance when the effect on the process of developing programs in Berlin and Bonn and the leverage on the Bonn government in the grants of Federal Republic funds is considered. These now average more than the DM equivalent of half a billion dollars a year.

Of special importance are the tax provisions that, because the

The Strength of Berlin

value of new investment can be deducted from taxable profits, make the location of new plants in Berlin highly advantageous. There is also aid with insurance, under the Hermes plan,[11] to offset the considerable risks of delay to shipments.

These supports are given because the city would not be viable without help. The partnership that has developed with the American and German aid programs and with the negotiations over the major problems has touched the vital nerves of both countries. These are stronger manifestations of intention than oral declarations. The very success of the efforts led Khrushchev to his determination to smash the "Berlin showcase," in 1958. While signs of a Communist retreat are not always obvious, there are indications that they now think the "soft sell," to encourage a sense of security, might be better than the more brutal approach of the Stalin and early Khrushchev period. If they were to play upon the restlessness of youth, as earlier Soviet savagery is partially blurred with time, they still might find a weak place in the armor of the city.

In 1965 and 1966, the remarkable economic vitality of the city was manifest in many ways. Of particular interest in the sixfold increase of trade between the city and the outside world. Since 1950, for instance, the exports of goods and services have gone from more than 1 billion DM to more than 12 billion DM. A small segment of trade has gone to the Soviet bloc. The term "the balance of trade" is frequently used, but it is an artificial concept as applied to a city. Nevertheless, the decline in the "deficit" is significant.

The rise in the total production, of which more than 60 per cent is exported, shows the unusual increase from four to fifteen million DM. This rate of growth amounts to over 10 per cent in almost every year since 1950. The figures for GNP are: 1950: 3,862; 1955: 7,379; 1960: 12,000; 1963: 14,805.[12] There is every indication that they will be higher in newly available statistics.

Growth in production in the major industries has, in many cases, greatly exceeded the base year of 1936. In the case of chemical and iron and steel production, such increase has averaged 300 per cent beyond the base year, while the production of electrical equipment, clothing, and ceramics and glass has reached almost twofold. Significant growth also marks other areas of production.

---

11. A special joint government and insurance company program.
12. *Handbook of Economic Statistics*, pp. 58–59.

TABLE 6. WEST BERLIN BALANCE OF TRADE AND GOODS AND SERVICES
(Million of DM at Current Prices)

	1950	1960	1961	1962	1963	1964	1965
IMPORTS:							
Goods and services	2,511	8,887	9,399	9,676	10,220	11,430	12,815
Goods	2,415	8,164	8,600	8,810	9,250	10,300	11,600
From Federal Republic and other Western countries	2,340	7,882	8,356	8,581	8,988	10,020	n.a.
Soviet Zone and Bloc countries	75	282	244	229	262	280	n.a.
EXPORTS:							
Goods and services	1,276	8,377	9,412	9,743	9,910	10,990	12,080
From Federal Republic and other Western countries	1,100	7,802	8,811	9,141	9,292	10,296	n.a.
Soviet Zone and Bloc countries	70	147	136	134	108	134	n.a.
Balance (Import Surplus)	−1,235	−510	+13	+67	−310	−440	−735
Exports—% of Total Imports	51	94	100.1	100.7	97.0	96.2	94.3
Import or Export Surplus—% of GNP	32	4	0.1	0.5	2.1	2.7	4.2

n.a. Data not available.
Source: Handbook of Economic Statistics, p. 65.

TABLE 7. WEST BERLIN INDUSTRIAL PRODUCTION, SELECTED INDICES
(1936 = 100)

	1960	1962	1964	1965
Iron and steel	280	250	275	277
Sawmills and woodworking	57	95	107	83
Machinery	108	122	153	170
Electrical equipment	173	201	204	218
Chemicals	244	290	350	406
Ceramics and glass	189	190	192	195
Clothing	223	225	198	219

Source: Handbook of Economic Statistics, p. 62.

Growth of Educational Institutions

The economic strength that resulted from varied types of support has surprised the Soviets and has impressed the noncommitted countries. The stimulus from the expanding economy has carried Berlin in directions not at first anticipated. The development of

The Strength of Berlin

educational and cultural resources had also been most gratifying.

A basic optimism about the future is reflected in the intellectual life of West Berlin. People are proud of their heritage in science and art. They wish to gain the reputation as the capital of culture of West Germany. The enthusiasm with which Berliners delve into creative pursuits is a good indication of their faith in the future. No one claims that any great renaissance is taking place either in educational procedures, art, music, dancing, or in literary pursuits, but there is an impressive spiritual vitality.

Perhaps the leading educational institution to make rapid progress since the war has been the Free University, located in the wooded residential area of Dahlem. This university has six faculties and fifteen thousand students, including some four thousand from the Federal Republic and one thousand from abroad. New buildings are constantly going up to accommodate the teaching faculty and the student body that is expected to grow to twenty-five thousand students in the next twenty-five years.

Among the more famous teaching and research groups of the Free University is the Otto Suhr Institute of Political Science. There is also in the University a library of ninety thousand books; the East Europe Institute; the America Institute, and the gigantic new University Hospital, or Klinikum, still under construction.

The University, founded in 1948, is one of the newest in Germany. It grew out of a protest of the students at Humboldt University in East Berlin who resented the restrictions on their academic freedom.

There are some in Berlin who now consider the Free University students to be notably leftist. Others say the current explosive temperament of the students, reflected in demonstrations for better housing and more academic freedom, is a passing phase.

The Technical University (Technische Universität), which was heavily bombed in the war, survived to rebuild its massive structure and offers courses in nuclear, aeronautical, and electrical engineering as well as in other fields. As a teaching and research institute, the Technical University has always been considered of first rank in Germany.

As part of a continuing effort to make Berlin a research center, support—including U.S. counterpart funds—has been extended for rehabilitating the Max-Planck-Gesellschaft, which carries on experiments in nuclear research, hydraulics, and navigation. In addition, the Max-Planck-Institut für Forschungen auf dem Gebiet des Bildungswesen (educational research) carries on surveys of the curriculum in West Berlin schools.

Young leaders from Asian, African, and Latin American nations take advantage in ever increasing numbers of the other unique educational institution—the Deutsche Stiftung für Entwicklungsländer at the Villa Borsig. They spend six weeks with international experts, provided through UNESCO, in their field of specialty such as public administration or public health. As they gaze out on the Tegel Lake and the old majestic trees on this estate formerly owned by one of Germany's leading industrialists, the visitors from developing lands have an opportunity to become acquainted with each other as well as to learn the techniques most useful to their own countries. These foreign visitors also have an opportunity to visit various points of personal interest in West Berlin and see Communism at work in East Berlin.

Development in Art

Berlin as an art center revolves around the work of young artists connected to the Akademie der Kunst. Members of this academy engage in poetry reading, lectures, concerts, and sponsor art exhibits. Before long, the Neue Nationalgalerie designed by Mies van der Rohe will add to the city's resources.

To encourage and stimulate young West Berlin artists, the Berlin art prizes, established in 1948, are given annually—six 10,000 DM awards in six branches of modern art; six other 5,000 DM prizes for younger artists. West Berlin has maintained its great tradition in sculpture, with the works of Bernhard Heiliger, Karl Hartung, Erich F. Reuter, Hans Uhlmann, Karl Heinz Droste, Ursula Forster, and Alexander Gonda widely hailed. The Nierendorf and Schuler galleries try to help new artists by showing their works in one-man shows with wide publicity. The Galerie Springer on the Kurfürstendamm is the most famous West Berlin art gallery for modern painting and sculpture.

The Berlin Cultural Festival salutes a different area of the world each year. In 1964, the fourteenth annual festival was dedicated to

The Strength of Berlin

"The Reciprocal Influence of Western and African Culture." The 1965 festival was devoted to Japanese culture. Some 1,626 artists from twelve nations took part, and 60,000 patrons, among them 500 journalists, saw plays of first quality, art, and music dedicated to the culture and traditions of the Negro. This cultural festival tends to focus world attention on West Berlin.

East Berlin's answer to this festival has been to hold one of its own. It lasts sixteen days, and in 1965 it featured artists not only from Communist countries but also from France, Belgium, and Western Germany. In East Berlin there is a tendency, for political reasons, to withdraw into the classical eighteenth-century style.

We find present-day Berlin a city of many trees; perhaps it has more than any other great city of the world. A place of considerable natural beauty, it has benefited from impressive town planning. The Hansaviertel, designed by a number of international architects in 1957, was the first large housing project to be constructed in Berlin after the war.

Few would have dreamed, as they looked at the destroyed Berlin of 1945, that in 1965 the city would have such stimulating architectural beauty contributed to by so many international architects.

A project for the next few years is Gropius Stadt Berlin-Buckow-Rudow which is being built from the designs of Walter Gropius, the Bauhaus architect now in Cambridge, Massachusetts. Many new office buildings, shops, and stores, some approaching skyscraper heights, give the Western half of Berlin a dignity particularly important to a city under strain.

Building styles vary, ranging from the "pregnant oyster," the Congress Hall with its curving roof, the American contribution, and continuing with the strange irregular angles of the new Philharmonic, and the brilliant blue of the new glass-enclosed church adjoining the Kaiser-Wilhelm-Gedächtniskirche, to more traditional structures.

One can be critical of a particular building, but visitors look with awe at what a city can do in just a few years to take on a new image along the most functional modern lines. Berliners build with optimism in the face of continuing harassment.

In another area of creative art—music—Berlin has become once again a home for opera with the Deutsche Oper Berlin and its world-famous conductors Karl Böhm, Heinrich Hollreiser, Eugen Jochum, and Lorin Maazel. Berlin's large musical community enthusiastically supports the Berlin Philharmonic Orchestra—conducted by the flamboyant and renowned Herbert von Karajan—as well as the Berlin Chamber Orchestra, the Doric Quartet, and others. The Hochschule für Musik turns out well-qualified musicians, composers, and teachers.

The Press and the News

Some with whom I talked in Berlin, in 1965 strongly critical of today's press, insisted it had deteriorated in style and content. During my short stay, it was hard for me to gain a clear picture.

Thus, while the press has been accused of failing to maintain standards, the city has nine daily newspapers (contrasted with three in Washington, D.C.), varying in opinion from far left to far right. The *Berliner Zeitung* maintains the largest circulation. *Der Tagesspiegel*, an independent morning paper, is noted for sober, well-balanced news coverage, and its general objective reporting. *Der Tag* and *Der Abend* are also considered constructive forces. *Telegraf* is the SPD party paper. *Berliner Morgenpost* is independent, pro-Bonn, and appeals to a broad middle class with its dramatic treatment of news.

West Berlin has one radio-television network of its own, Sender Freies Berlin (SFB), as well as the American RIAS; American Forces Network (AFN); British Forces Network (BFN); Forces Françaises Berlin (FFB); and SFB-Fernsehen television.

The cultural life is more than a consequence of economic recovery. It shows a vitality of spirit which has great significance for the future. Now there is both material and moral strength.

In 1965 industry flourishes. There is relatively little poverty. There is a dynamic cultural and educational life and a lively interest in politics. The presence of the three occupying powers is not under attack. There is no evident weakness in the political, social, or economic life of the city. Vulnerable though it is to Communist military attack—likely to be subjected to recurring diplomatic pressures, fearful at times over access routes—its life is balanced, healthy, and gay. This is the city that has been rebuilt in a new pattern by Allied help, political understanding, foreign money, and

The Strength of Berlin

German hard work. Its voting percentages of eligible citizens are extraordinarily high, with the Communist vote less than 2 per cent in 1961. This is strength in democracy.

There can be no complete security in the modern world where the collision of philosophies, of systems, of doctrines is actual or at least threatens from day to day. There is here a constant contrast of systems.

Berlin could not maintain its financial position, could not keep up production, could not hold its population, could not maintain its position if it were not for the continuing political support from Bonn, from Washington, and from NATO. The fact that other cities and nations have come to the help of the city in the time of need would have been without meaning if these centers of strength were to end their support. The manner in which the safety of one country is dependent on the unity of aims of many nations is widely understood. In the case of Berlin, it is glaringly apparent. If the NATO countries were to find that there were no meaning to the accepted and classical position, if the United States were to abandon the nation's commitments and break the time-honored promises, then the essential weakness of the small area, the isolated city, the helpless people would be manifest in an instant.

A political or military tidal wave would sweep over the city. The streets would be empty, the factories silent, the signs of desolation would be appalling. This is the situation faced by all small nations, by most large nations, and by any part of the free world which is left to shrivel under the impact of hostile influences.[13] There is not enough strength to stand alone. The appearance of independence is in this day and age an illusion.

A balance sheet of the strengths and weaknesses of the city of Berlin has many lessons to convey to the atomic age, to the years of jet transport and space exploration. Only those who have lived in the period when oceans were barriers to political aggression, and formed at least temporary protections from sudden assault, can recognize the meaning of the assimilation of the interests of remote small countries to the strategy and the security of great nations—an Okinawa for the United States, a Laos, a Lebanon, Iran, Zanzibar—or Berlin. The question of power has become infinitely more

13. It is an issue similar to that in Vietnam, the Berliners frequently said in 1965.

complex. It is not enough to count the soldiers, add up tonnage, list the tanks and guns, as signs of victory or defeat. A Liechtenstein can conceivably launch a nuclear bomb. France, weakened in two wars, can threaten the balance of power with a minor atomic *force de frappe*.

The final analysis of the plus and minus of endurance, of survival, shows many intangibles: the will of the people, the understanding between leaders of the free world, the sense of mutual involvement, alliances, and the binding force of a promise. In all of these essentials of strength, Berlin has the moral force, developed by a close partnership, sanctioned by tradition and rooted in good faith and friendship. Weakness will not invade this structure unless the acids of doubt, suspicion, and intolerance corrode the oncoming generation. To combat this possibility, continued effort to develop a perceptive and inspired belief in the basic soundness of the German youth is necessary.

To those who are familiar with the facts, a complete turnabout in Washington, with a reversal of the policy on Germany, Europe and Berlin, is unthinkable. There are some who question aspects of the present policy, but their questions point the way to the significant answers. For a time, a decade or more ago, the world was in doubt as to the meaning of the clash with tyranny, between those striving for representative government and those in the police state. This doubt can no longer exist for those who see the Wall, or for those who are imprisoned in the East Zone.

Even if erosion has altered the conditions of access in minor respects—and it is conceivable that further changes might occur—the surrender of Berlin by the Berliner, or by the friends of the city, could only come with a drastic reversal of the policy of NATO countries. Before such a change could develop and be accepted by the leaders, there would be a look at the alternatives to defending Berlin, and these alternatives are awesome and bleak.

VIII. The Young Men

The Students Protest

The young people of West Berlin are probably more like Americans than they were before the War. They are more restive in the face of rules, tradition, and authority than they used to be.

In recent months, following some American traditions, they have set up a system of student evaluation of professors. They are looking for a change in the system. At the Free University in protest meetings, they shouted, "The University is not free." They aired their grievances with stomping and pounding their knuckles on the desk. They had proposed in the spring that the "Student Village" invite some three or four professors from Humboldt University in East Berlin to give lectures. They proposed debates between these men and selected professors at the Free University. These debates would not have been sponsored by the University but would have been a part of the *Studentendorf's* cultural program planned by the students.

The decision by the authorities to postpone this program seemed to the students a denial of free speech. "How can we justify such suppression in talking to our fellows from Communist countries?" they asked. "Was the refusal by the authorities because they feared that Americans with money to give Germany might object?"

They were indignant over the decision of the University to deny Professor Erich Kuby from Munich the use of the Theatre Maxima of the University for an address. He had criticized the University and had called it "unfree."

The "strikes" on the campus in the spring and summer of 1965 were a new phenomenon. They shocked the Rector and the governing body. In further comment, the students criticized the University for becoming too rigid in administration and curriculum. As elsewhere in Germany, large classes and an authoritarian attitude tended to increase the distance between the students and the professors. Even though there was agreement that some reforms were needed, the students were driving the administration into a position where co-operation and understanding were difficult.

One trouble in the German university system is the rotation of the position of rector. While this arrangement spreads the burden, it does not commend itself to those who consider that the presidency of a big university is an important, time-consuming job that can only be learned with several years of experience. It is difficult for a scholar whose main interest is in his specialized profession to shift suddenly to the administrative and psychological problems. Moreover, the choice of the rector is influenced by many factors of a political nature, and the election is in some cases skillfully maneuvered on the part of cliques and special interest groups.

While the rectors of the Free University have been of high caliber, it is still thought that the office has suffered from the difficulties of making the major readjustment in points of view and taking on many obligations that are not completely palatable. It is possible that the Free University, which has been passing through several transition periods since its founding in 1948, has suffered more acutely from this arrangement than some other universities. The experience that I have had in some six or eight universities and colleges leads me to conclude that the weakness of the system could well be examined with special attention to recent troubles in the Free University.

In 1965, when I was in Berlin, there were frequent arguments heard in West Berlin academic circles about the quality of higher education. One leading Free University administrator and professor has explained the problem as follows: "Before the war in all of Germany there were 70,000 university students. Since the war, the total has reached 250,000 students in West Germany and West Berlin. There are too many students and not enough qualified professors." This difficulty for the schools and universities cannot be easily solved. In secondary education West Berlin has a total of 460 other schools compared to the 394 in 1938. One hundred and fifty schools were completely rebuilt after the war, but the need for elementary and high school facilities is still great.

The possible return of an old tradition to the German universities has brought concern to some of the professors and students of the Free University. The "corporation," or duelling society, is still a part of student life although to a lesser degree than before the war. A majority of the students are against them, but some still take pride in belonging, such as the young man who recently returned to the Free University Student Village with more than a dozen head wounds. He had duelled with a saber, with only his eyes and neck protected and gained admittance to a corporation on this, his sixth such duel. In these student duels with sabers, the young men wear leather padded collars in order to make it impossible to receive a cut in the neck, and they wear heavy goggles made out of steel to protect the eyes—the cheeks, forehead, and the top of the head are unprotected. Bloody but gallant, the student only regretted that he had not received the most distinguished of all marks, the slash on the cheek.

There are also the leftist leanings to consider. One prominent Federal Republic leader recently commented when asked about leftist university students: "The fact that there are a few Communists in a university does not set the tone for the institution as a whole." There are many who conclude that the University has not yet reached its goal of academic superiority. Most educators confidently hope that with the years it will grow in stature. A tribute to its reputation is the fact that there are several thousand applicants from West Germany above the number that can be admitted.

In order to get a direct impression of opinion among the students, I sought several opportunities to talk with them.

One occasion was a visit to the Student Village in Zehlendorf, where some seven hundred students live in small buildings in a green rural setting. The separate two-story dormitories are clustered around a community center with music rooms, a little theater, meeting rooms, and a cafeteria. Here there is a small coffee room or "night club."

On the evening of June 24, 1965, there was a gathering of some hundred or more students to exchange views with me and two other American visitors. The discussion was heated. "Did we believe in free speech?" they asked over and over. Why should their cultural program not include professors from the Humboldt University in East Berlin? Why should the Rector and the governing body prohibit discussion and debate between the Communists and the Free University professors? Could democracy justify such "repression?" Was it not difficult to explain to friends in the East the restrictions in the Free University?

The preoccupation with this question for an hour seemed to overshadow their interest in German reunification, but, when they did speak of this burning question, they said: "Twenty years without progress—must we wait for fifty years? We must find some course of action now." Their repeated theme was a demand for a "policy of movement."

With regard to the meaning of the Student Village, the young Mayor and Vice-Mayor said they wished more student control over financing and administration. They wanted to administer justice to the delinquent students themselves. Above all, they wished to control their program of lectures and debate without interference from the authorities. The reasons for restrictions, they implied, were probably a general feeling of sensitivity in Germany motivated by a fear that foundation money—wanted for fellowships and other help—might be frightened away. In fact, there is relatively little such money now.

The criticism in discussing the problems of their life and work was linked with several episodes: not only the denial of a speech by Professor Erich Kuby, already referred to, but also the uncertain attitude of the University officials toward the corporations, and the negative response to the plan to invite the East Berlin professors. They were interested in political problems, but it was difficult to direct the discussion away from their local issues. They indicated that the developing tutorial system in the Student Village offered them welcome opportunities to discuss informally with the professors. Some instructors live in the Village, and there are a number of "cultural" groups airing diverse intellectual problems. The students thanked the Americans for their contribution to these developments.

At eleven o'clock some of the most active and interested of the audience adjourned to the club for more discussion. Outside in the summer night, in twos and threes, less politically minded students strolled in relaxed enjoyment of the warm air. The zonal boundary was a mile away.

Another of several student meetings I had was downtown—close to the Hansaviertel with its twelve- and fourteen-story apartments, in Siegmunds Hof. This dormitory for the Technical University was also built with American money. It is close to the Ernst-Reuter-Platz with its new business structures, with the modern *plastic*, stark in symbolic outline, with wings spread, a bronze dedicated to the memory of the former Mayor.

More than a hundred students gathered first in the conference room and later thirty or so met over coffee in the art gallery in another building, and engaged in lively discussion. They raised questions of broad scope. They asked for more action by the Allies for German reunification, a bolder response to cruelty at the border, a willingness to take risks, a show of force. They declared that the city would stand firm if there were a new blockade. If there were interference with access, the Allies must act quickly, they said—"Could there not be plans for all likely contingencies, with local orders going into effect within hours without reference to Washington? Why must all three commands consult their home governments, thus losing three or four days to gain a co-ordinated position?"

They told the story of the little dog dying in the barbed wire and the Germans trying to rescue it, while American soldiers stood idly by. "Could such restraint impress the Soviets or the Vopos?" A few days before, these Communists had shot a pleasure seeking couple in a small boat—drifting near the boundary in the Teltow Canal. "Why did no one shoot the murderers guarding this line?"

NATO they said was important, but for most Germans reunification was the prime consideration. "If we could have reunification with free elections, we would pay the price of relinquishing NATO membership." "Perhaps money could be added to political concessions made elsewhere to increase the price offered for freedom of the Zone." "The policy of small steps would help." "More contacts would prevent the widening gap between the East Zone and the Federal Republic." In this view, the two student groups agreed.

Criticism of the Allies, while not always sharp, was persistent, and virtually unanimous—the United States had the power but was not using it.

Free speech for the students, particularly for the men from the Free University, was a major concern; they joined with other students at the Free University in their will to protest.

New Currents of Opinion

On July 16, the young men in the largest classroom in the law school were crowded in, spilling into the corridors, standing against the wall. The leader of the association spoke. "This is the University founded by students," he said. "This is the 'Free University.' The faculty did not start it, students did, and we want to run it."

A professor was given his turn to speak—or almost. There were interruptions from the floor. He protested, "You asked me to come and to discuss the University's problem—now you won't let me speak." Several booed, but he spoke for another ten minutes. Some of the faculty stood with the students along the wall, everyone sweltering in the crowded hall.

The meeting went on. "There are at the University fifteen thousand students," the young men said. "We should have more than 15 per cent of the vote on the University *Senat*. It's our University." The women joined them in stamping and pounding.

The immediate issue was the "dismissal" or the reinstatement of a young assistant, Ekkehardt Krippendorf, in the Political Science Institute. He had printed severe criticism of Rector Lueurs for his action in regard to a proposed speech by Professor Jazy of Basel, Switzerland. His letter was considered to verge on the insulting. Rector Lueurs had written a reply to young Krippendorf which reflected his strong reaction. When one examined the facts, it appeared that even before the exchange of arguments, it had been decided that Krippendorf was not to teach in the coming year, but there was still talk of a research grant. The sharpness of the debate had led to a divided faculty and to an expression of revolt by the students. The campus leaders were demanding a significant share in the appointment and dismissal of the professors and also in determining the curriculum. They were staging another of a series of protests on that hot July evening.

The precise merits of the Krippendorf case may never be clar-

The Young Men

ified. There were allegations of bad faith, of distortion of facts, of improper conduct on the part of the young assistant, intemperate demands by the students, inadvisable statements by the Rector and faculty—altogether a confused situation. There did not seem to have been a show of constructive diplomacy, there had been more noise than wisdom in several quarters.

The salient point was then, and is now, that the students no longer stand in awe of authority. They speak frequently of revolt in Berkeley. They asked about "teach-ins." They clamor for free speech, "the right to say anything at any time on any subject." They wish to have the Communist professors debate. They object to having the authorities of the University put limits on who should speak. They do not admit that the faculty is uniquely qualified to run their affairs. The students, they say, have rights that cannot be limited. A new era has come for the universities.

In all this stir and discussion, the issue for those on the periphery of the specific conflicts was not who was right and who was wrong, but the fact that youth insist that, rather than submitting to authority and system, they should press for new ideas. In contrast to the present group, those who founded the Free University in 1948 were older students. Many had had the experience of war, and all had lived through the first miserable days of the postwar struggle. They had a bitter knowledge of Communism. They knew that the political foundations of the new Berlin were laid for them by leaders in Germany and abroad to whom they owed a large debt. Their perspective was at the same time wider and also colored by memories of a national guilt in which they feared they had a share. Even those who had been brave enough to protest or who were in the underground, still felt this burden.

Today, the young men have few of these memories. They recognize the chaotic conditions of the world and feel that those of their elders who survived Nazism owe them an explanation for the past. They will not accept any pronouncement if they do not agree to its inherent validity. They are suspicious of tradition. They discard slogans, they are strong in their conviction that they have the intellectual, physical, and economic capacity to view political relations from a fresh point of view. For them, the older men have lost the authoritative voice that went formerly with their years and their station. The Rector has no more right to decide university issues than the students; he, too, must prove himself and win a fight in which abstract theory can outweigh decades of experience. The old days are gone, a new spirit prevails.

Their political fears make them restless. Many of the young men are concerned that the United States has become so committed in Vietnam that Americans are no longer bothering enough with Berlin. However, if the United States were to leave Vietnam tomorrow the effect on West Berlin would be a tremendous shock. The majority in West Berlin stand firmly behind the U.S. position despite some worries that the United States might be temporarily distracted from Berlin by commitments elsewhere.

The students, with rare exceptions, are not Communists, but they do not fear Communism as do older Germans with more experience. They say "let us have a look at the people and consider the arguments." They have a passion for experimentation and adventure in the political field. Some of their attitudes are in part the result of their inverted sense of guilt. Because some think Germans should feel shame even if not guilty, they are belligerent in rejecting any part of this. For many reasons, there is a widening gulf between generations which will not be bridged even when these young men and women grow older. Those who were born after World War II think they owe little to the past; in a sense, they are people without parents. They are intense in their desire for freedom, and they take a position that is designed to prevent a new authoritarianism. There must be no second Hitler. The new type of nationalist feeling, which they do not clearly recognize, can become a strong political force unless they are kept in tune with internationalism.

In spite of their frequent protests against existing conditions, the youth of Berlin have plans for the future which are similar to those found in the West, in America, or in the Federal Republic. They expect to lead profitable lives as lawyers, teachers, doctors, and businessmen. Many hope to visit America. Some expect to leave Berlin to seek opportunities elsewhere.

It is well known that the students from abroad and from West Germany go frequently to East Berlin, partly out of curiosity, partly for a clearer political understanding of the sector and the Zone.

The Young Men

Some even attend classes at the Humboldt University. There may be a measure of connivance which makes it possible for students who are West Berliners to cross the line to go to the Communist university. Some of the students feel that they should explore the doctrines of Communism and see how it diverges from Western democracy. "Why should we fear the debate," they say. "If we are strong, we can at least listen.

The young men must be heard. The clamor from many countries alarms the timorous and inspires the more courageous. To those who fear change, and there are many, the independence of vigorous young men everywhere about them is a startling phenomenon that they do not associate with their own youth.

In Berlin, the stirrings and the protests are loud as the new politicians are trying to break the mold of past thinking. The slogan "no experiments" is rejected. The difference between the past manner of behavior and the present has been said to be that youth revolt not within the system but to change it. In Germany, the recent past has no aura to make it acceptable to the majority of the postwar generation. They see it as a time of tactical error and of moral degradation. They must create a new environment as their world.

Neither the educational resources, the political system, nor the international relations that confront the average German seem to them adequate. Looking back to the Nazi era and the War, they say their parents have failed them, they do not want to listen to the sounds from the past. The problems of Nazism cannot be understood. In the freer atmosphere of the present day, they do not fully appreciate the weight and control of the governmental apparatus as it was shaped and reinforced by Hitler and his circle of close associates. They vaguely sense the heavy hand of authority and the unanswerable command of the man in uniform. The past is as remote to the Germans of the new generation as the stories of the American Indian wars to Americans. The distance of time is untraveled and unbridgeable. There are nonetheless moments when the young are devastated with shame. Now, in the aversion to old authoritarianism, even the more reasonable aspects of authority are challenged.

The students acknowledge few debts—they have received

considerable help from America, from the Federal Republic, and from the city. The University buildings have been financed from extraordinary resources, partly from the American aid programs, partly by Henry Ford II. Scholarships and other subventions have come from the Ford Foundation.

Help to the students and to young people takes various forms. The Berlin *Senat* lends young married couples 3,000 DM to set up housekeeping. It is not repayable for five years. These couples are also presented with a gift of 700 DM for every child. A survey conducted by an enterprising educator shows that a majority of couples have three children in five years—thus the amount of the initial loan made to them is substantially reduced, and if there are more children, could be wiped out altogether.

Because they have become so articulate in recent months, attention is usually focused on the universities. It is probable that the lower grades of education may be even more important, however, in shaping the future.

West Berlin must have more schools to accommodate a fast growing population. It is predicted that by 1970 the district of Schöneberg alone must have three large new schools or go out of the education business. The elementary and high schools are now conducted on a two-session-a-day basis, including Saturdays. Getting more schools in West Berlin has become a gigantic financial and political problem.

If the school shortage is acute, the effort to improve the curriculum and give West Berlin's coming generation a well-rounded education, particularly in civics and history—a touchy problem at best—has been well-intentioned and reasonably successful. Children in West Berlin are learning the truth about their own twentieth-century history. In 1960 the *Senator für Volksbildung* (Senator for Public Education) advised all West Berlin teachers that political information and education in the schools should instill in all young people the will and ability to make political judgments and awaken them to their democratic responsibilities in a democratic society and a democratic state.

A look at a typical West Berlin elementary or high school textbook would indicate that for the most part the advice has been heeded. Heerdt-Heumann in *Unser Weg durch die Geschichte* offers an objective view of the Hitler period, power, motives, and party manipulations. It covers the Jewish persecutions and war horrors with a combination of objectivity and realism. The downfall of Hitler, the aftereffects of the war, the formation of the United Nations and the Federal Republic are factually accounted for. Germany's commitment to NATO is underscored. Berlin, the key to freedom, is emphasized. And, although the section is sketchy in parts, there is also a comprehensive treatment on East Germany today with a brief discussion of the policy of reunification "within the framework of world politics."

One educator with whom I talked, however, believes the school textbooks do not go far enough to describe the major problems facing a new generation in a divided city. Nor, he contends, do the teachers have a broad enough schooling in political science or history to educate youngsters adequately. Political science has not been taught to teachers in German universities in the past, and only in the last three years has there been any broad opportunity in the field of political science. "You cannot teach history without a good grounding in Marxism-Leninism," he said. "Our teachers just don't know how to argue about Communism."

Some Berliners are disturbed that despite the conscientious effort made in elementary and high school to give children a broad-based education, not enough students are inspired to seek higher education. There is still much criticism of the fact that the decision as to whether a student can go on to higher education must be reached at the age of twelve or thereabouts.

Meanwhile, the East German Communists have been engaging in advertising campaigns to show the virtues of higher education and to encourage children of peasants to take advantage of educational opportunities offered by the regime.

No such concerted effort has been made in West Germany or West Berlin. The critics add that higher education is too often considered a hindrance to early earning of income in the West. In fact, they point to the limiting of higher education in West Germany and West Berlin largely to children of public servants and to those in certain social groups striving to be accepted in the middle classes. Some fear a growing conservatism along with irrationalism in higher education. They also blame industry for exerting strong pressure on West German educators not to extend educational opportunities beyond the ninth year of school in order to help alleviate the current labor shortage.

In East Germany, in contrast, a minimum of ten years of education is required, and, of those in the East Zone educated through the tenth year, it is reported that one half go on to higher education. But, despite Communist emphasis on education, the critics concede that there is greater danger to intellectual development in East Germany's forced educational system than all of the hurdles in the West. If a young person studying under Communism wants to be a chemist and teachers are needed, he is likely to wind up as a teacher and vice versa. In fields where people are urgently needed, the choice of the state has to be accepted.

One wing of West Berlin opinion holds that a new type of experimental school now being tried in the West Berlin districts of Wedding, Spandau, and Gropius Stadt may be the answer to helping more young people to qualify for higher education. Special attention is given to teenagers to help them qualify for the *Abitur* examination, the step to more schooling, at a stage comparable to the American junior college. A recent comparison showed that 40 per cent of U.S. high school students who qualify and take the examinations for university and college entrance go on to higher education, while up until recently only 10 per cent of all West German teenagers try to go on.

Some Berliners are highly critical of the old-fashioned German compartmentalized system of education. They view the opening of the new Bochum University in the Federal Republic as pointing the way to eventual abandonment of this harmful system. If the new teaching standards, which stress teamwork, often employed in institutions are accepted, it is felt that the over-all impact will be tremendous. The big question to many is whether such a system could ever be accepted by tradition-bound Germans.

Another educational experiment in West Berlin which has proven successful is the dual language—German and English—John F. Kennedy School. This has been much appreciated by families of various nationalities in the city.

A notable contribution to the intellectual life and to the contin-

The Young Men

uing enjoyment and education of special importance to Berliners old and young is found in the new or enlarged libraries. It has been claimed that more people read in Berlin than in any other German city (three books per person annually). There are one hundred municipal lending libraries. The American Memorial Library, which is reported to be the most used library in Europe, was built with a 5,400,000 DM gift made by the United States during the Blockade. It has a capacity for 600,000 to 700,000 books. A new library, the Staatsbibliothek, is currently under construction in the Tiergarten.

The young men in the Federal Republic, many of whom apply to the Free University for admission, are almost as active and independent as the students in this educational center behind the Iron Curtain. They, too, have protested. They, too, have challenged the authority of the governing bodies with marches and strikes. While the problem is more complex and acute in Berlin, where contacts with the Communists are so exciting, the same trends of thinking obtain.

Conversations with younger members of the working classes, however, indicate that they are less enticed by theoretical suppositions and more impressed by the practical dangers of dealing with the Communists. In Germany, it is still true that a vast majority of the people are aware of tyranny and oppression in the Zone and despise the rule that restrains the thought and action of their fellows. They have also begun to wonder about some of the episodes of the past which have come to them only second hand as tales of horror. Here lies the insidious danger of the present Communist "soft sell."

This possible entrapment comes at a time when there are discernible traces of criticism of America. These are limited by the knowledge that the United States was generous in laying the foundations of the new Germany. Appreciation of this, however, is not sufficient to prevent the young men from asking, "Should America limit German action with regard to the East Zone?" "Does the United States really care what happens to the Germans east of the Rhineland?"

These questions come from the children of those with whom we

Americans worked to restore a devastated Germany. These children are grown—they can ask questions not heard twenty years ago. They live in a land of prosperity and opportunity. They do not wish their rights and ambitions curtailed by an outside power. Within the framework of democracy, they have a desire for innovation and a will to take risks.

IX. The Mood and the Method

How Long Is the Sausage?

The mood of Berlin is a part of the strategic as well as the tactical situation. For those who regard any change in the face of Communist pressure as loss, it is hard to reconcile the buoyant attitude of the city, its economic strength, and its political stability with the warnings of catastrophe. The contrast that one finds in Berlin is a cause of the intense interest in the life of the people and a degree of expectancy which stimulates all who come there to question what shape the future will take.

Changes that have taken place since the surrender, the Blockade, the June 17 uprising, the Wall, and the end of the Adenauer era are considerable. The pessimists consider them signs of weakness in the face of continued Communist will to aggression. The more optimistic emphasize the realities of a prosperous, confident, and even gay city.

The more thoughtful, taking account of both extremes of opinion, consider it necessary to warn of the danger of erosion of policy. Here more than in most cities mistakes, a sudden weakening of courage, or recourse to an undependable compromise may bring about a sharp decline in conditions and a threat to the Allied ability to hold the position. There is no present prospect of such a development.

From a distance, and on the basis of casual tourist visits to Berlin, there is a tendency for Americans to take the present situation in Berlin for granted. They assume that the people will maintain their firmness, that industry will continue to prosper, and that the major troubles of the city are over. The situation appears somewhat different to the citizens of Berlin. They are aware of the fact that our financial aid has terminated. They note that we make fewer official visits to the city. They find few references in official announcements and formal speeches to the importance of Berlin to the United States.

The Berliners are extremely sensitive to any signs of lack of American interest. They become alarmed if, in the discussion of changes in NATO or escalation of the war in Vietnam, there is talk of reducing the number of American troops in Europe. While it is unlikely that the atmosphere in Berlin would change overnight, the people are highly alert to both the official attitude and to the chance remarks of prominent Americans. They are firmly convinced that without our interest and will to defend the city they cannot survive in freedom.

Today, even the residents of the East Zone, in some cases, want the Allies to maintain a resistance to attacks on Western rights. The withdrawal of the Western Powers would not necessarily be in their interest. Their hopes for the future are involved, their obstruction to Communism is subtle.

Since 1963, following the Cuban missile crisis, the activities of the East Zone authorities have gone into slow motion. There have been varied pressures, but they seem to have been mainly of local origin and not to have the serious intent of Moscow behind them. As probes rather than challenges, they have put the Western Powers somewhat on the defensive and have not been of such extensive character as to justify serious reprisals from the West.

These salami tactics have been disturbing to the more observant who fear that the Western Powers might not be sufficiently alert to the whittling away of rights. It is clear that there has been submission to interference or slight modifications of procedure in some instances. While this has been going on, Western protests have been aimed at maintaining the legal position and not conceding as rights what has been accepted for practical reasons and convenience. This process, which has been going on for more than ten years, has led some to ask, "How long is the sausage?" Since the

The Mood and the Method

Allies would hesitate to face world opinion with a use of nuclear arms over what seem like trivial accommodations to controls established over access to the city, since there has been hesitation in using small counter-measures, and since most observers do not notice minor changes in requirements, only formal objection or quiet negotiation has marked the request for a permit of a new color or a new type of identification paper.

Not long ago, it was reported to Allied missions in Berlin that the trains bringing Western troops into the city were displaying the East Zone flag. There was consternation, but when it was found that only a small metal plaque was attached to the locomotives, run and owned by the East Zone authorities, and not to the coaches in which the soldiers rode, it was agreed among the Western commandants that the matter was inconsequential and too trivial to be made the subject of a diplomatic episode. In every case where it is generally known that a procedure has been altered, there are some who reach the conclusion that an important right has been lost and there is considerable nervousness in Berlin. It is hard even for the most experienced expert to arrive at a positive judgment as to the significance of the change in procedure and to secure agreement among the British, French, Americans, and Germans as to when a strong stand is imperative. The situation is perplexing and is apt to lead to recriminations between those who think any change is a surrender and those who think that the practical issues—as in the case of the barge traffic—should be paramount. Even though the desire and intention to give no ground is essential to Berlin's survival, it is worth noting that none of the changes so far inaugurated has impaired the prosperity of West Berlin. Individuals and families have suffered, freedom of travel has been curtailed by fear of kidnapping, of seizures, and even of minor delays, but production and the standard of living have scarcely been affected. In every case where the pressure threatens to weaken confidence, some measure has been adopted to restore faith in the future. The city has shown almost uninterrupted progress.

The importance of these attempts to incite fear and win concessions should not be discounted, however. The capacity to resist attack does not lessen the provocation by the Communist authorities. The costs in strain and in money are not insignificant.

One of those areas where procedure is carefully watched by all the people has been the air rights. Some of the rights have been left unused for reasons which observers have attributed to timorous and unnecessary caution. In July, 1965, when East Zone helicopters intruded into the air space after the low flights of Soviet planes over the Congress Hall in April, there were demands for the renewal of Western Allied flights over East Berlin.

The Berliners knew that the Four Powers in occupation have the right, periodically exercised, to fly over the entire city. The fact that such flights have not taken place recently was thought to set an undesirable pattern of restraint which was neither expected by the Soviets nor in the interests of the Berlin policy. The slow reaction of the Allies to the illegal flights was regarded as indicating a flagging interest on the part of the United States. While there is a tendency for the West to say, "What will the Germans pay for reunification?"—there is a corresponding attitude in Berlin and Bonn to ask what the Allies will do in a time of stress.

What is at issue is the relation of both the resistance to salami tactics and of little steps to over-all policy. It is concerned with the manner in which to exist with a divided Germany. One could say coexist since the Federal Republic must coexist with the East Zone, but coexist has assumed a special meaning in the Communist vocabulary. Some think in terms of the next ten years, some in terms of the next twenty years. The time perspective of commentators varies according to a number of elements: the estimate of the speed with which China gains strength, the economic realities manifest in Communist countries, the rise of new generations with fresh attitudes, and as the whole nature of security, space, weaponry, and psychological waves of opinion take new forms. There are some people so imperceptive of change around them that they assume the future will be like the past. There are others who expect miracles. One has only to look at the developments in the past five years to judge which group is nearer the truth. More of the prevention of erosion later.

There is clearly a considerable time period during which, in the light of the strong positions taken and held by the Kremlin and by Washington, only minor modifications of the German situation are probable. The question is, then, whether there is a gain from

The Mood and the Method

experiments and small actions which do not undermine the holding operation. Those who recommend little steps have concluded that a stern and inflexible policy is likely to widen an existing gap between the East Zone and the Federal Republic. Others think that the appearance of yielding can invite further aggression. In any case, the advocacy of minor action now is sufficiently widespread to merit careful attention.

A special aspect, then, of East-West relations is the emerging policy of little steps, now corresponding to the mood in West Berlin. It can be considered to be the Western counterpart of the salami tactics of the East by which the Communists gain small, almost unnoticed, concessions or acquire, without serious counter-pressure, rights that infringe on the West. Just as it is obvious that small concessions are bad, so it is arguable that little gains, measured by the same standard, improve both the lot and the attitude of people in the Soviet Zone—and so are to be favored. There is in both cases a large element of political judgment that is not subject to statistical appraisal and that cannot be fully assessed even after the event. The psychological elements that can be decisive as they bear on the Communist appraisal of the Western policy, and as they influence the population in the Zone are, nonetheless, illusive aspects of Communist maneuvers. Current knowledge of what people are saying and doing helps in arriving at opinions but still brings us only part way on the road to firm conclusions.

There is a wealth of comment in the West on attitudes in the Zone, and those who live in Communist-held Germany are well informed about the outside world. This knowledge comes in considerable measure from the radio. RIAS is heard by many. There are numerous signs of its importance, in letters and in reports of visitors. When lightning knocked two RIAS FM transmitters off the air for two weeks in May, 1965, letters poured in from East Germans asking anxiously about the station. One listener wrote that he had called a local radio shop to ask for emergency repairs on his set, only to get the answer that they had already had dozens of similar calls and that the trouble was not with his radio but with RIAS. In addition to RIAS, Radio Vienna is a good channel for broadcasting comments and events to East Germany. Other stations, including the Voice of America and Radio Free Europe in German and other languages, are available for those who know the languages used. It is not possible to keep out the words of the free world, and the acute political consciousness of the people makes them eager listeners.

The conditions under which visits from West Germany are permitted vary from time to time. In the summer of 1965 a considerable number of persons were permitted to visit relatives in the Zone. The visitors from the West reported that conditions were tolerable. But lack of choice as to jobs, the inability to travel without hard-won permission, and the sense of supervision and control persist even though there are some areas of independence.

The continuing awareness of the community of interests which are German has been fostered by the programs of the Ministry of All German Affairs, by travel back and forth, by correspondence, and in a few cases by roundabout means such as meetings of West and East Berliners in Prague, Warsaw, or elsewhere abroad. The *Passierscheine* have been significant to those who wish to cross, but many have not gone over to the East since the Wall. The conflict of emotions *in* the Zone and *about* the Zone derive from the depth of feeling the Germans have for their homeland—even when under Communist domination. For the first time, there is developing in the East something that is akin to national pride as industry expands. This somewhat inconsistent complex of attitudes is noteworthy and is being carefully watched. How long will the dichotomy of Germans thinking about Germans resist the effect of daily habit and of continuing propaganda? This is the question that concerns many in Berlin and in the Federal Republic. Will the memories of the united fatherland dim as daily routine essentially governs the lives of the East Zone people? More informally stated—some ask, as they think Allied rights are whittled away or new claims made by the Communist regime—"How long is the sausage?"

The Search for Independent Action

Leading personalities in Germany concerned with the Berlin policy have recently engaged in an interesting series of debates which

The Mood and the Method

accelerated in tempo after the 1965 elections. In the spring of 1966, the question of an exchange of speakers between East and West was actively considered by Mayor Brandt and Chancellor Erhard. Bonn and Berlin worked for an agreement about newspapers and debates. These efforts, referred to as all-German discussions, were to apply on both sides of the partition. Considerable progress seems to have been made, but on June 29 Albert Norden, propaganda chief of the SED, in a conference in East Berlin rejected the proposals. It is probable that Willy Brandt gained some prestige in this episode.

The thought of action independent of the West had been growing in Berlin for several years. It was said in 1965 that the August, 1962, death of Peter Fechter, caught in the barbed wire as he tried to scale the Wall and bleeding to death in the sight of the American military, West Berlin police, and the East German Vopos, led to the bitter conclusion that the Americans—their strongest friends—did not care. There were then angry protests against the United States not before heard in Berlin. They did not know that the emerging Cuban missile crisis increased the danger of an attack on Berlin. They did not realize how deeply concerned Kennedy was with the risks of two simultaneous challenges from Khrushchev. Washington in August and September was anxiously watching the Soviet military contribution to Cuba's Castro. At this time there were protests in Germany against "ritualistic repetition of empty formulae" and the fog of illusion which could deceive no one as to early prospects of success.

The seeming firmness of the West left Berlin unconvinced, and limits on new experiments or contacts led to frustration in some quarters. In September, Heinrich Albertz and Willy Brandt gave interviews to *Der Spiegel* on the subject of "contacts."[1]

Policy of "Little Steps"

There is a strong emotional response to the policy of "little steps," which is reported to have originated at the time of the Tutzing speech of Egon Bahr in July, 1963. Willy Brandt made a talk at approximately the same date to the conference there.[2] The phrase

1. Shell, *Bedrohung und Bewährung*, p. 291.
2. The ten-year meeting of the Political Club of the Evangelical Academy in Tutzing.

does not acutally occur in either speech but seems to have been developed in informal conversation at about that time. The same theme was again used in Hamburg a year later by Egon Bahr. The concept has become a rallying point for those who want action now. It takes various forms and is bound to be controversial because it opens the door for possible concessions and because its implication is that those who favor these steps are for progress and that those who fear them are holding back from opportunities of great human importance.

The sponsors of the general idea vary considerably as to the specific application. Professor Shell, in his authoritative treatment of the problems of division and the threat to Berlin, analyzes the argument between Heinrich Albertz, assistant Mayor, and Franz Amrehn, who earlier held this same position for several years when the CDU-SPD coalition governed the city.[3]

The reasoning of those who urge that reunification is a German goal that can only be reached by sacrifice and a "step by step (*Schritt für Schritt*) progress" is that the "all or nothing" policy has been mainly negative so far.

They vary in their appraisal of Allied cold war policy. Some overlook the extent to which it has rebuffed the Soviets' aggressive intentions in 1948, 1954, 1955, and 1958, placing Germany in an honored position among partners and making Berlin a key issue in Western defense.

Nevertheless, to those who saw a generation dying and new men coming forward, the seeming inaction was difficult to justify. For me, a visitor from Washington, it was not easy to defend to the younger critics the policy of no apparent action for reunification.

The more experienced leaders in Germany recognize fully the frustrations that they face. They cannot and do not expect the Western Allies to engage in any warlike action to free the Soviet-occupied Zone. Under present conditions they would fear such a move almost as much as would the NATO Allies, the nonaligned countries, and others who have come to know the aggressive tendencies and nuclear capabilities of the Soviet Union.

In 1966, they find themselves faced with the unhappy choice of, one, waiting for the more powerful nations to take action that will

3. Shell, *Bedrohung und Bewährung*, especially pp. 293–96.

The Mood and the Method

induce Moscow to relinquish the Zone; two, relying on some unexpected and unpredictable event to alter the basic power situation; or, three, working out minor measures that will help keep the divided parts of Germany in close contact. The recognition of the limitations and time factors of these three main lines of policy—which are not mutually exclusive—is what has led some of the leaders to support a policy of little steps.

The theory behind this policy is a complex of several motives. It is not everywhere accepted, and it obviously holds a number of dangers. For this reason, some leaders are gravely concerned over this tendency. Almost everyone agrees that it is good for Germany and for the Germans on both sides of the Iron Curtain to keep alive the feeling of identity with the West, which still prevails in the population of the East. This awareness of the national community of interests has been fostered by the personal contacts that have been maintained throughout the twenty-year period since the war. The estimates of direct individual contact between individuals runs between five and ten million persons a year. This includes those who come to East Berlin to meet friends from the West, the visitors from the West who have relatives in the Zone, the older people who, as pensioners, are allowed to visit families in the West and still return to the Zone, and others who by various means make contact in an unofficial manner. There is, in addition, considerable mail going both ways; packages, the radio, television, and the more rare reunions in other Eastern countries.

The debate implicitly concerns itself with the degree to which America would move toward a policy of *détente* and the extent to which the concerns of Germany and Berlin continue to matter.[4] The argument put forward by Deputy Mayor Albertz moves to the logical conclusion that the time has come for Germany to develop initiative and to take whatever the occasion offers to bring forward proposals for action. The determination to avoid recognition should not be permitted to immobilize the West. Perhaps, the quibbling over the significance of *de facto* recognition can actually enhance the status of Ulbricht.

The importance of these comments has increased as they have become widely accepted after the speeches of Bahr and Brandt in

4. *Ibid.*, p. 293. See also Egon Bahr speech.

Tutzing. Some considered the speeches to be trial balloons, to test the views of the Bonn government and the three Western occupying powers. The men closely associated with Brandt had been working on the idea of "change through rapprochement." Egon Bahr, having put forward this idea, then said, "Having done whatever is possible within our accepted limits, we can achieve practical results—otherwise we must wait for a miracle—and the Germans are not now inclined to wait."

The growing interest in a policy of involvement is natural and characteristic of the new sense of strength in the Federal Republic and in West Berlin. Germans are no longer astonished to find themselves a major power in Europe but have accepted the fact as a mandate for more independence and a more active program. There is no present danger of Bonn abandoning the co-ordinated policy of holding the line against Communism. Ulbricht, in his mid-seventies, is still hated and feared, but he will not hold his position forever. Nonrecognition is the accepted policy, but the legal aspects leave many of the young men cold. The sympathy of German residents on both sides of the Iron Curtain for each other is deep and real, but it needs to be nourished in years to come.

This is a period in which the failure to appreciate the essence of the German problem might push some of the right and left groups to extremes. Cynicism as to the future of the Germans, or indifference in America, is immediately noted in Germany.

It is possible that the Germans forget that our public opinion also is sensitive to their attitudes. A personal note may illustrate the points made here. In a discussion in Berlin in July, 1965, an eager young political leader was urging an increase of 100 or 200 per cent, or even more, in credits to the East Zone—either through the "swing," the uncompensated imports in the Interzonal Trade Agreement (IZT) or by other means. He also said he advocated varied and more permanent contacts, perhaps a major commission on each side of the line.

I asked, "Would you then expect American soldiers to remain in Berlin?"

He said, "Of course."

I replied, "President Johnson would advocate it. I would advocate it, but are you sure the Congress and the American people

The Mood and the Method

would want to maintain the same extended, wholehearted commitment?"

We in America are not the only ones to puzzle over the Berlin problem. Berlin gives the psychological warfare experts in the Kremlin a great deal of trouble. Leonid Brezhnev and Alexei Kosygin must get a volume of conflicting advice. Walter Ulbricht's associates flounder as they quote the West Berlin newspapers in grotesque fashion. West Berlin is a complex city, and there are no signs that the Communists understand it. Their zigs and zags of policy vary more sharply in Germany than in most places that interest them. Their tactics are frequently inept. Their estimates of German reactions have been misleading in many instances. Their frequent harassment hardens the anti-Communist sentiment just when there is talk of relaxation of tensions, when *rapprochement* seems possible.

The Communists do not understand that the men and women of present-day Berlin are very different from the Prussians and the Saxons—that they are at the same time more cynical, tougher, and gayer than many other German types, that they are both less sentimental and less serious. They are pleased by the Berlin Bear and the Freedom Bell alike. They are not inclined to solemnity unless the times are grave. Their passion for jazz comes from envy, frustration, and a feverish desire to live more hours of the day because the number of days is always threatened by Eastern armies.

This combination of qualities is an enigma to the Soviets and baffles the stubby, heavy-handed, Moscow-trained Ulbricht, clever though he is. There is surprise throughout Europe about the nature of the citizenry that weeps in candlelight processions for a dead hero and dances all night in the hottest sports of Europe.

Neues Deutschland, the main Communist daily in East Berlin, is full of absurdities that make the jokes on the Kudamm more spicy. If the West Germans find no way to approach the East, the fault will not be solely their firm hold on democratic ideology: the awkward barriers and conditions that rebuff the wish for contacts create an almost insuperable psychological wall.

The reactions to the Eastern helicopters over West Berlin in June, 1965, the new demands for barge documentation in early

July, shock at the shooting of the young and old in the dead zone by the Wall, the blandness of the election issues, the negotiations over the passes did not make a pattern that the Communists could recognize. With minds fixed on the Marxist-Leninist dialectic, the decline of the West, the inevitable conquest of socialism, they cannot add up the business, sports, romance, pleasure, and cynicism of a city they have threatened with destruction.

The Berliner *Luft* blows fresh. The words of Communist propaganda have little resonance in West Berlin. Serious response to danger is reserved for action in times of genuine peril. At other times they laugh.

The moods of Berlin are various. June and July, 1965, were cold, but there were warm days when thousands swarmed the beaches of Wannsee. The traffic to the lakes and parks was bumper to bumper. The cafés along the sidewalks were crowded. The people strolled along the streets late into the night and returned from the night clubs at dawn. The days were much like the previous weeks and months in a city grown accustomed to danger. More than two million people went about their business in workshops and factories remote from the Wall, seemingly unaware of the barbed wire that hemmed them in where the Zone bordered on their parks and woodlands.

Yet these days were not without their alarms and excursions, many of which have already been described. There had been shootings at the Wall and escapes by some who dared to crash the barrier. The *Tagesspiegel* of June 22 reported that over the weekend five residents of the zone fled to West Germany: three young men, a forty-five-year-old plasterer, and a twenty-four-year-old soldier of the Border Guards. The latter was in uniform and carried his machine gun. Several shootings in the night, and star shells revealed men seized and dragged away by the Border Police. A watchman shot from the Communist sector into a house in West Berlin. In the same issue there were stories of several flights from Hungary and Poland. Berlin was still a half-opened gateway for those in the East.

On July 2 the East German newspapers announced "improvements at the Wall, near the West Berlin district of Wedding,

The Mood and the Method

because of provocative discussions of West Berlin terrorists and underground organizations against the city border." Nationalist China's Traffic Minister Shen Yi, educated in Dresden, visited the Wall on July 3 and later noted: "This Wall is the shame of all mankind in the twentieth century. It is a sad and ostentatious display of a prison regime that I shall never forget."

The people were deeply stirred by the June 16 murder of Herman Dobler and the wounding of his young woman companion. The protests of Ambassador McGhee against the brutal and inhuman shooting of the innocent couple on the Teltow Canal went unanswered by Moscow.

Some, of necessity, took seriously the challenge of new demands in connection with barge traffic. The shipment of freight over inland waterways was of major importance to both East and West;[5] the main concern was limited to official and industrial circles but few in Berlin expected a long interruption of this essential traffic. Even the uninitiated knew that the East Zone needed the trade as well as the West.

A more alarming episode was the intrusion of helicopters into West Berlin air space. Because of these new provocations, Chancellor Erhard demanded that the Allies slap Ulbricht's wrists and called on the three Western Powers to react strongly to this new situation.

Public criticism increased in several quarters. The occupying Powers were caught in a dilemma. They knew better than the Berliners that military or diplomatic steps to halt these inexcusable actions might lead to an incident that would be followed by a violent encounter. The incidents against the Berliners could not go unnoticed, even though it was difficult for the casual observer to estimate the effect of shootings or how far the East Zone aircraft had intruded into West Berlin air space. After protest had been sent to Moscow, it was reported that the American helicopters flying over West Berlin were armed with machine guns. This gave some satisfaction, as did the knowledge that an additional helicopter was brought into the city by Americans to join in patrolling the sector border. After the first few hours of the various incidents,

5. See above, Chapter VI.

except for a few articulate critics of Western policy, the Berliners usually forgot the episodes and went about their business.

Another source of tension resulting from new conversations on visitors passes to East Berlin was mainly confined to those who were officially concerned. The negotiations that had been conducted on a lower level and that were closely associated with the conversation on IZT were complicated by the increased preoccupation with the election prospects of Willy Brandt and Ludwig Erhard. Although a great number had benefited from the 1963 agreement, the citizens did not hesitate to say that the passes should be turned down if the price demanded by the East were raised.

One formula used to ease negotiation of the many contacts between the two Germanys in this strange situation has been the use of special phraseology to designate the authority of the signers of documents. For example, under the signatures on the annual trade agreement renewals are the words "West German Currency District" and "East German Currency District"—the wording thus avoided the term "German Democratic Republic" on official documents. The formula was never palatable to Ulbricht.

Willy Brandt who had begun the second phase of his election campaign and was frequently away from Berlin, was concerned about all the causes of increased tension: the question of the barges, the passes, the helicopters, the shootings. He asked for a positive Allied reaction to the harassment and unacceptable demands.

At this time an American airman from Indiana and a soldier from Texas were recommended for decorations for superior bravery in the face of a violent Communist mob that had attacked the American military mission in Potsdam in June. The situation of Potsdam is unique—much more restricted for Western officers than Berlin itself. The town lies to the south just beyond the sector-zonal border in the Communist-held territory. The Western military mission there, which deals with the Soviets on a small number of questions, has been limited to a handful of officers.

Trouble arose when rioters protesting American fighting in Vietnam stormed the mission quarters and tore down the American flag. The soldiers, who had held out on the third floor of the

The Mood and the Method

building, risked their lives when they restored the flag as the East Germans tried to climb the outside of the building.

In this summer season, as usual, there was widespread speculation about the significance of the Communist demands and pressures. Was there a major Communist effort to increase tension over Berlin? Did the Kremlin, and Ulbricht, wish to impress China? Was awareness of U.S. preoccupation with Vietnam a factor? Was the disarray of NATO currently influencing Communist tactics in Berlin?

The United States should act promptly, people said: "Act quickly, talk less." Then after each episode the anxiety melted. The fear vanished. The surface calm had been little disturbed in any case. The holidays were at hand.

A Time for Entertainment

In the week of the Fourth of July, so many families began their summer vacations that hardly an airplane seat was left for those who had not made advance reservations for the mountains or seaside resorts.

Snow fell over the hills surrounding East Berlin as the temperature dropped below the fifties. Nevertheless, families and clubs of young people swarmed to the Wannsee area. Walkers enjoyed the air at Grunewald. Window shoppers strolled down the Kurfürstendamm, seemingly without a care in the world, chatting agreeably.

There was plenty of action for those who stayed in Berlin. There were many sporting events. Rowing, swimming, sailing, tennis, golf, and special contests were the focus of interest. Berlin children, 161 of them, participated in a soapbox derby; the top 5 would be sent to the all-German derby in Duisburg later in the summer. More than 100 children from Neukölln were flown to summer vacations in Bavaria.

West Berlin sports fans were thrilled when one of their favorites, young Schroter, won the European sprinting championship in Zurich.

The International Film Festival opened at the Congress Hall on John-Foster-Dulles-Allee on June 25 with a spectacular reception and an avant-garde French movie, *Paris Stories*, which left most of the spectators somewhat puzzled.

One evening in early July, Rolf Schwedler, the able, gay official, third in rank in Berlin,[6] accompanied by another official, sought refreshment in a beer hall in the district of Wedding. After midnight, about to go home, he saw an empty police car. Turning on the cold-fire-blue light, which usually meant an emergency mission, he began a debonair conversation over the two-way radio. The resultant convergence of several security officers led to a sudden official embarrassment. Schwedler's chagrin and the newspaper publicity gave the people of Berlin good-natured delight. Recognizing the human impulse, they sympathized more than condemned his escapade. His political prospects were clearly damaged, although no one was genuinely shocked by his evening diversion.

To know Berlin well, one must read the little inconsequential notices and consider the small happenings as well as the more momentous. One must read that the police stopped 838 speeding drivers on July 2, and that the Institute of Demoskopie of Allensbach reported in the Congress Hall that 43 per cent of the West Germans had decided that the Germans are the cleanest people in Europe and that 77 per cent of the German population are "especially clean."

Some four hundred children from Wedding and Reinickendorf were guests at the German-French Volksfest where they were treated to cocoa and cake.

The German Lottery Bureau reported that Berliners are the most active gamblers in the Federal Republic, the average annual contribution to the lottery being 55.66 DM.

Interestingly enough, the consumption of ice cream in Berlin has doubled in recent years—according to a poll of West Berlin housewives, restaurants, and inns. They insisted that the quality of the ice cream had continually improved.

A young rhinoceros named Miris arrived at its new home in the West Berlin zoo, having been shipped in from Basel, Switzerland.

---

6. Rolf Schwedler was temporarily serving as head of government in the absence of Mayor Brandt and Deputy Mayor Albertz.

The Mood and the Method

A Time for Conversation

Before the Directors of Schools left for their summer vacations, the West Berlin Commissioner for Education spoke to them: "We must always remember that we carry with us historical baggage. We can never take a vacation from our history. The younger German generation will never overcome their past if they do not share some of the blame. . . . That is why they must have a clear understanding about our city in the history of the German people and understanding of people in other lands."

The featured discussion on a West Berlin television program was on "What is a good German?" There were guests on the panel from England, Holland, Israel, and Austria.

In connection with exchanges in the field of commodities, a group of legal experts from Colombia and a number of trade union leaders from Kenya and Ethiopia arrived for visits of several days.

The Cologne professor, Boris Meissner, addressed the Otto Suhr-Institute of the Free University on "Soviet Power and East European Integration."

Robert Margulies, European Commissioner of EURATOM, came briefly to confer with officials. A delegation of Tanzanian police officers began a five-day visit to West Berlin. Thirty-two Latin American educators paid a visit to West Berlin. A new seminar, one of a series at the Institute for Developing Countries, began its meetings at the Villa Borsig on the shores of Tegel Lake.

Some of the other visitors to Berlin that week in July were President Heinrich Lübke, Italian President Giuseppe Saragat, Philippine General Carlos Romulo, members of the French delegation of the Inter-Parliamentary Union, and a group of American Boy Scouts.

The Bundestag was ending its session. The universities were preparing to close down. The students and professors had been feuding over ideas and responsibilities. The term ended in a spirit of rebellion.

There were discussions of political matters in the coffeehouses and restaurants. Across the line an East German party member published a Brown Book describing eighteen hundred leading Nazis in World War II.

There was a scholarly address by Professor Byrnes of Indiana University on the origins of Russian concepts of government in the last century.

A group of American political scientists met with the leaders of the political parties in the city to discuss the present situation.

For the most part, normal life went on with its stories of romance, crime, and tragedy.

"How free is free," was the question in many minds, while the politicians were asking, "How secure is secure."

The talk in Berlin is always good. It shows perspective on Communism, on Nazism, on Europe. It is concerned with the underdeveloped nations, with economics, and with political tendencies. The recent ferment among the youth liberates ideas to flourish in the pressurized atmosphere of this community.

A Normal City

The city was in a period of varied activity. Industry and construction were booming. The lure of vacation was tempting those who could not leave the city to enjoy its parks and lakes.

There was unusually heavy traffic. The most serious accident in fifty-seven years occurred in the subway when there was a collision of U-Bahn trains near the sector border. Ninety-seven persons were hurt and several died.

In the Kreuzburg district, which borders the wall, plans were developing to plant 243 trees to beautify the area.

In the quiet suburb of Dahlem, celebrating for the Fourth of July, the American soldiers of the Berlin brigade were on parade on Clay Allee. They were part of the small force that, along with the British and the French, continues to occupy the city. Several thousand men—spit and polish—passed in long columns before the reviewing stand. A part of the show which delighted the Berliners was the salute to the flags of the fifty states of the United States in front of American Headquarters, scarcely remembered as the former Nazi Air Force office. An impressive display of tanks preceded the floats the soldiers made to represent aspects of their mission in Berlin.

It was a good show, and the officials in the stands and the people on the streets enjoyed it. They knew that these men came into the city over the autobahns and continued to patrol inside the Soviet sector even after the Wall. They were a part of the defense of the city, exerting their rights and keeping access routes open. They revered the generals from the time of Generals Frank Howley and Lucius D. Clay in 1946 and 1947 to the days of Generals Polk and Franklin in 1965.

This is the city that does not conform to the political realities of its position except when called on for a show of normal strength, a city of wit in both words and actions. This is where humor may save a people from the threats of the Communist world.

This is the Berlin that Khrushchev had called "abnormal," which the Kremlin still harasses, which Ulbricht abuses with blunt thrusts of propaganda. A mecca for tourists and a political prize, it has become, because of its people, in spite of occupation by Allied soldiers, a city like any other. The answer to "how long"—is "as long as need be."

X. The Germans Vote in the New Era

The 1965 election on September 19 marked the end of the era dominated by Adenauer as chancellor. He had been the most significant figure in shaping both external and internal policies since the time in 1949 when the Allies had cleared the way for him to be chosen as leader. This election was the fifth time the Germans voted in the Federal Republic. The large number voting, 87 per cent of the eligible voters, evidenced the political responsibility of the postwar period even though the issues had not excited the imagination. Willy Brandt had run an energetic campaign against Ludwig Erhard, who had served as chancellor since October, 1963, but had not succeeded in establishing himself in the minds of the electorate as a leader of national scope. Erhard won for his party as a recognized economist and a man who inspired confidence. The Christian Democratic Union (CDU) and the Christian Social Union (CSU) together won a total of 245 seats, the Social Democratic Party (SPD) 202, and the Free Democratic Party (FDP) 49.

The results confounded prophets and distressed many hopeful Socialists. The new situation did not reveal clear-cut results for the SPD. Generally speaking, they gained what the FDP lost, but the meaning of this gain will become clear only with a gradual unfolding of various German and European issues. The immediate reconstruction period dominated by the strong rule of the Chancellor which brought the Federal Republic into NATO and the EEC had given way to a less dramatic phase of political life. This phase posed

The Germans Vote in the New Era

highly complex issues still unresolved. The growing strength of the Socialists in North Rhine–Westphalia did not emerge immediately, and, in the first ten months before the provincial election, no new SPD personality of outstanding capabilities came to the forefront.

The margin for the Christian Democratic Union and for Chancellor Erhard was greater than the political pundits had expected. He proved to be more Santa Claus than "rubber lion," as his foes had suggested. The German people had expressed their confidence by giving him a vote substantially above that for the Christian Democratic party in 1961. This was a turning point in the post-Adenauer era.

After it became evident that *Der Alte* could no longer act as head of government, there was much discussion of the political capacities of Erhard. Frequent comments were made that he lacked political adroitness and could not keep control of the party after the style of Adenauer. This view was held by some of the more sophisticated observers, but the people of Germany, influenced by the continuing prosperity and with a sense of confidence, gave him at the polls the right to govern in his own name. The general lines of policy remained the same, but new power for Erhard also brought him new problems as he selected his Cabinet and adjusted to a changing Europe and new attitudes toward reunification.

The election did not settle political questions so much as it altered leadership. It was surprising that, in a country where so many hot issues are debated in private circles, those brought out in the campaign were dull and unprovocative, even though there are many circles of opinion seething with a restless search for new ideas in security, in contacts with other nations, in Germany's future, in the East-West struggle. None of the problems raised by these questions came out clearly in the debates. In fact, it is hard to imagine a contest in which it would be so difficult to point out significant disagreements between the major candidates.

Many have asked why it is that Willy Brandt, the young, photogenic, attractive Mayor, had not succeeded in projecting an acceptable image to the majority of the people. He was the only candidate known by his first name; he came from one of the most exciting arenas of the times—Berlin—but he failed to gain the vote predicted for him. It was true that the Social Democrats got a higher percentage of the votes than in the previous elections, but it was the verdict of the average German to continue to endorse Ludwig Erhard's policy. Brandt's appeal was shadowed for many by a fear of unknown possibilities. In Berlin, he had shown the ability to elicit a warm response, and the city had improved in many important respects under his stewardship. Unfortunately for him, he was thought by the more conservative to be seeking new avenues of action which might upset the status quo. Moreover, the Berliners themselves could not vote. Even if they had, they could not have overcome the wide margin by which the CDU won.

There were marked differences in personalities which entered into the struggle and, in this rivalry, the well-known and comfortable figure of Ludwig Erhard fared better than the more dynamic, and less experienced younger man, Willy Brandt. Although in this case, damaging criticism of the candidates was kept in a lower key than in 1961, there were still many who spoke of the more experimental and less traditional attitudes of Brandt, and of the alleged mystery of his years in Norway during the war where he became an anti-Nazi leader. Thus, behind the public campaign of the SPD leader there were hints, not fully attributable to him, of a Socialist desire to flirt with the Communist leaders and to try new approaches to cold war problems. These were little steps and may have damaged the Socialists in their efforts to win the majority. Here, then, is one of the open questions for the future.

Because of the limitations imposed by the Allies on the relations of Berlin to the Federal Republic, the Berliners themselves could not vote in the election. The city's delegates in Bonn are chosen by the Berlin House of Representatives and they are not full members of either of the parliamentary bodies there, the Bundesrat and the Bundestag, because they are not allowed to vote in plenary sessions.

Few had predicted the large vote accorded to Ludwig Erhard. In spite of his strength at the polls, the formation of his government was not easy. Erhard depended on the co-operation of the CSU members who were elected by the CSU—the Bavarian affiliate of the CDU—as well as on achieving a coalition. There were compromises of various types required to arrive at a workable majority. He did not have to go so far as to include Franz-Josef Strauss (CSU) in the cabinet—a move which would have made the agreement with his rival Mende (FDP) impossible. He did retain Gerhart Schröder as Foreign Minister. This coalition performed with considerable confidence until the July 10, 1966, elections in North Rhine–Westphalia resulted in local losses for the CDU and gave the SPD 49 per cent of the vote.

The shifts in percentages also indicate a degree of fluidity in the political situation in Germany. The decline of the Christian Democrat's majority in 1961 was partially reversed by Erhard's strong mandate in 1965. At the same time, the Social Democratic Party showed an upward trend at the expense of the Free Democratic Party.

TABLE 8. OFFICIAL RESULTS OF GERMAN ELECTIONS FROM 1957 TO 1965

	1965[a]		1961[b]		1957[c]	
	(000)	%	(000)	%	(000)	%
Political parties:						
CDU/CSU	15,524	47.6	14,298	45.3	15,008	50.2
SPD	12,813	39.3	11,427	36.2	9,495	31.8
FDP	3,097	9.5	4,028	12.8	2,307	7.7
Seven minor parties	1,186	3.6	1,796	5.7	3,094	10.3
Qualified voters	38,510		37,440		35,226	
Votes cast	33,416	86.8	32,849	87.8	31,072	88.2

a. Add 22 Berlin deputies: 66 CDU; 15 SPD; 1 FDP.
b. Add 22 Berlin deputies: 9 CDU; 13 SPD.
c. Add 22 Berlin deputies: 7 CDU; 12 SPD; 3 FPD.

Key to party symbols: CDU/CSU—Christian Democratic Union/Christian Social Union; SPD—Social Democratic Party; FDP—Free Democratic Party.

In mid-October, 1965, Eugen Gerstenmaier, President of the Bundestag, administered the oath of office to Chancellor Ludwig Erhard. The Chancellor was formally re-elected in the lower house on the first vote by a majority of 272 to 200, with 15 abstentions, on October 20.

Congratulations poured in to Erhard from around the world. Greetings came from President Johnson, British Prime Minister

Wilson, French President Charles de Gaulle, and Soviet Prime Minister Alexei Kosygin, representing the four countries most directly concerned with postwar Germany, as well as from other leaders. The press, radio, and television generally hailed the Erhard victory and the new coalition with relief; after having severely criticized the conduct of the campaign and the discussions that preceded the vote, they took a sanguine view of the outcome. They referred to Erhard as "the clear victor," a person in an enviable position who plainly intended to assume his duties using his full powers to formulate basic policy.

As new personalities emerged from the election, former Chancellor Adenauer took his place on a list of deputies as third in alphabetical order, following Dr. Manfred Abelein and Dr. Ernst Achenbach.

The Bundestag has been transformed into a youthful body, having an average age range of from forty-five to sixty-four, with seventeen deputies under thirty-five, and the number of deputies between ages sixty-five and seventy-four falling from forty-five to twenty-four. One of the outstanding new leaders was Federal Defense Minister Kai Uwe von Hassel, who won his seat from Schleswig-Holstein. Another was Dr. Felix von Eckhardt, for many years the chief CDU spokesman in Bonn and recently Federal Republic representative in Berlin. He made a strong showing in Wilhelmshaven, commonly supposed to be a safe SPD seat. Also seated was a young woman economist, Dr. Ursula Krips, a SPD deputy in her early thirties. Prince Konstantin of Bavaria, a journalist, won the only CSU place in five Munich constituencies; all the rest went to the SPD.

A review of the Bundestag showed that there were 120 white-collar workers, 90 "public servants," 26 from the trade unions and professional associations.

The most challenging future problem for consideration, as stated by Gerstenmaier, is German reunification. He promised more lively debate on all major issues as the new Bundestag began its work.

Erhard's Problems

The decisions confronting Erhard were almost equally divided between external and internal problems. The foreign issues are central to the shifting trends in Europe's struggle for unity and security. There is little basis for the talk of choice between international partners which has been discussed in the American press, although there is a strongly persistent talk of Erhard's preference for Washington over Paris.

Since the domestic issues of the recent German election were muted by the major candidates because of fear of disturbing a balance that each thought was in his favor, international issues have been emphasized by those who now endeavor to interpret the outcome. Actually, for those who have been in Germany and are trying to appraise the views of the average citizen, this attempt to sharpen the divergence of views seems artificial. There are few Germans outside of Bonn who consider that the relations between German leaders and President de Gaulle will affect their personal lives. There are relatively few who consider that Minister Schröder's alleged pro-Americanism is a matter of interest. For the most part, the voter takes for granted the close relationship with the United States and has accepted the new friendship with France as a dependable constructive postwar development achieved by the Christian Democratic Party.

The statement by Thomas Hamilton under the headline "Erhard Is Facing Choice on Allies" is one of the more moderate analyses, but it gives an unreal twist to the problems that lie ahead.

He says that "the principal decision facing West Germany is how far to go to conciliate Paris at the risk of impairing relations with Washington."[1] No such dilemma exists. The issues for the professional politician have subtle aspects that escape the rank and file. Excitement over the proliferation issue, allegations that Germany wishes to join the nuclear club, and the questions raised by Franz-Josef Strauss as to whether the "special relationship" between the United States and England is bad for a United Europe, which could become "a pillar of the same size and solidity as the American pillar," are largely unrealistic speculation.

Many of these comments have an esoteric sound in a Germany growing in strength. More real, according to conversations in the summer of 1965, seem the questions of trade between East and West Germany and the contacts that might foster later moves

1. *New York Times*, October 24, 1965.

toward reunification of areas whose long border of separation plagues the Germans every day.

It is in this question that domestic and foreign problems combine to give those groups not having majority strength in the Bundestag an opportunity to challenge the new government.

Without an absolute majority in Parliament, and with the division of views and personalities within the CSU/CDU raising special problems, the task of maintaining a viable government requires skillful compromise. Irrespective of his personal feeling about the shrewd and vigorous CSU leader Franz-Josef Strauss, Erhard was required to make account more than before of the large Bavarian vote, which manifests the importance of the following that Strauss can command in some parts of Germany.

The first negotiations and earlier arrangements of the Cabinet may not supply the lasting elements to assure a strong government which Erhard indicated was essential if he was to remain in the Chancellorship. It is thought that the well-known conflict between Gerhard Schröder and Strauss would be resolved, but there remained many thorny questions for Erhard to handle. A few forecast that the Chancellorship might change before the four-year term is completed.

Strauss, a challenging personality, while recognized as vigorous and more right-wing than most of the outstanding German leaders, is also known to be one of the most intelligent of their political figures. The fears that his statements engender abroad result in part from the mythology that has its roots in the past and that confuses opinion on postwar Germany. Those who recognize the importance of maintaining close German-American relations realize that hasty assumptions as to current trends can disturb a partnership essential to security, and that rumors circulated during and after the election should be sifted and scrutinized in order to separate evidence from prejudice.

Brandt's Problems

Willy Brandt's problems were close to those of Berlin. It is here that he grew to national stature in the Social Democratic Party, it is here that he built his circle of close associates. And yet it is here

The Germans Vote in the New Era

that his participation in Federal Republic politics was limited by the voteless status of the city's representatives in the Bundestag.

Here, too, he has been criticized for the diversion of his interests from local problems to the fight to become Chancellor.

Some comments in the Berlin newspapers indicated a latent sense of neglect in 1965 by some in the city. Commenting on Mayor Brandt's announced withdrawal from national politics, the Berlin newspaper *Morgenpost* stated on September 23 that "Too often during the past few months Willy Brandt has spent time far from Berlin; too often his responsibilities as candidate for Chancellor and as leader of the Opposition commanded his time; too seldom did the Governing Mayor of Berlin have a chance to give his greatest energies to his difficult office in Berlin."

However, *Recklinghäuser Zeitung*, also in September, commented on the gains he made in the nation: "The man who is returning to his Berlin office did not really fail. In spite of all, with him, the SPD gained a breakthrough. As with the late Adlai Stevenson, who was defeated twice in Presidential elections, it was not the lesser of the two who lost, it was the one with the less luck."

Meanwhile, in the absence of a clear indication of who might be a future candidate, the position of Brandt as a leading government figure remained uncertain, in spite of any decision he might make. His power within the party could either decline as his failure to gain the majority leads to a conclusion that his future does not hold promise, or, depending on his performance in Berlin and the nature of the crises that might arise, he may gain in stature by his temporary withdrawal from the national political scene. Inevitably, however, as Mayor of Berlin he was in the spotlight of world opinion and of Federal Republic decisions in regard to the future of Germany.

Perhaps events that kept Brandt from the Chancellorship will lead him to increased efforts in the field of contacts with the East and of programs designed to develop new relationships with the Zone. The question arises as to whether he will be tempted to diverge from the parallelism with the CDU and swing the SPD in a new direction. If he should do so, there would be a considerable number of the younger men both in West Germany and in Berlin who might be active workers for a new approach. The temptation is clearly there, at a time when SPD participation is limited to a minority position in the Federal government.

Brandt himself and many of his co-party members recognize a deep debt of gratitude to the United States in assuring the security of Berlin as well as for future German development. Some of those, however, who have newly arrived on the political scene, are not so sure that identification of German and American interests determines the course they want to follow. There is a definite drive for independence and rejection of the familiar phrase "no experiments." There is in this situation no present reason for apprehension with regard to German-American relations, but an element of warning which should lead to special attention to new and sometimes neglected currents in German thinking. The late sixties do not bring a period in which attitudes can be taken for granted.

As the issues clarify in the months ahead, there is time for Brandt to construct a sound political image and to convince the West Germans that along with his ambitions he has an attractive political philosophy and an understanding of the broader problems of the country.

With the suggestions that he adopt a more experimental course, and bid for the votes of the oncoming generation, he has difficult choices to make. In his group of close associates are several who wish to move rapidly in the increasing economic relations with the East. Some think that there is a growth of mutual interest and understanding between the Federal Republic and the Zone which should be fostered.

Washington's Problem

Washington's problem is to allay doubts and fears and to demonstrate that its German partner is helping to reinforce the NATO alliance, does not wish to produce nuclear arms, and is a staunch supporter of the programs of unity and arms control.

The men in the White House and the State Department know that, in all important matters, the new government will follow the same line of co-operation as the Adenauer government. It will share in the task of maintaining security forces, and will be moderate in questions related to the control of the atom. Its economic policy will be helpful to those Americans who wish to avoid the threats of instability or inflation.

There are, however, changing issues that Washington will come to recognize increasingly as Germans have more responsibility and strive to follow in a constructive manner the new approaches to the troubling division of Europe. The temperature of the cold war and the manner of adjustment to the Communist threat are intimate and internal problems for the Germans, and have been at times remote for Americans. This difference in involvement can yield to a conscious effort in Washington circles.

Some in the United States believe that Germany wants the atomic bomb. This statement is not borne out by either the campaign speeches, public pronouncements, or the German position in NATO councils. They do not wish either to produce or to control nuclear weapons. The furor stirred up in July, 1965, when American Deputy Secretary of Defense Roswell Gilpatrick was quoted as "scrapping the multilateral nuclear force and opposing the 'spread of atomic weapons,'" has led to confusion in some quarters about the German position, as reflected by some of the statements of the leaders. The position that has been held and is likely to continue is that Germany does not wish to produce or to stockpile nuclear weapons, but that the Federal Republic would press for equality of treatment in other respects, and wishes the protection that comes with tactical nuclear weapons. Unlike France, Germany does not wish a *force de frappe*. In fact, most Germans—now more sophisticated than a few years ago when they demonstrated against "atomic death"—are aware of the fact that security in the present-day world has to take account of all the recent scientific developments. There is now a strong determination to gain equality with other non-nuclear powers.

Many discussions of these issues confuse rather than clarify the trends in German policy. There is little doubt that the thinking in the Federal Republic is taking a new course. There will be a much more independent search for actions which will promise future strength for the nation in its relations with the United States, with Europe, with the Soviets, with China and in Africa and Asia.

The sense of reliance on other nations which was inevitable in the years of postwar struggle has shifted, and a new awareness of power, as Bonn looks afresh at old problems, has developed. This shift in balance means that there can be a diplomatic ingenuity in the associations and agreements of the near future and a look towards new partnerships, and a path which brings Bonn closer to East Europe with its increasing economic potential and its varied attitudes towards the Western world, a policy that aims at reunification in a decade is not to be ruled out.

The Elections and Berlin

The years after the fourth election in the German Republic will have a different tone, new issues, and new personalities. While the world looks to the continuing problem of Berlin, it knows that the crises of the future will be vastly different from those of 1948, 1953, 1958, and 1961. There is in the nation and in the city a new sense of independence and a separation from the past.

As attention turns to the East as well as the West, it is colored by the changes outside Germany and also by the election of 1965, the first in a decade to be conducted almost uninfluenced by the Western occupying powers. The inevitable re-examination of issues, including the future of NATO, the Hallstein doctrine,[2] the Berlin clause,[3] and other political and economic matters which grow out of Germany's divided status, will come with a growing sense of economic capacity and a constant preoccupation with security.

The election scarcely affected Berlin, except as it influenced the plans of Willy Brandt. It did increase the need for our awareness of an unpredictable future. The ramparts are sound, but the view of those who watch the area beyond focuses on a changing scene.

2. The Hallstein doctrine, instituted by Walter Hallstein, now President of the European Economic Community, precludes diplomatic relations with governments that recognize the GDR. There are, however, trade missions in some countries with East Zone representation. There was an exchange of diplomatic representatives with Rumania early in 1967.

3. The Berlin clause carries over agreements with the Federal Republic automatically to Berlin.

XI. The Wall
Is Not Forever

History Yields to the Future

The ghosts of history still walk the streets of this great city. No one can see its ruined towers and crumbling palaces and churches without feeling the winds that stir the dust of the past. Not even the shining new buildings, the wide sweep of the city's autobahns, and the restored parks cleared of rubble can hide the traces of the ancient villages or wipe out the memories of the proud and sometimes brutal rulers. So much has happened here that the city remains a scar on the surface of a troubled Europe. The Germans know that more has been buried in the wreckage than the ashes of Hitler. More has been scorched by fire than the thousand-year Reich.

Yet nature has already covered the ashes with flowers. Trees have grown tall in the Tiergarten. The Trümmerberg is green with pine and shrubs. People have rebuilt stone on stone so that by their works they might redeem and remake a place where children can play and young men can learn to live in hope and dignity.

In Berlin as elsewhere a generation born since the end of World War II is coming of age. Their ideas are bound to differ from those of men born earlier. They will bring to bear new aims and expectations. The demonstrations of the students against authority, the new and sometimes shocking statements of iconoclasts must be viewed as more than the result of a psychological malaise. They are expressions of a growing force which will be healthy if it can be guided into the more constructive channels of a new Germany—a land that knows no Hitler, that seeks increasing opportunity, and that feels the pulse of a new vitality in a world largely divorced from the wartime past.

Looking to these changes in 1965, I journeyed to Berlin with two young assistants mentioned earlier, Blythe Finke and William Allen, to take a fresh view and to talk to old and new friends in order to examine critically present trends, in terms of weakness and strength. I was convinced that our policy needed to be shored up and perhaps altered by directing more attention to present attitudes in the East and in the West. At least its freshness could be restored. This policy has not gone unscathed through the time of the building of the Wall, the death of Peter Fechter, the controversies over foreign policy in Bonn, and the uncertainty over the future of Mayor Brandt. While some have talked of *détente,* we have permitted the meaning of the security issues to be blurred for some of the Germans. Our presence is less visible to the younger Berliners as the prosperity and strength of the city is taken for granted.

The past twenty years have brought many unexpected events, in space and on the earth. Not the least of these have been the changing attitudes in Germany and the new aspects of Europe's problems—both modifications of underlying trends which have become even more apparent in 1966 than they were in 1965.

The people of Germany feel that twenty years is a long time to tolerate a divided country. Often they discount the extent of economic and political progress which has taken place in their own country in this period. They underestimate the achievements of a responsible government that has gained respect and power in the Western world. They are beginning to press impatiently for the solution of the problems that remain, not realizing how far they have come in acquiring influence in the community of free nations, although the gains made by a defeated Germany have been much greater than anyone in the United States, in England, in France, or in the center of Europe could have anticipated in 1945.

In Berlin progress continues, but in the third postwar decade the city is distracted by new proposals. With regard to the threat from the East, the atmosphere has recently become less tense. Although there are no indications of a basic change in Communist strategy, there are those who think the aggressive intent of the Zone is not as

The Wall Is Not Forever

menacing as before. The shock of August 13, 1961, has been surmounted, and confidence has returned as economic well-being has become general. "We are now strong in our own right," they claim. Even the continuing possibility of new harassment does not preclude a growing sense of security. As this feeling grows, the pressure for innovation increases. Recently, in response to this concern, which appears to be on the increase in the Federal Republic as well as in West Berlin, Rainer Barzel said that his speech on June 17, the Day of German Unity, was "a stone thrown into stagnant water."

The course pursued by the West may indeed seem stagnant, but there is, in fact, little possibility of turning policy in a new direction and at a more rapid tempo as Germany follows the narrow path between two kinds of danger. On the one hand, there are risky experiments; on the other, paralyzing inaction. Nevertheless, the impulse to act increases as patience proves less palatable to oncoming politicians.

The desire for movement increases in an atmosphere of restlessness that has invaded NATO and the EEC as well as the network of political alignments of Germany. The continuing signs of firm Western commitments to Bonn and the constructive international developments of the past decades cannot silence doubts about Berlin occasionally expressed outside Germany.

Within the nation the ferment that came with a changing of the guard in the CDU and the growing desire for more governmental responsibility in the SPD open the door for those who say, "We must try new measures." The young political leaders who cross an imaginary threshold leaving the postwar period behind, demand a louder voice in those issues that affect relations with the East Zone.

While those who have watched the gradual increase in strength in West Germany and West Berlin, and are mindful of the continuing chain of agreements, of legal positions, and of commitments, know better than those who come new to the problem, they are sometimes unheeded. There is a delicate balance in the formulation of Berlin policy which calls for recognition. The dangers surrounding access procedures and the significance of America's responding to harassment or blockade were evident to me years ago from the vantage point of another occupied country, Austria. Even now, twenty years later, the importance of respecting the precise wording of commitments keeps us bound to a recognized course of action. Any change is likely to bring a shock to confidence, and yet change must at times be contemplated.

Decades of experience have led older statesmen to a certain caution with regard to innovations in policy. In judging new ideas, it is possible that those who know the secret contingency plans for maintaining access or defending Berlin and how these fit the global American policy have special insight. Others, however, conversant in the general nature of security measures with which NATO shields the city, can make useful comment and raise pertinent questions. Even outsiders, and everyone not working with official and classified papers is an outsider, can on occasion propose plans of value to those whose daily work is occupied with Berlin. While, on the one hand, those remote from the flow of confidential information hesitate to urge any modification of the Berlin program or to develop new solutions for a divided Germany, on the other hand, they recognize that those immersed in daily tasks may fail to judge the longer-range implications of changing moods. This is a danger that increases with the passage of time. Moreover, those who have grown old together may fail to be receptive to the new and freshly emerging suggestions that seem constructive to men who know no war and who barely remember the years of reconstruction. A time factor telescopes and dims the outlines of events between World Wars I and II for the oncoming generations.

What Must Now Be Done

American financial aid is no longer needed, but understanding and intellectual co-operation are of increasing importance. There are new problems and new personalities, old problems appearing in new forms after the Wall. The sensation of urgency mounts for those Germans who see increasing industrial and political consolidation in the Zone; this has impressed many who are reaching positions of mature responsibility in the present era and who want to renew their contacts with their fellows in the Eastern provinces.

In 1965, I was struck with a sense of unrest and desire to break out of established molds. I found that among the young people with whom I talked in June and July, there was a number who were sufficiently vigorous in their approach to Berlin's problems to give promise of future leadership. Along with this capacity I found a failure to understand the part played over the past two decades by Western aid and support in holding back Communism and accomplishing a massive reconstruction. This lack of appreciation could lead to undervaluing Western ties.

These experiences and these conversations led me to conclude that there was need for further study and more intensive exchange of views in Washington, but particularly in Germany, between those who understand the essence of American aims and those Germans who are increasingly anxious to grapple with the problem of reunification. Such studies should be oriented to bear on policy, with further examination and evaluation of what is going on in the Zone of Soviet occupation. They should lead to greater availability in America of the findings about the Zone which appear in various writings in Germany. New consideration of changing conditions and new aspirations may be the basis for dispelling outworn assumptions and substituting a more realistic approach to proposals that are being made outside of Germany.

There is also, in Germany, insufficient appreciation among the young people of the interrelationship of the three-power occupation of Berlin with the maintenance of the NATO alliance and the future destiny of Germany as a major partner in the defense of the free world. Recent conversations in Berlin imply that Americans are becoming accustomed to the division of Germany to an extent that dulls initiative and paralyzes action. This leads to a cynicism that could open a gap of misunderstanding of the long-run problems. It is more important therefore, at this time, that the United States continue, and even accentuate, the indications of its determination to honor our pledges to protect Berlin. Old phrases that are worn and tired can be given a new vigor if they are brought more in harmony with thinking and discussion in the schools and universities. Progress in this respect depends on a sensitive approach to the psychological dilemma of post-Hitler youth.

The importance of Germany as our partner is well expressed by McGeorge Bundy in testimony before the Senate Committee on Foreign Relations on June 20, 1966:

> The Federal Republic of Germany is one of the great political, social, and economic triumphs of the last twenty years. My generation of Americans passed much of its youth in the struggle against the Nazis;

we know something of what Germany was in 1945. This experience reinforces our admiration—in my case at least—for what the new Germany has achieved. The German economic miracle is familiar—but it is less significant than two tremendous political decisions: for democratic process at home and for Western community abroad. Initially we had a major—perhaps even a decisive—role in both choices, but they have been repeatedly confirmed and renewed by the people of the Federal Republic themselves.

Germany remains divided and limited in her strength. She is immediately dependent upon American strength—and cannot afford the luxurious and expensive pretenses of others. She is also plainly and inescapably debarred from access to nuclear weapons. This position the Germans accept, although they naturally seek to limit its costs. In their desire to wring some political advantage from their non-nuclear status, some in Germany have suggested that they could somehow bargain with Moscow on the topic of their nuclear restraint. There is no bargain here—certainly none that Americans can support. Germany is well and wisely—and permanently—out of the national nuclear business.

But the real point about this dependence on us and this limitation in the nuclear field is that neither of them—and not both together—can make Germany less than what she is: the second power of the Alliance—and a nation whose self-respect and self-confidence are deeply needed for peace.

Thinking along these lines suggests that the fear of a future "German problem," so easily associated in some quarters with reunification, or nuclear ambitions, should rather be directed to the dangers of isolation. Germany is persistently seeking closer ties with the other leaders of the free world. Discrimination against a vigorous and dynamic nation could drive the people down a road in the direction of Moscow. This is a course that they do not now wish to travel. There is no inclination to compromise with the Communists, but some may think profitable bargains are available to the astute. This inclination might lead toward neutralism. Only the ability to see the issues and preconceptions from the angle of Berlin, and Bonn, can weld together a Europe puzzled by de Gaulle, apprehensive over nuclear proliferation, and desperately seeking peace. It should take account of the economic changes and the growing prosperity in both East and West Germany.

Since Germany does not want to produce the bomb but wishes a limited participation in decisions, the alarm of the few who cite the

The Wall Is Not Forever

past as evidence of aggressive tendencies should give way to more constructive thinking. Those Americans who have had a part in postwar reconstruction are for the most part determined to co-operate with Germany on various intellectual, economic, and security measures.

If it is necessary to stimulate new studies, take new measures, institute new exchanges and special seminars in Berlin and elsewhere, it would be well worth the cost. If there is need for further exchanges of views in Washington, London, and Paris, there are many ready and able to assist in such an effort.

I have not found in my work on Germany, since the end of my official responsibilities in that field, that the communications between interested groups have been severed. It is true, however, that preoccupation with pressing issues in other regions in the Far East and in Latin America has led to a measure of competition for the interests of policy-makers. A tendency of this kind, if carried too far, could bring dangers to those central positions of European strength which have been developing since World War II. The fate of the United States will depend not so much on outlying regions and new nations, where dangers and opportunities are clearly evident, but on those citadels of strength and common tradition for which we have fought on the continent of Europe. I do not believe there has been a time in history when the city of Berlin has played a more crucial role.

In the third postwar decade, Europe is entering a new phase, with the shifting of opinion and the re-examination of values. Attention has focused on changes in NATO, new aspects regarding German-French relations, and on the questioning of various styles and methods of co-operation. In this time of reappraisal, complacency about Berlin is bound to be dangerous. Whoever thinks the city can be ignored, or its defense compromised, should look again to the meaning of the early commitments. It has been the firm belief of heads of state and wise men that Germans would consider the surrender of the city a betrayal. If it were to occur, the temptation to gamble for reunification would appeal to many Germans. The risk would appear justified, and the trap might be cleverly baited for those who seek to create a greater Germany. Who can say what ingenious inducements might then attract the unwary?

The division of Germany has been long, and the end is not in sight. For those now living, there is a demand for tangible goals and realistic action. They do not accept failure. They are not ready to turn blind eyes to the East. Some new doctrines, experiments, and proposals are emerging. Some think these can work miracles. Others think these measures will be of little significance. The wiser and the battle-scarred think progress will be achieved only over a long period of time.

The present situation can satisfy no one. It presents a continuing political, financial, and diplomatic problem to Chancellor Kiesinger. It is exasperating and even threatening for Walter Ulbricht. He sees the city almost within his grasp, but always eluding him—a city that his masters in the Kremlin cannot win for him. This is where the signs of freedom can be seen in spite of the Wall. This is where every brightly lighted building, every chime of the Freedom Bell,[1] carries a message Ulbricht does not wish to hear.

Because Berlin is a rallying point for all Germans and is a key to the future of the center of Europe, its continued security and welfare are substantial and meaningful elements in the conflict of East and West. This reality cannot be ignored in the long struggle that lies ahead. There will come a time when those who press to subjugate its people may find the game not worth the candle.

There are times for holding firm. There are times for experiment and movement. In 1966, the spirit of the city and the talk of the young men suggest a new attitude. The phrase *kein Experiment* is held to mean defeat. The suggestion of increasing East-West contacts arouses enthusiasm. There is an attraction to the idea that attitudes might have changed in the Kremlin, even in Pankow.

Some of the men who had learned the hard lessons of 1948, 1953, 1958, and 1961 have disappeared from the scene. To some now debating the issue, the word "confederation" is no longer anathema. The high price that had been paid for freedom in the West was partially forgotten. The manner in which the compromises with Communism had bound men over into slavery was not fully remembered. "There must be a price," some said, "which can be paid for reunification." They insist that the Western world in general, and the United States in particular, can use its strength

---

1. The Freedom Bell was paid for by the contributions of several million American school children in 1954.

and its wealth to strike a bargain. Dreams are compounded of theory and a desire to outline new courses of action.

The division is a new challenge to both the Eastern and Western centers of power. Eventually it will bring a reappraisal even in Communist circles of the outrage of the Wall. It poses economic problems for the Kremlin as well as for Bonn and Washington. The emerging will of Germans to unite with Germans is a major factor to influence the policy of the future.

Those who caution against concessions have a hard task in persuading the less experienced of the possible aggressive Communist intent. These, who say the struggle is long and requires many years of patience, are put on the defensive. Not only to the young, but also to a man growing old, the conclusion that reunification may not come in his lifetime is a bitter thought. But even if this is a hard doctrine, it does not exclude hope.

The building of great nations has been full of tragedy and long periods of discouragement. The United States required more than a century and a half to grow from thirteen to fifty states. It developed its understanding of world problems and its military might only well along in the twentieth century.

Europe has been divided and reunited over long periods. It still remains the center of science and culture, and fosters the precious values of law and order, humanism, and freedom. New nations are emerging, uniting, disintegrating, and dividing. New ideas of government, new goals in space and on the earth are appearing to astonish and confound. Moreover, we move towards an unpredictable future guided by both logic and experience and prepared for the unexpected. In 1966, there are many unanswered questions that call for an open mind.

The year 1966 has been one in which Germany and Berlin have been taken for granted, in spite of the unusual problems that continue to confront them. The Federal Republic is well established in NATO, solidly entrenched in the EEC, has assumed a recognized role in relation to the developing countries, and has played an important part in the financial and economic councils of the Western world. De Gaulle's withdrawal from NATO has brought an informal three-nation directorate with Germany sitting in the place France earlier wished to occupy. No longer do most political leaders consider the Federal Republic a special case requiring extraordinary restraints or emergency help. The tragic and heroic days are over. Internal political conflicts and economic adjustments are less exciting but no less demanding.

The German economy has come into a period of more sluggish movement. There is little talk of miracles and more realization that expansion brings dangers. The economy still has strength though some of the dynamic qualities are dampened after twenty years of rapid recovery. The currency is strong, and the Federal Republic remains an attractive place to hold funds with interest rates in line with other major centers. In fact, the co-operation of the Bundesbank is of significance for Wall Street and Washington.

Erhard's first year of leadership was not an entirely happy one. When he came to Washington in September, he sought evidence of his close relation with President Johnson. In fact, his success was limited. Internal struggles have confronted him with the type of difficulties for which he is reputed to be least equipped. Criticism has mounted. It has even been said that economic stability is endangered. The elections in the important *Land*, North Rhine–Westphalia, which cut sharply into support of the CDU, gave the SPD 49 per cent of the votes and showed a reversal of the trend of the 1965 national election. This manifestation of the weakness of the Erhard contingents led to some chipping away at his influence both within and without his party. By the Socialists, Erhard was called an inept fencer, and some in his own party echoed the phrase. The increasing ambitions of Rainer Barzel, considered by some as a potential head of the CDU, were spurred on by events in the summer and fall, but Kurt Georg Kiesinger was chosen.

In military circles there was occasional trouble. The beginning of the German postwar army was something I observed at first hand. When the leading generals and Minister Blank came to the United States in the early fifties, I was asked by Jimmy Riddleberger to invite them for a swim in my pool. As was hoped, their reserve and stiffness vanished as they bobbed around in the water talking to their American hosts. The more serious aspects of their mission were touched on informally and the ground laid for the next day's discussion. For us in the State Department, the manner in which a new military tradition would be developed seemed of great importance and was thought to hinge on a new attitude in the officer corps. The gratifying progress was interrupted occasionally by minor problems.

Political trouble growing in the military ranks was evident in late August and September when several of the top Generals resigned. Their action shook the position of the Defense Minister Kai Uwe von Hassel and threatened the continuity of the cabinet. The issues being fought were in two widely different areas—in the technical and personnel fields. There had been extraordinary and deplorable losses of the starfighter airplanes and pilots in the course of training and test flying. Doubts as to the wisdom of the defense program caused criticism of the management of the air force. At this time the indignation in officers quarters over the decision to permit labor union organizers to come into the camps to recruit further upset the government's coalition. There were demands for the resignation of the Defense Minister which Erhard resisted, but the ominous political stirrings led some to raise the question as to whether the Erhard government had the durability to last the next three years.

The role of the military forces in German life has always been a delicate matter. The determination after the war to reduce the relative importance of the soldiers in the life of the nation was an aim fostered by the Western Allies—though not so clearly visualized in the army-dominated East Zone—and willingly adopted by the postwar German leaders. There was a comprehensive program of subjecting the military to the civilian as a part of the new democratic tradition. Berlin had no military problem since neither the recruitment nor the stationing of troops of the Federal Republic was permitted under the conditions of occupation still in force. There, even more than in the rest of the Federal Republic, the desire to remain apart from the problems of rearmament was paramount with some evidence of the pacificism expressed by elements of the SPD, the majority party in the city.

In spite of the old tradition and the war years, the army in the Federal Republic had developed along what were considered healthy lines. The troubles of 1966 were likely to be a minor phase of the adjustment to the new situation that had come with the frustrations of defeat, of the special status in the postwar security system, and the necessity to rebuild on new foundations after the destruction of the old regime. The struggle was mainly internal and did not notably affect Germany in Europe.

Consideration of East-West Debates

Influences originating mainly in Berlin's desire for contacts, and sponsored by Mayor Willy Brandt, placed Erhard in a delicate position as the issue of debates with East German leaders was raised. He could not well oppose such a suggestion even though it held dangers both internally and externally. The representatives of the SDP in Berlin had a special opportunity to act more freely than the government in power. Already in 1965, in connection with little steps, the possibilities of discussion between leaders in the Zone and in the Republic had been raised. The young men in particular were fascinated by the idea that it held a chance for intellectual adventure and seemed to break out of a fixed mold of restraining prohibitions. In considering the prospects of a clash of wits, they did not recognize the extent to which the more subtle arguments of democracy might appear to be on the defensive to those who held a harder and more disciplined political doctrine. They were eager for the fray. Thus Willy Brandt had many backers in putting forward the idea and few who opposed the project.

The outside world looked on with interest as the exchange of letters between Ulbricht's headquarters and the Berlin government in 1966 gave promise of a new chapter, or at least a new footnote, in the history of the cold war. Active consideration of the manner in which the debates would be conducted had been going from the time of the SPD letter to the SED in February until the rejection of the plan by the East Zone authorities in June. The main difference in approach seemed for a time to center on the preference of the SPD for emphasis on the specific and the wish of the men in the East Zone to avoid concrete questions. They chose rather to discuss such global matters as peace, atomic weapons, the war in Vietnam and issues that would be more appropriate for the end than for the beginning of a series of interchanges. The SPD holds that a start should be made with the consideration of questions where the disparity of views was not apparently unbridgeable. The failure to meet in Hanover in the FRG and in Chemnitz (or Karl Marx Stadt) in the Zone, resulted not from a disagreement on detail but from a flat no from Ulbricht and the labor leader Norden. It has been assumed that Ulbricht feared the mounting interest in the prospect of these discussions. He may have thought the events would have stirred new ideas among the people who would inevitably be aware of the confrontation. The first phase of this effort was closed and some months are likely to pass before it is reopened. The proposal is of such a nature that it is not likely to be forgotten on either side of the Wall. The Social Democrats are in a favorable position to bring forward later some modification of the plan. It is in line with their pressure for movement and for breaking off shackles that inhibit activity designed to bring the two parts of Germany closer.

Little is known as to what the Russians in the Kremlin thought of the proposed exchange. They probably exercised some restraint in the matter, for if they had not, Ulbricht would almost certainly have prolonged the consideration. They are certainly aware of the possibilities of unrest in the Communist circles in East Germany. Faced with the possibility that there may be modifications to the conduct of the cold war, they are likely to rethink their German policy as time goes on, taking account of the new feelers which the SPD has put out and new questions being raised by the Western world.

The Hallstein Doctrine and Diplomacy

One of the doctrines recently under quiet review has been the Hallstein doctrine. This has been strained to the breaking point in dealings with nations in the center of Europe and in Africa. There is an increasing tendency in Bonn to urge that it is against the commercial, and perhaps against the diplomatic interests, of the Federal Republic to hold to the rule that there can be no embassies in nations that recognize the GDR as a sovereign state. In fact, there can be no ideal solution of this question, as there can be no easy answer to the two China questions. Nowhere in the West is there serious acceptance of the Ulbricht regime as an independent, freely chosen, government, but the cutting off of large areas and the curtailing of trade and cultural relations is not satisfactory to those who have a realistic and immediate interest in dealing with these nations. Many in Germany are now restive over the limits to their expanding commerce and to their influence particularly in Africa and in Central Europe.

The trade missions that have been established are a partial substitute for the more conventional diplomatic missions. These can help to establish useful contacts with Czechoslovakia, Rumania, Tanzania, and Egypt, but they leave a gap in the structure that some political leaders wish to see filled. Present-day tendencies suggest that the Hallstein doctrine is not now of wide effectiveness as a deterrent and that the likelihood of a major modification may increase in the near future.

Various changes lie in the offing that Berlin will urge on Bonn and that Bonn will be forced to consider in the interests of political co-operation. These are the more acceptable because of the growing strength of the German share in NATO. Contrary to the general direction of de Gaulle's policy, the most clearly visible result of the French attack on existing security arrangements is to increase Bonn's influence relative to that of the other members of the Alliance. Since it is clear that the Germans—because of their resources, their productivity, their location, and their attitude—are valued members of NATO, they have gained a position, without nuclear potential, which makes them of prime importance to the United States.

While the first result of this change in relationships in Europe is to consolidate the position of Germany as a key country in the Western Alliance and in the EEC, later consequences may drive it toward new ventures. It is difficult for Germany to turn its back on the happenings to the east. It has many reasons for thinking that it can cultivate old contacts and develop new ones with satellite nations which are more difficult for powerful America to engage in without endangering the whole purpose and principles of the Western Alliance. With considerable potential, but less global responsibility, Germany might be tempted to bargain with Russia. How soon, or how far, such tendencies might develop, it is impossible to forecast. The only element in the situation that stands out boldly is that the present generation of young men cannot deny their ties with the areas that lie across the "green border" and that surround Berlin.

It is this problem, this dilemma, that forces on the United States a careful consideration of its links with various factions in Germany. America, like Russia, must consider how best its long-run interests can be served while the West will continue to hold an unfaltering defense of Berlin. Neither side can ignore completely the will of a dynamic Germany for reunification—a concern that might drive some of the more restless to extremes. Neither can assume that it is dealing with a static situation. The people in the territory that was the old Reich are not inclined to Communism. By the same token, they are not willing to be kept within narrow bounds. Moreover, they do not wish the future to be like the past.

Barzel's Proposal

It was with a knowledge of the 1966 situation that Rainer Barzel made his speech on June 17 in New York. In this address he put together a number of well-known suggestions that related to the neutralization and co-operative arrangements through a mixed commission dealing with technical matters in the now divided parts of Germany. He urged that neither the military, economic, nor ideological aims of the Soviets were best served by the division of Germany.

In addition to familiar and frequently discussed possibilities, he added a new element. This idea was presumably intended to attract the attention of the Kremlin and give a new evidence of sincerity in the will to keep the peace in the center of Europe. This was the offer to permit the Soviet soldiers to remain on German territory. While by its novelty it added spice to the total plan, this possibility did not enhance the proposal for most of its hearers. Except among the hardened Communists, there was no desire in any part of Germany to prolong the stay of the Communist troops. In fact, the basic dilemma is evidenced by this part of the speech. It is reasonably clear that either Soviet troops would exercise an influence over the workings of the democratic process in the areas occupied, and thus prevent genuine reunification, or they would be ineffective and therefore frustrated, from the Soviet point of view. It is not in the nature of the Communist system to permit dilution of its methods and its doctrine.

The significance of the speech by Rainer Barzel, the rising young CDU leader, is not so much its contents as the fact that he chose to give it at what must have seemed to him an important phase of his political career. The atmosphere in Germany was sufficiently receptive to new ideas and to an attempt to improve relations with the East to cause him to seize on an opportunity for discussion of a matter that would have been considered political dynamite some years back. The fact that he did not receive either loud praise or sharp condemnation indicated movement toward a new stage of analysis and a reshaping of political notions.

Reunification and Berlin

As long as Berlin remains free, the question of reunification will be in the forefront of political thinking. As long as Germans seek reunification, Berlin will constitute a stepping stone and a key for a forward policy. Moreover, until there is a reasonable solution of the divisions, such as this, which plague the peaceloving nations, there will be danger and apprehension. The peace will not be secure.

In considering reunification, it is necessary to contemplate the nature of the forces that pull a nation together or that lead to fragmentation. It is not easy to say what makes unity so important in the United States, in India, in Russia, in China, in Germany. What leads to separation of an Ireland, the division of Nigeria, the breaking up of empires, the dissolution of kingdoms? Any attempt to look ahead in the case of Germany must be guided by an analysis of the centrifugal and the centripetal forces. What are the gravitational political forces pulling the parts together? How durable are they—how strong? These are central questions.

There are elements of historical necessity which govern in some cases, including the geographic position of a land mass which makes it almost intolerable to divide it and which render unity constructive. Questions of race and tradition are often overriding. Religion unites in some cases, divides in others. Deliberate efforts to build strong new nations by bringing in outlying regions have played a part. There is no repeated pattern that makes diagnosis or prediction easy. Speculation in a particular case pursues a cautious path where the number of variables is almost infinite and where dominating forces from within or without may determine the structure and the organization of national life. Neither the psychologist, the political scientist, nor the historian can say when, how, or if Germany will be reunited.

The signs of forces preventing the joining of the East Zone to the Federal Republic are impressive. It is clear that only the firm stand in Berlin has held back those influences that would have engulfed the occupied area. It is in the political interests of the USSR to see that this edge of the satellite complex remains strong and unbroken. In spite of Barzel's suggestion, it is also of considerable economic advantage to have the industry of the Zone producing for the Communist military establishment and raising the level of production. Prestige is involved and so is money.

Only occasionally, perhaps, do the men in the Kremlin wonder if they are losing in their strategic battle for gains in a partially uncommitted world by holding an unwilling vassal of this nature. It must be difficult for any realist to think of relaxation of tensions, let alone friendly Russo-German relations, while the bitter division, emphasized by a shining Berlin, reminds all Germans of what they have been denied. The time may come when they wish their unnatural hold over the Zone to end, but the terms of such a shift in policy are not easy to visualize.

The reasons why the drive for reunification can be expected to persist lie mainly in the German character.

More than some nations and races, they hold many attitudes in common. They came together as a nation something over a century ago, and despite the disparity between Prussians and Bavarians, Saxons and Rhinelanders, they have presented a united front to the outsider—the Russian and to the rest of Europe. They appear to have much in common. There have always been strong family ties in Germany, ties that have been partially frustrated but not completely destroyed. There have been similar attitudes toward business, property, trade, and money. There have been persistent strains in culture, in architecture, in music, in sport. The social fabric, while varying by region, has had many elements in common. There has been a national pride and a sense of destiny. In fact, the centripetal forces have been strong and will not soon vanish. In the unpredictable future, the configuration of Europe cannot be forecast. All that one can reasonably say at this time is that Germany, more than many other portions of the globe, has the characteristics to make it a united nation. For this reason, division can bring out the less benign characteristic and a possible dangerous irredentism.

Ulbricht's grim attempt to celebrate the Wall on its fifth anniversary represents the abyss of misunderstanding which still separates the Communist world from the democratic West. This event, five years after the grotesque barrier began to slash its line across the city streets, manifests a strange concept of human attitudes. Neither the pain nor the humor of the Berliners is taken into account in the actions of the Pankow regime. The management of the area shows little appreciation of the German character. Only recently have they begun to appeal to the pride of workmanship which is a national characteristic. They have done little to respond to their desire to beautify their towns and cities. They have been unable to create an impelling image of the East German worker or leader. Individualism does not flourish in the Zone. The hard lines of the Wall reflect the rigidity of the system. The question remains as to whether they can create a new type of German.

A major part of their dilemma is the existence of Berlin. It is a pressure point that they can use against the West anywhere in the world. It is also a place where warnings of danger are flashed to the Western capitals. If the Communists restore it to its typical position in the heart of Europe, they are inevitably looking toward the West, toward its standards and its ways. They either face the solid concrete barrier or they look over and beyond to a rich and varied culture that capitalism has created. They cannot obliterate this vivid fact—made more real to all Europe by their attempt to honor the shameful act of August 13, 1961.

The Diplomacy in Slow Motion

Neither de Gaulle in Moscow nor Erhard in Washington brought significant influences to bear on Europe and on conditions in Germany or in Berlin. There seems to be a pause in which no clear sense of direction and no impressive will for change are evident. No strong voices have been raised to advocate a new strategy. The need to accept the withdrawal of NATO installations from France and the redeployment of troops has distracted leaders from more substantive questions. In the lull that characterized the end of the year in Europe, the issue of Franco-German relations subsided. The changes in the satellite nations seemed gradual rather than dramatic. The direction of Communist thinking was obscure. Those who wished to speed the course of international events seemed for the moment to be muscle-bound. Even the modest efforts to knock new holes in the Wall are temporarily at a reduced pace. Kiesinger in early 1967 faced a growing challenge.

The future is still hidden—there are in the world dark areas of doubt and fear, but in Berlin the lights still shine, lit by heroes of other days. One sees the dark bulk of the Wall. But the Wall is not forever.

BIBLIOGRAPHY

This list of sources does not, in all cases, duplicate the bibliography in some of the major sources, such as Jean Smith, *The Defense of Berlin*, Kurt Shell, *Bedrohung und Bewährung*, and Alois Riklin, *Das Berlinproblem*. A considerable number of newspapers and journals in the Federal Republic of Germany have been consulted. Some have been cited in footnotes, but a complete list is not included here. Documentary sources additional to those cited have been consulted. Where not otherwise indicated, the source is personal interview or notes made in the course of my work.

Apel, Hans. *Ohne Begleiter: 287 Gespräche jenseits der Zonengrenze.* Cologne: Wissenschaft und Politik, 1965.

Adenauer, Konrad. *Erinnerungen: 1945–1953.* Stuttgart: Deutsche Verlags Anstalt, 1965.

Bender, Peter. *Offensive Entspannung: Möglichkeit für Deutschland.* Cologne: Kiepenheuer & Witsch, 1964.

Berlin Press and Information Office. *Berlin: Anspruch und Leistung.* Berlin: 1965.

———. *Berlin Faces Facts.* Berlin: 1962.

———. *Berlin: Facts and Figures, 1960.* Berlin: 1960.

———. *Berlin: Figures, Headings, Charts.* 1962–63 Edition. Berlin: 1963.

———. *Berlin: Zahlen, Stichworte, Tabellen.* Ausgabe 1964–1965. Berlin: 1965.

———. *Reference: Berlin.* Berlin: c. 1964.

———. *Zur Passierscheinfrage: Erklärung des Regierenden Bürgermeisters Willy Brandt vom 9. Januar 1964 vor dem Abgeordnetenhaus von Berlin.* Berlin: 1964.

———. *Zur Passierscheinfrage, II: Die Verwaltungs-vereinbarung vom 24. September 1964.* Berlin: 1964.

Brandt, Willy. *Denke ich an Deutschland.* Berlin: Berlin Press and Information Office, 1963.

———, and Richard Lowenthal. *Ernst Reuter: Ein Leben für die Freiheit: Eine Politische Biographie.* Munich: Kindler, 1957.

Brandt, Willy. *Helfen: Ja! Sprengen: Nein!: Eine Erklärung des Regierendum Bürgermeister von Berlin Willy Brandt*. Berlin: Berlin Press and Information Office, 1962.
———, with Leo Lania. *My Road to Berlin*. Garden City: Doubleday, 1960.
———. *Plädoyer für die Zukunft: Zwölf Beiträge zu deutschen Fragen*. Frankfurt: Europäische Verlagsanstalt, 1961.
———. *Von Bonn nach Berlin: Eine Dokumentation zur Hauptstadtfrage*. Berlin: Arani, 1957.
———, et al. "West-Berlin stark durch seine Wirtschaft," *Der Volkswirt* (Frankfurt), XXX, (May, 1963).
Brant, Stefan. *The East German Rising*. New York: Praeger, 1957.
Bundesministerium für gesamtdeutsche Fragen. *SBZ von A bis Z: Ein Taschen-und Nachschlagebuch über die Sowjetische Besatzungszone Deutschlands*. Bonn: Deutscher Bundes-Verlag, 1965.
Bundesministerium für Gesamtdeutsche Fragen. *Vierter Tätigkeitsbericht 1961–1965: (Gradl-Mende Report)*. Bonn: 1965.
Clay, Lucius D. *Decision in Germany*. Garden City: Doubleday, 1950.
Combat (Paris). "The Five Germanys" [as quoted in *Sudeten Bulletin: Central European Review*, XIII (March, 1965), 85–87].
Conant, James B., U.S. High Commissioner Berlin. *Deutsch-Amerikanische Zusammenarbeit in West-Berlin*. Bad Godesberg: US-Informationsdienst, 1956.
Davison, W. Phillips. *The Berlin Blockade: A Study in Cold War Politics*. Princeton: The Princeton University Press, 1958.
Der Spiegel. Hamburg.
Deutsches Institut für Wirtschaftsforschung. "The Foreign Trade of East Germany with the USSR from 1955 to 1963," *Economic Bulletin*, II No. 5 (1965), 37–39.
Deutsche Stiftung für Entwicklungsländer. *Annual Report 1962–1963*. Berlin: 1964.
Dönhoff, Marion Gräfin, Rudolf Walter Leonhardt, and Theo Sommer. *Reise in ein fernes Land: Bericht über Kultur, Wirtschaft und Politik in der DDR*. Hamburg: Nannen, 1965.
Dulles, Allen. *The Craft of Intelligence*. New York: Harper & Row, 1963.
Dulles, Eleanor Lansing. "Berlin and Soviet Methods in Germany," *The Department of State Bulletin*, XXXVI (June 17, 1957), 978–83.
———. "Concerted Efforts Against Tyranny," *The Department of State Bulletin*, XXXIII (September 12, 1955), 422–26.
——— and Robert Dickson Crane (ed.). *Détente: Cold War Strategies in Transition*. New York: Praeger, 1965.
———. "Education—Communist Style, American Style," *The Department of State Bulletin*, XXXVII (July 1, 1957), 25–29.

———. *John Foster Dulles: The Last Year*. New York: Harcourt-Brace, 1963.
———. "The Meaning of the Division of Germany," *The Department of State Bulletin*, XLI (November 30, 1959), 790–95.
———. "The Soviet Occupied Zone of Germany: A Case Study in Communist Control," *The Department of State Bulletin*, XXXVI (April 15, 1957), 605–10.
Dulles, John Foster. *War or Peace*. New York: Macmillan, 1950.
———. *War, Peace and Change*. New York: Harper, 1939.
Epstein, Julius. "The Tragedy in Churchill's Relationship to Roosevelt and Stalin," *Sudeten Bulletin: Central European Review*, XIII (July–August, 1965), 223–27.
Erler, Fritz. *Democracy in Germany*. Cambridge: Harvard University Press, 1965.
———. "The Struggle for German Reunification," *Foreign Affairs*, XXXIV (April, 1956).
Evers, Carl-Heinz, Senator für Schulwesen. *Das Bildungswesen des Landes Berlin*. Berlin: c. 1962.
———. *Wege zur Schule von Morgen: Entwicklungen und Versuche in der Berliner Schule*. Berlin: 1965.
Friedensburg, Ferdinand. *Berlin: Schicksal und Aufgabe*. Berlin: Berthold Schulz, 1953.
Galante, Pierre. *The Berlin Wall*. New York: Doubleday & Co., 1965.
German Information Center. *Berlin: Crisis and Challenge*. New York: c. 1962.
Guttenberg, Karl Theodor, Freiherr von und zu. *Wenn der Western will: Plädoyer für eine mutige Politik*. Stuttgart: Seewald, 1964.
Hangen, Welles. *The Muted Revolution*. New York: Alfred A. Knopf, 1966.
Hartmann, Frederick H. *Germany between East and West: The Reunification Problem*. Englewood Cliffs, N.J.: Prentice-Hall, Inc., 1965.
Heidelmeyer, Wolfgang, and Günter Hindrichs, *Documents on Berlin: 1943–1963*. Munich: R. Oldenbourg, 1963.
Heller, Deane and David Heller. *The Berlin Wall*. New York: Walker, 1962.
Hildebrandt, Dieter. *Die Mauer ist keine Grenze: Menschen in Ostberlin*. Düsseldorf: Eugen Diederichs, 1964.
Hildebrandt, Rainer. *Als die Fesseln fielen . . . Die Geschichte einer Schicksalsverkettung in einem Aufstand*. Berlin: Grunewald, 1960.
———. *Was Lehrte der 17. Juni?* 1954.
Holbik, Karel, and Henry Myers. *Postwar Trade in Divided Germany: The Internal and International Issues*. Baltimore: The Johns Hopkins Press, 1964.
Hoppe, Hans-Günter, Senator für Finanzen. *Berlin: im Spiegel seiner öffentlichen Finanzplanung für das Jahr 1965*. Berlin: 1965.

Howley, Frank. *Berlin Command.* New York: G. P. Putnam's Sons, 1950.
International Commission of Jurists. *The Berlin Wall: A Defiance of Human Rights.* Geneva: 1962.
Internationes. *Berlin Book List.* Bonn: 1963.
Jänicke, Martin. *Der dritte Weg: Die antistalinistische Opposition gegen Ulbricht seit 1953.* Cologne: Neuer Deutscher, 1964.
Jaesrich, Hellmut. "West-Berlin: Ein verwegener Menschenschlag?" *Der Monat,* May, 1965.
Keller, John W. *Germany, the Wall and Berlin.* New York: Vantage Press, 1964.
Legien, R. *The Four Power Agreements on Berlin: Alternative Solutions to the Status Quo?.* 2nd ed. Berlin: Carl Heymanns, 1961.
Leopold, Dr. Kurt. *Quick* (Munich), July 11, 1965.
Lohmar, Ulrich. *Deutschland 1975: Analysen, Prognosen, Perspektiven.* Munich: Kindler, 1965.
Ludz, Peter Christian (ed.). *Studien und Materialien zur Soziologie der DDR.* Cologne: Westdeutscher Verlag, 1964.
Mampel, Siegfried. *Der Sowjetsektor von Berlin: Eine Analyse seines äusseren und inneren Status.* Frankfurt: Alfred Metzner, 1963.
Mander, John. *Berlin: Unterpfand der Freiheit.* Frankfurt: Athenäum, 1962.
Merian-Brevier von Berlin, II (November, 1959). Hamburg: Hoffmann und Campe, 1959.
Mosely, Philip E. *The Kremlin and World Politics.* New York: Vintage, 1960.
Moser, Fritz. *Die Amerika-Gedenkbibliothek Berlin.* Wiesbaden: Otto Harrassowitz, 1694.
Ost-West-Kurier (Frankfurt), Special Edition, May 5, 1965.
Paul, Wolfgang. *Kampf um Berlin.* Munich: Langen-Müller, 1962.
Plischke, Elmer. *Contemporary Government of Germany.* Boston: Houghton-Mifflin, 1961.
———. *Government and Politics of Contemporary Berlin.* The Hague: Martinus Nijhoff, 1963.
———. "Integrating Berlin and the Federal Republic of Germany," *The Journal of Politics* (February, 1965), 35–65.
Press Office of the Embassy of the Federal Republic of Germany in Washington, D.C. *German Press Review.*
Pritzkoleit, Kurt. *Berlin: Ein Kampf ums Leben.* Düsseldorf: Karl Rauch, 1962.
Redslob, Edwin. *Freie Universität Berlin.* Berlin: Wolfgang Stapp, 1963.
Research Institute of the German Society for Foreign Affairs. *The Berlin Question in its Relations to World Politics.* Munich: R. Oldenbourg, 1964.

Bibliography

Rhode, Gotthold and Wolfgang Wagner (ed.). *The Genesis of the Oder-Neisse Line: Sources and Documents*. Stuttgart: Brentano, 1959.
Riklin, Alois. *Das Berlinproblem*. Cologne: Wissenschaft und Politik, 1964.
Robson, Charles B. and Werner Zohlnhöfer. "Berlinproblem und 'Deutsche Frage' im Spiegel des Englischsprachigen Schrifttums der Nachkriegszeit: Ein Literaturbericht," in *Jahrbuch für die Geschichte Mittel-und Ostdeutschlands*. Berlin: Walter de Gruyter, 1962.
——— (ed. and trans). *Berlin: Pivot of German Destiny*. Chapel Hill: University of North Carolina Press, 1960.
Sanger, Fritz and Eugen Silbmann (ed.) *Politik für Deutschland: Sozialdemokratische Beiträge 1962–1964*. Bonn: Vorstand der SPD, 1964.
Schadewaldt, Wolfgang, et al. *Berliner Geist: Fünf Vorträge der Bayerischen Akademie der Schönen Künste*. Berlin: Propyläen, 1963.
Schenk, Fritz. *Im Vorzimmer der Diktatur: 12 Jahre Pankow*. Cologne: Kiepenheuer & Witsch, 1962.
Schiller, Karl. "Berlin-Deutschland-Europa," *Tatsachen-Argumente*, No. 125 (March, 1965).
———. *Berliner Wirtschaft und Deutsche Politik*. Stuttgart: Seewald, 1964.
———, Senator für Wirtschaft. *Daten zur Entwicklung der Berliner Wirtschaft (West) 1950–1959*. Berlin: c. 1960.
———. *Die Industrie in Berlin (West) 1964*. Berlin: 1964.
———. *Es Lohnt sich . . . Investieren Produzieren in Berlin*. Berlin: 1965.
Schiller, Dr. Karl. *The Wall in Berlin*. Berlin: 1964.
Schindler, Dr. Hans-Georg, et al. *Berlin Sowjet Sektor*. Berlin: Colloquim Verlag, 1965.
Scholz, Arno, Werner Nieke, and Gottfried Vetter, *Panzer am Potsdamer Platz*. Berlin: Grunewald, 1954.
Senat von Berlin. *Berlin: Quellen und Dokumente 1945–1951 (vol. 1 & 2)*. Berlin: Heinz Spitzing, 1964.
Shell, Kurt L. *Bedrohung und Bewährung: Führung und Bevölkerung in der Berlin-Krise*. Cologne: Westdeutscher Verlag, 1965.
———. "Totalitarianism in Retreat: The Example of the DDR," *World Politics*, XVIII (October, 1965), 105–16.
Siegler, Heinrich von. *Wiedervereinigung und Sicherheit Deutschlands*. Bonn: Siegler & Co., 1964.
Smith, Jean E. *The Defense of Berlin*. Baltimore: The Johns Hopkins Press, 1963.
Speier, Hans. *Die Bedrohung Berlins: Eine Analyse der Berlin-Krise von 1958 bis heute*. Cologne: Kiepenheuer & Witsch, 1964.

Speier, Hans. *Divided Berlin.* New York: Praeger, 1961.
Stammer, Otto. *Verbände und Gesetzgebung: Die Einflussnahme der Verbände auf die Gestaltung des Personalvertretungsgesetzes.* Köln Westdeutscher Verlag, 1965.
Stanger, Roland J. *West Berlin: The Legal Context.* Ohio University Press, 1966.
Statistisches Landesamt Berlin. *Statistisches Jahrbuch Berlin: 1964.* Berlin: Kulturbuch, 1964.
Stingl, Josef. "Is Berlin a Myth?" *Sudeten Bulletin: Central European Review,* XII (September, 1964), 235–37.
Storbeck, Dietrich. *Berlin: Bestand und Möglichleiten.* Köln: Westdeutscher Verlag, 1964.
[Strausz-Hupe, Robert, et al.]. "Reflections on the Quarter," *Orbis,* V (Summer, 1961), 127–38.
Tagesspiegel (Berlin), June 23, 1965; August 11, 1965; and September 22, 1965.
Thalheim, Karl C. *Die Wirtschaft der Sowjetzone in Krise und Umbau.* Berlin: Duncker and Humblot, 1964.
Tiburtius, Joachim, Senator für Volksbildung. *Die Politische Bildung und Erziehung an der Berliner Schule.* Berlin: Kulturbuch Verlag, 1960.
―――. *Schools in Berlin (West).* Berlin: 1961.
Tondel, Lyman M. (ed.). *The Hammarskjold Forums: The Issues in the Berlin-German Crisis.* New York: Oceana, 1963.
U.S. Department of State. *American Foreign Policy-Current Documents: 1958.* Washington, D.C.: U.S. Government Printing Office, 1962.
―――. "Berlin-1961," *Background* (August, 1961).
―――. "Berlin: City Between Two Worlds," *Background* (November, 1952).
―――. "Flight From 'Paradise' the East German Exodus," *Background* (June, 1953).
―――. *Germany 1947–1949: The Story in Documents.* Washington, D.C.: U.S. Government Printing Office, 1950.
―――. *Occupation of Germany: Policy and Progress, 1945–46.* Washington, D.C.: U.S. Government Printing Office, 1947.
U.S. Embassy-Bonn, Economic Affairs Section. *Handbook of Economic Statistics: Federal Republic of Germany and Western Sectors of Berlin.* Bonn: March, 1965.
U.S. High Commissioner for Germany. *Quarterly Reports on Germany: October, 1949–December, 1950.* Washington, D.C.: U.S. Government Printing Office, 1950.
―――. *Western German Economic Recovery, 1945–1952.* Washington, D.C.: U.S. Government Printing Office, 1952.
U.S. Mission Berlin. *Regional Economic Characteristics of West Berlin.* Berlin: 1964.

Bibliography

U.S. Department of Commerce. "Investing in West Berlin: A Special Report," *Foreign Commerce Weekly*, LXVII (May 28, 1962), 949–992.

U.S. Senate, Committee on Foreign Relations. *A Decade of American Foreign Policy: Basic Documents, 1941–1949.* Washington, D.C.: U.S. Government Printing Office, 1950.

———. *Documents on Germany, 1944–1961.* Washington, D.C.: U.S. Government Printing Office, 1961.

Vardys, V. Stanley. "Germany's Postwar Socialism: Nationalism and Kurt Schumacher (1945–52)," *The Review of Politics*, XXVII (April, 1965), 220–44.

Vicker, Ray. "East Germany Leads the Way in Red Scramble for Economic Reform," *The Wall Street Journal*, October 4, 1965.

Windsor, Philip. *City on Leave: A History of Berlin, 1945–1962.* London: Chatto & Windus, 1963.

Woodward, Margaret Rupli. "Berlin Rebuilds: Economic Reconstruction of West Berlin, 1948–1953," *The Department of State Bulletin*, XXX (April 19, 1954).

INDEX

A

Abeken, Gerhard, 127n
Abend, Der, 162
Abgeordnetenhaus. See House of Representatives
Abitur, 176
Abshire, David M., x
Access, 32, 133–45; air, 138–45; land, 133–35; military, 32, 212; water, 135–38. See also Paris Agreement, 1949; Blockade of 1948–49
Adenauer, Konrad, 4, 11, 12, 45, 54, 59–64 passim, 90, 198, 199, 202; Adenauer chosen as Chancellor, 37
Adenauer-Dulles friendship, 101
Adenauer era, 79; post-Adenauer era, 79, 86
African visitors, 52. See also Visits, to Berlin
Aid, American, 79, 145, 146, 147–58; airlift, 148; Government Administration and Relief in Occupied Areas, 149; success of, 156–58; total, 156
Air corridor, 139
Air incidents, 191. See also Access
Airlift, 18, 138, 140. See also Blockade of 1948–49; Clay, Lucius D.; Aid, American

Akademie der Kunst, 160
Albertz, Heinrich, x, 46, 185, 186, 187
All German Affairs Ministry. See Bundesministerium für gesamtdeutsche Fragen
Allen, William L., xi, 77, 78, 210
Allgemeine Elektrizitäts Gesellschaft (AEG), 151
America Institute, 159
American Forces Network (AFN), 162
American Memorial Library, 152, 177
American Military Police, 67
Amrehn, Franz, 46, 186
Anderson, Omer, 76
Architectural exhibit, 1957. See Building exhibit
Atlantic Community. See North Atlantic Treaty Organization
Atomic bomb, 23; German attitude, 207
Attlee, Clement, 27
Aubrey, Albertine, 134n
August 13, 1961, 60, 103. See also Wall
Austria, 4, 8, 9, 24, 25, 32, 34
Austrian State Treaty, 10, 41
Azocar, Patricia, x

B

Baedeker's Berlin, 47
Bahr, Egon, 46, 187, 188; Hamburg

[237]

speech, 186; Tutzing speech, 1963, 185
Bainbridge, John, 69n
Balkans, 25, 28
Barge traffic, 40, 84, 191; halting of, 84; permits, 136, 137
Barzel, Rainer, 211; plan, 218; 223–24
Basel, 7
Basic Law, May 8, 1949, 37, 39
Bay of Pigs, 55, 77
Bender, Peter, 85, 86, 92, 101
Benjamin Franklin Foundation, 17, 153
Bergstrasse Ecke Haupstrasse, 69
Berkeley (California) revolt, 171
Berlin, 3, 4; age of population, 148; between the wars, 5, 6; Blockade of 1948–49, 9, 10; conversations, 196, 113; crisis, 42; economy, 65; incidents, 191; inability to vote in national elections, 200; morale, 134, 141–48 *passim*, 159; Nazi years, 6, 7; postwar, 8, 9; reconstruction, 150–58; "show case," 157. *See also* Blockade of 1948–49, Crises, Escapes, Harassment, June 17, Production, Refugees, Stockpiles, Unemployment, Visits
Berlin Air Safety Center (BASC), 36, 139
Berlin Conference, 1954, 18, 19, 41
Berlin, Constitution, Article 87. *See* Constitution
Berlin Desk, U.S. Department of State, 4, 150
Berlin, *Senat*. See *Senat*
Berliner Morgenpost, 162
Berliner Zeitung, 162
Bernauer Strasse, 59, 60, 65, 71
Bernstein, Bernard, 31
Berolina Hotel, 125
Berta, West German Police substation, 60
Blank, Theodor, 218
Blockade of 1948–49, 9, 22, 35, 56, 90, 131, 138, 155; end of, 133
Bochum, speech by Brandt in September, 1964, 96
Bochum University, 176
Bode Museum, 126
Böhm, Karl, 162
Bolz-Zorin correspondence, on "GDR sovereignty," 140
Bonn. *See* Federal Republic of Germany
Border closing of August 13, 1961, 53

Border-crossers. See *Grenzgänger*
Borsig plant, 151
Boy Scouts, 195
Brandenburg Gate, 15, 18, 60, 61, 65, 68, 77
Brandt, Willy, 12, 17, 46, 54, 87n, 90, 185, 187, 192; August 13, 1961, 58–62; debates proposal, 171, 220, with Dulles, 1958, 19; with Dulles, 1959, 43; dedication John-Foster-Dulles-Allee, 20; election campaign, 192, 198–200; *Passierschein* negotiations, 93–98, 108; problem of, 204–6; stopped by Communists, 144
Brandt, Stefan, 16n
Brezhnev, Leonid, 189
British Forces Network (BFN), 162
Brown Book on Nazis (East German), 195
Buchwald, Art, 133n
Building exhibit, 1957, 17, 161
Bulgaria, treaty, 26
Bundesbank, 218
Bundeshaus, 45
Bundesministerium für gesamtdeutsche Fragen, 103, 110n, 111, 114, 184
Bundesrat, 38
Bundestag, 37, 45, 58, 87, 144, 145
Bundy, McGeorge, 213
Bureau of the Budget, 13
Burke, Arleigh, x
Busack, Otto, 46
Byrnes, James F., 32, speech, 33, 34

C

Caddenabia, Italy, 59
Cairo Conference, 27
Camp David, 44
Canal system, 135, Havel, 135, 137. *See also* Access, water
Carthaginian peace, 31–33
Castro, Fidel, 185
Catudal, Marc, xi
CBS (tunnel). *See* Columbia Broadcasting System
Checkpoints, five, 93
Checkpoint Bravo, 77
Checkpoint Charlie, 47, 66, 67, 68, 72, 93
Christian Democratic Union (CDU), 34, 198
Christian Social Union (CSU), 198
Churchill, Winston, 23, 26
Clark, Mark, 8, 32

Index [239]

Clay Allee, 196
Clay, Lucius D., 18, 31, 35n, 64, 65, 197
Columbia Broadcasting System, 73
Commandants, Allied, 67
Commandatura. *See* Kommandatura
Communism, 32, 54, 78, 105; doctrine, 88; error, 134; intention, 62; party (KPD) Berlin, 34; policy, 53; "soft sell," 177; no change in strategy, 210; vote in Berlin, 163
Congress, U.S., 13
Congress Hall, 17, 20, 145, 150, 153, 161, 182, 193, 194
Constitution, Berlin, 39
"Contacts," East-West, 82, 85, 86, 92, 96, 169, 187
Contingency planning, 141
"Corporations" (duelling), 167
Council of Foreign Ministers (CFM), 36
Counter-measures, 181
Counterpart funds, 151
Crane, Robert D., 50n
Crises, June, 1948, 131; November, 1958, 42, 55, 131; August, 1961, 45, 131. *See also* June 17, 1953
Cuban missile crisis, 1962, 58, 63, 77, 102, 140, 180, 185
Cultural Festival (Berlin), 160
Czechoslovakia, x, 24, 32, 35, 90
Czechoslovakians, 105, 142

D

Davison, W. Phillips, 149n
DDR. *See* German Democratic Republic, East Zone
"Dealings," 107
"Death strip," 47, 65
"Debates with Communists (proposal), 171
De Gaulle, Charles, 30, 203, 214, 217, 226
Department of Defense, 13
Department of State, objection to tunnel story, 73
Détente, 187
Deutsche Oper (West Berlin), 161
Deutsche Stiftung für Entwicklungsländer, 160
Dewey, Thomas, 18
Dibelius, Bishop Otto, 123
Directive 1067, 31, 32, 33
"Disease and unrest" formula, 30
Division of Germany, 79
Dobler, Herman, 77, 169, 191

Dönhoff, Marion Gräfin, 108n
Doric Quartet, 162
Drain of skilled labor from East Zone, 109
Droste, Karl Heinz, 160
Dulles, Allen W., 5, 16, 18
Dulles, David, xi
Dulles, Eleanor Lansing, 16, 43n, 16–104, 104n, 136n, 146n; visits to Waldbühne, 104; work on Berlin aid, 149
Dulles, John Foster, 5, 8, 11, 12, 14, 16, 18, 42, 43; death of, 43
Dulles, Pamela, xi
Duppel-Kleinmachow crossing point, 59

E

East Europe Institute. *See* Ost-Europa Institut
East German Currency District (as formula), 98
East Germany. *See* East Zone
East Prussia, 81
East Sector (Berlin), 63
East Zone, 28, 35, 47, 74, 79, 103–28; agriculture, 120–21 (table 121); barges, 135; Communist control, 110; credits to, 113, 188; education, 118; economic conditions, 51, 52, 103; flag on trains, 181; food rationing, 122; labor force, 109; labor shortage, 119; living standard, 100; planning, 118–19; press agency, 59; production, 106, 111; radio, 59; revolt in (*see* June 17, 1953); trade, 92, 113; "sovereignty," 41, 42
Ebert, Friedrich, 36
Eckhardt, Felix von, 202
Eisenhower, Dwight D., 11; views on Berlin, 29n, 35n, 44
Elbe river, 142
Elbe, Joachim von, 38
Election campaign, 1965, 87, 198; compared with past years, 201 (table)
Election in North Rhine–Westphalia (1966), 201, 218
England. *See* United Kingdom
Erhard, Ludwig, 90, 94, 96, 185, 191–201 *passim*, 218, 220, 226; problem of, 202–4
Erhardt, John G., 8, 192
Erler, Fritz, 46, 90
Escapes through the Wall, 61, 75, 78, 190. *See also* Tunnels; Fechter, Peter; Puhl, Hans; Refugees

Europe, changes over years, 217
European Advisory Commission (EAC), 24, 29, 30, 132
European Alliance. See North Atlantic Treaty Organization
European Defense Community (EDC), 37
European Economic Community (EEC), 33, 88, 90

F

FDGB. See Freier Deutscher Gewerkshaftsbund
FDP. See Free Democratic Pary
Fechter, Peter, 65–69, 210
Federal Republic of Germany, 11, 37, 40, 96; attitudes towards contacts, 83; contribution to Europe, 147; subsidies to Berlin, 45, 149, 151, 155
Film Festival, 150
Finke, Blythe, xi, 77, 210
Finland, Treaty, 26
Fischerstrasse, 14
Flohr-Otis plant, 151
Food package program, 16, 154
Forces Françaises Berlin (FFB), 162
Ford, Henry II, 153, 174
Foreign Ministers Conference. See Council of Foreign Ministers; Berlin Conference, 1954
Foreign Policy Association, 7
Forster, Ursula, 160
Foster, John W., 43
Fourth of July, 131, 196
France, 92, 132, 149, 164, 181; airplanes, 138
Frankfurt am Main, 83
Franklin, John F., 197
Free Democratic Party (FDP), 44, 89n
Free University of Berlin, x, 90, 159, 165, 166; founders, 171; Senat, 170; students from Federal Republic, 177; student protest, 170. See also Students
Freedom Bell, 19, 189, 216
Frei Deutsche Partei (FDP), 44, 89n
Freier Deutscher Gewerkschaftsbund (FDGB), 34
FRG. See Federal Republic of Germany
Friedensburg, Ferdinand, 36, 46
Friedrichstrasse, 47, 126
Friedrichstrasse Checkpoint. See Checkpoint Charlie
Fulbright, J. William, 48, 50, 54, 62

G

Galante, Pierre, 48n, 66
Garcia, Maria, x
Garden of Remembrance, 126
GARIOA. See Government Administration and Relief in Occupied Areas
Geneva Conference, 1955, 41, 132, 140; communiqué, 140n
Geneva Conference of Foreign Ministers, 1959, 45; East German presence, 107
Georgi, Rudi, 116
Gerhartz, Elizabeth, 14
German Democratic Republic (GDR), 74, 85, 96, 99; "GDR consciousness," 115. See also East Zone
German-French Volksfest, 194
German occupation, 24
Germany, 32, 34; importance to U.S., 213, 214
Gerstenmaier, Eugen, 63, 201
Gilpatrick, Roswell, 207
Globke, Hans, 60
Goebbels, Paul Joseph, 7
Goerz, Renata, xi
Gonda, Alexander, 160
Government Administration and Relief in Occupied Areas (GARIOA), 25, 149. See also Aid, American
Gradl, Johann Baptist, 46
Gradl-Mende Report, 110, 112. See also Bundesministerium für gesamtdeutsche Fragen
Grenzgänger, 58, 124. See also Bordercrossers
Grenzpolizei (Grepos), 66, 67, 68, 72, 78, 124
Gropius Stadt, 161
Gropius, Walter, 161
Gross National Product (GNP), 130n, 157
Grunewald, 193
Guilt feeling (German), 148, 172
Gusev, Fedor Tarasovich, 30
Guttenberg, Karl Theodor, Freiherr von und zu, 87

H

Hallstein doctrine, 208, 221
Hamburg, 60, 142
Hamburg Waterways Directorate, 136
Hamilton, Thomas, 203
Hanover, 60
Hansaviertel, 161, 169

Index

Harassment, 133–42, 145. *See also* Access
Harriman, Averell, 18
Hartley, David, 17
Hartung, Karl, 160
Harvard, 7
Hassel, Kai Uwe von, 202, 219
Havel. *See* Canal system
Heerdt-Heumann, 174
Heidelmeyer, Wolfgang, 30n
Heiliger, Bernhard, 160
Helicopters, East Zone, 84, 139, 182, 191
Helicopter incident, 1958, 84, 107
Helicopters, U.S., 84
Helmstedt, 40
Henry-Ford-Bau, 152, 153
Hermes plan, 157
Herter, Christian, 20
Hertz, Paul, 12, 13, 46, 130n
Herz, Hans-Peter, 127n
Hildebrandt, Dieter, 50n
Hildebrandt, Rainer, 52n
Hilton Hotel, 78
Hindrichs, Guenter, 30n
Hitler, Adolf, 7, 21, 172, 173, 175, 209, 210
Hitler's Beer Hall Putsch, 6
Hochschule für Musik, 162
Hof (Bavaria), 48, 115
Hollreiser, Heinrich, 162
Holt, John, 8
House of Representatives, 44, 62, 96
Howley, Frank, 31, 197
Hulick, Charles, 67
Humboldt University, 127, 165, 168, 173
Hungary, x, 25, 35, 42, 101, 190; Hungarian treaty, 26
Hungary, 1956 Revolt, 42, 77, 80, 90
Hungarians, 105
Hyannisport, Massachusetts, 59

I

Impact Programs, 152–54
Industrie-Bank, 151. *See also* Aid, American
Institute of Demoskopie, 194
"Interhotel," 125
International Co-operation Administration (ICA), 13
International Film Festival, 193
Inter-Parliamentary Union delegation, 195
Interzonal Trade Agreement, 188. *See also* East Zone, credits to

Interzonal trade, 86, 92, 192
Iron Curtain, 24, 79, 87, 108
Italian treaty, 26

J

Jazy, Professor, 170
Jessup, Philip, 36
Jewish persecution, 175
Jochum, Eugen, 162
John-Foster-Dulles-Allee, 193
John F. Kennedy School, 176
Johnson, Lyndon B., 64
Joyce, Edward, xi
Jugendweihe, 122
June 17, 1953 Uprising (also June 16), 14, 15, 17, 41, 42, 52, 90, 103, 154

K

Kaiser, Jacob, 46
Kaiser-Wilhelm-Gedächtniskirche, 161
Kaiser Wilhelm Research Institute, 154
Karajan, Herbert von, 162
Karl-Marx-Allee (formerly Stalinallee), 125
Kennedy, John F., 22, 59, 61, 63, 64, 185; July 1961 speech, 50; June 1963 Berlin visit, 102, 154
Kennedy-Khrushchev Vienna meeting, 51, 54, 55
Khrushchev, Nikita, 20, 22, 42, 43, 49, 50, 61, 64, 133, 135n, 140, 144, 153, 157, 185, 197
Khrushchev's ultimatum, 1958, 22, 90. *See also* Crises, November, 1958
Kiesinger, Kurt Georg, x, 216, 218, 227
Kinderlift, 154
Kirchentag, 123
Klein, Günther, 46
Kleine Schritte. See "Little steps"
Klieforth, Alex, 7
Klinikum, 17, 153
Kohl, 97
Kommandatura, Allied, 32, 34, 37, 39
Konev, Marshal Ivan, 48, 144n
Konstantin, Prince (Bavaria), 202
Korber, Horst, 97
Korea, 140
Kosygin, Alexei, 189
Kremlin, 27, 34, 49, 53, 193; attitude, 104; promises, 132. *See also* Union of Soviet Socialist Republics; Khrushchev, Nikita
Kreutzer, Heinz, 39n
Krippendorf, Ekkehardt, 170, 171
Krips, Ursula, 202
Kuby, Erich, 165, 168

[242]

The Kudamm. *See* Kurfürstendamm
Kulbeik, Helmut, 66
Kurfürstendamm (Kudamm), 59, 193

L

Labor force, East Zone, 109
"Land Berlin," 38; land status, 36, 37, 40
Lansing, Robert, 5, 43
League of Nations, 27
Leber, Annedore, 9
Leipzig Fair, 106
Lemmer, Ernst, 46
Lenin-Marxist doctrine. *See* Marxist-Lenin doctrine
Leonhardt, Rudolf Walter, 108n
Leopold, Kurt, 114, 115
Liechtenstein, 164
Lipschitz, Joachim, 46, 58
Little blockade, 1963, 144
"Little steps," 81, 82, 101, 183, 185-88, 200
Lochner, Robert, 55
London School of Economics, 6
Lübke, Heinrich, 195
Ludendorff, Erich, 6
Lueurs, Rector, 170
Ludz, Peter Christian, 114

M

Maazel, Lorin, 162
Maier, escapee, 69
Malik, Jacob, 36
Malta Conference, 27
Mander, John, 50n
Mansfield, Mike, 50, 54, 63
Mantelgesetz, 39
Margulies, Robert, 195
Marienfelde, 14n, 15, 52, 58
Marshall, George C., 8
Marshall Plan, 18, 25, 33, 35, 106
Marxist-Lenin doctrine, 110, 114, 175
Max-Planck-Gessellschaft, 160
Max-Planck-Institut für Forschung auf dem Gebiet des Bildungswesen, 154, 160
McCarthy, Mary Catherine, x
McGhee, George C., 136n, 191
Macmillan, Harold, 59
Mehring Platz, 152
Meissner, Boris, 195
Mende, Erich, 54, 91n, 201
Mende (Gradl) Report, 110
Middle Germany, 116, 138. *See* East Zone

Military convoys, 150
Ministry of all German Affairs, 111, 184
Mochen, Franz, 153
Molotov, Vyacheslav, 3
Moran, Lord Charles, 28
Morgenthau, Henry, Jr., 31
Morgenthau Plan, 27-30
Morse, Wayne, 50, 63
Moscow Conference, 27
Mosel river, 6
Mosley, Philip, 31n
Munich, 6
Murphy, Robert D., 35n

N

National Broadcasting Company (NBC), 71, 73
National Socialism (NAZI), 6, 7, 171, 173. *See also* Hitler, Adolf
NATO. *See* North Atlantic Treaty Organization
Neues Deutschland, 55, 189
Neukölln, 61
"New Course," 106
Newsweek magazine, tunnel story, 72, 73
Niemoeller, Martin, 76
Nierendorf gallery, 160
Nonrecognition, 188. *See also* Recognition
Norden, Albert, 185, 221
North Atlantic Treaty Organization (NATO), 3, 4, 16, 33, 40, 41, 42, 45, 54, 64, 77, 79, 86, 87, 88, 89, 90, 101, 102, 129, 131, 147, 163, 164, 169; Germany's commitment, 175
North Atlantic Treaty Organization allies, 132, 186
North Atlantic Treaty Organization meeting, 1958, 19
Notstands Programm, 152

O

Occupation costs, 39
Occupation policy, 33. *See also* Germany, Austria, Morgenthau Plan
Oder-Niesse line, 76, 81
Orlopp, East Zone representative, 115
Ost-Europa Institut (Berlin), 114, 159
Ost-West Kurier, 124n
Otto-Suhr-Bau, 153, 154
Otto Suhr Institute of Political Science, 159

Index

P

Pan American Airlines, 59, 150
Pankow, 53, 58, 83, 93. *See also* Ulbricht, Walter
Paris Agreement, 1949, 40, 140, 141
Paris meeting, 1949, 132
Paris Peace Conference, 5, 29. *See also* Versailles Treaty
Paris protocol ending occupation (1955), 41
Parker, Jameson, xi
Parker, Sydney, xi
"Passengers" for escape from East Germany, 72
Passes. *See Passierscheine*
Passierschein Agreement, 93–96
Passierscheine, 84, 86, 97, 108, 142, 184
Pasvolsky, Leo, 29
Paul, Wolfgang, 50n
Peaceful coexistence, 98
Pensioners, from East Zone, 97
Pergamon Museum, 126
Philharmonic, Berlin (West), 161
Pitterman, Bruno, 43
Plischke, Elmer, 39
Pohl, Wolfram, 41n, 155
Poland, x, 25, 28, 101, 190
Poles, 105
Polish control over East Prussia, 81
Pollack, Alfred, 142
Polk, James H., 197
Potsdam, 1945, 27
Potsdam, Bahnhof, 58
Potsdam Mission, 36; Communist attack, 192, 193
Potsdamer Platz, 60
Prague, 184
Production, East Zone, 106; *See also* East Zone
Production, West Berlin, 158 (table)
Prussian spirit, 106
Puhl, Hans, 69

Q

Quebec conference, 1944, 29
Quick magazine (Munich), 114

R

Radcliffe, 7
Radio Free Berlin. *See* Sender Freies Berlin
Radio Free Europe, 184
Radio in American Sector (RIAS), 55, 153, 156; struck by lightning (1965), 183
Radio Vienna, 183
Rapacki, Adam, 42
Reber, Sam, 11
Recognition of East Zone (GDR), 86. *See also* Hallstein doctrine
Rector of Free University, 166–68, 172
Red Cross flag, 68
Refugees, 53, 56, 57, 62, 103, 109, 122, 124, 139
Reichstag, 18, 127
Reunification, 79–102, 113, 132, 147, 186, 224–26; four views, 100, 101; opportunity for, 80, price of, 182. *See also* East Zone, "Little steps," Recognition
Reuter, Erich F., 160
Reuter, Ernst, 4, 12, 16, 36, 44, 45, 155; death of, 41
Reuter, Hannah, 9
Riddleberger, James W., 4, 218
Riklin, Alois, 80n, 135n, 140, 145n
Robson, Charles B., xi, 4n, 39n
Romulo, Carlos, 195
Roosevelt, Franklin D., 23, 26, 27, 28; death of, 31
Rosen, Edgar, R., 4n
Rotter, Aurelie, 18
Rotter, Gertrude, 18
"Rubble mountain," 150, 209
Rumania, x, 101; treaty, 26
Rusk, Dean, 49, 60, 63
Russians, 105. *See also* Union of Soviet Socialist Republics
Russian War Memorial, Berlin, 68

S

Saale-Autobahn bridge, 115
Salami tactics, 180–81. *See also* Harassment
Salzufer Camp, 13
Sandkrug bridge, 68
San Francisco conference, UN 1945, 26
Saragat, Guiseppe, 195
Saxons, 109
S-Bahn, 8
SBZ von A-Z, 114
Schacht, Hjalmar Greeley, 7
Scherer, Ray, 56n
Schering plant, 151
Schiller, Karl, 130n, 138n, 147
Schmidt, Helmut, 89n
Scholz, Arno, 16n
Schöneberg District, 174
Schöneberg Rathaus, 19
Schools, new type, 176
Schreiber, Walter, 17, 44

Schröder, Gerhard, 89n, 201, 203, 204
Schröder, Louisa, 46
Schroter (athlete), 193
Schuler gallery, 160
Schumacher, Kurt, 34, 45
Schwedler, Rolf, 194
"Security and welfare" of Berlin, 21, 37n
Senat, Berlin, 95, 96, 98, 174; loans to students, 174
Senator for public education, 174
Senator für Wirtschaft (Senator for economic affairs). See Schiller, Karl
Sender Freies Berlin, 162
Sender Freies Berlin-Fernsehen, 162
Seven Year Plan, East Zone, 106, 112
Shell, Kurt, 48n, 49, 50, 54, 57, 60, 66n, 95n, 144n, 185n, 186n
Shen Yi, 191
Sieckmann, Ida, 65
Siegmunds Hof, 169
Siemens plant, 151
Smirnov, Andrei, 63, 64
Smith, Jean E., 48n
Soapbox derby, 193
Social Democratic Party (SPD), 34, 35, 44, 199
Socialist Unity Party (SED), 34, 44, 58
Sommer, Theo, 108n
Soviet-American airflights, 50
Soviet Embassy, East Berlin, 59
Soviet Revolution, 25
Spandau, prison, 139
Spiegel, Der, 185
Spree River, 70
Springer gallery, 160
Sputnik (October, 1957), 42, 53
Stalin, Joseph, 23, 26, 27, 28, 32, 157; death of, 11, 41
Stalinallee, 125
State, War, Navy Committee (SWNC), 29
Stockpile, 14, 16, 139, 140, 155
Stoph, Willi, 95
Strang, William, 30
Strauss, Franz-Josef, 90, 150, 201, 203, 204
Stubbins, Hugh, 153
Students, 70, 74, 165–70; protests, 170; restlessness, 84; tunnel building, 70
"Student Village," 152, 165, 167, 168
Studentendorf. See "Student Village"
Stuttgart Speech. See Byrnes, James F.
Suhr, Otto, 17, 36, 46
"Swing credits," 113, 188. See also East Zone, credits to

SWNC. See State, War, Navy Committee

T

Tag, Der, 162
Tagesspiegel, Der, 57, 58, 61, 162, 190
"Teach-ins," 171
Technical University, 159, 169
Tegel Lake, 160
Teheran, 28, 31
Telefunken plant, 151
Telegraf, 162
Telephone communications, with East Zone, 83
Teltow Canal, x, 169
Templehof Airport, 18, 19
Thalheim, Karl C., 106, 110n, 114, 119n, 127n
Thälmannplatz, 66
Third Reich, 23
Thompson, Christa, x
Thompson, Dorothy, 7
Time magazine, 73
Trade, East-West, 92, 142, 143 (table) See also Interzonal trade
Trade, West Berlin, 157, 158 (table)
Travel. See Visits
Truman, Harry, 18, 26, 27
Truman doctrine, 33, 35
Trummerberg. See "Rubble mountain"
Tunnels (under the Wall), 70–74
Tunnel intelligence, 17
Tutzing, 187, 188
Tutzing, Brandt speech of July, 1963, 97n, 185

U

U-Bahn, 47n
Uhlmann, Hans, 160
Ulbricht, Walter, 47, 49, 62, 64, 88, 93, 99, 114, 126, 145, 188, 189, 191, 192, 193; decision to raise Wall, 52; dilemma, 107, 216; economic concern, 51, 53; Passierschein negotiations, 98; revolt against, 117; Soviet relations, 133; status, 108, 187; view of Wall, 110; visit to Moscow, 1961, 48. See also Pankow; German Democratic Republic; East Zone, labor force; Refugees
Ulbricht regime, 104, 114, 118, 220
Unconditional surrender, 30
Unemployment, 131, 147, 148
Union of Soviet Socialist Republics (USSR), 25, 28, 34, 37; planes, 145;

Index   [245]

removals, 148; troops, 104. *See also* Kremlin; Khrushchev, Nikita
United Kingdom, 92, 132, 149, 181; airplanes, 138
United Nations Organization, 26
Unter den Linden, 125, 127
U.S. Commandant, 67
U.S. commitments, 1, 24, 80, 99, 132, 146
U.S. High Commissioner (Germany), 152
Unter den Zelten, 19

V

Van der Rohe, Mies, 160
Versailles Treaty, 1919, 5, 24. *See also* Paris Peace Conference
Vienna meeting, 1961, 22. *See also* Kennedy-Khrushchev meeting
Vietnam, 140, 163n, 172
Villa Borsig, 160
Visits, to Berlin, 65, 195; to East Zone, 92, 93, 108
Voice of America, 184
Volkspolizei (Vopos), 52, 58, 59, 60–69, 72, 78, 109, 124, 169, 185

W

Waldbühne, 104
Wall, the, *Abgeordnetenhaus* condemnation, 62; Adenauer's denunciation, 64; advance indications on, 54, 55, 57, 61; August 13, 1961, 41, 47–48; "improvements," 191; Khrushchev's expectation, 64; short term success, 51, 110; Ulbricht's problem, 51; Washington's policy, 50, 61, 62, 63. *See also* Brandt, Willy; Escapes; June 17, 1953; Tunnels; Ulbricht, Walter; Visits
Wannsee, 135, 190, 193
Warsaw, 184
Warsaw Pact countries, 35, 42n, 48, 54, 57
"Washington's problem," 206, 207
Weber, Heinz, 11
Wehner, Herbert, 54, 90
Weimar Republic, 83
Wendt, Erich, 97
Werner, Fritz, 151
Wertheimer, Mildred, 7
"*West* Berlin," 49
West German Currency District (formula), 98. *See also* Berlin
Western Alliance, 86. *See also* North Atlantic Treaty Organization
Western Allies, 62
Western guarantee, 37
Wier, Richard, x
Williams, Elwood, xi
Wilson, Woodrow, 5
Winant, John G., 30, 31
Windsor, Philip, 34n, 57n, 145n
Wohlfahrt, Dieter, 69, 70
Women's Organization, Berlin, 34
Woodward, Margaret, 152n, 156n
Work relief program, 152. *See also* Aid

Y

Yalta, 22–24, 27, 28, 31, 35n, 80, 132

Z

Zhukov, Georgi, 123
Zohlnhöfer, Werner, 39n
Zoo (West Berlin), 194

www.ingramcontent.com/pod-product-compliance
Lightning Source LLC
Chambersburg PA
CBHW021359290426
44108CB00010B/304